Principles of Publicity
and Press Freedom

CRITICAL MEDIA STUDIES
INSTITUTIONS, POLITICS, AND CULTURE

Series Editor
Andrew Calabrese, University of Colorado

Advisory Board
Patricia Aufderheide, American University
Vincent Mosco, Carleton University
Jean-Claude Burgelman, Free University of Brussel
Janice Peck, University of Colorado
Simone Chambers, University of Colorado
Manjunath Pendakur, Southern Illinois University
Nicholas Garnham, University of Westminster
Arvind Rajagopal, New York University
Hanno Hardt, University of Iowa
Kevin Robins, Goldsmiths College
Gay Hawkins, The University of New South Wales
Saskia Sassen, University of Chicago
Maria Heller, Eötvös Loránd University
Colin Sparks, University of Westminster
Robert Horwitz, University of California at San Diego
Slavko Splichal, University of Ljubljana
Douglas Kellner, University of California at Los Angeles
Thomas Streeter, University of Vermont
Gary Marx, Massachusetts Institute of Technology
Liesbet van Zoonen, University of Amsterdam
Toby Miller, New York University
Janet Wasko, University of Oregon

Recent Titles in the Series
Floating Lives: The Media and Asian Diasporas, edited by Stuart
    Cunningham and John Sinclair
Continental Order? Integrating North America for Cybercapitalism, edited
    by Vincent Mosco and Dan Schiller
*Social Theories of the Press: Constituents of Communication Research,
    1840s to 1920s, second edition,* Hanno Hardt
Privacy and the Information Age, Serge Gutwirth
Global Media Governance: A Beginner's Guide, Seán Ó Siochrú and
    Bruce Girard
*The Global and the National: Media and Communications in
    Post-Communist Russia,* Terhi Rantanen

Principles of Publicity and Press Freedom

Slavko Splichal

ROWMAN & LITTLEFIELD PUBLISHERS, INC.
Lanham • *Boulder* • *New York* • *Oxford*

ROWMAN & LITTLEFIELD PUBLISHERS, INC.

Published in the United States of America
by Rowman & Littlefield Publishers, Inc.
A Member of the Rowman & Littlefield Publishing Group
4720 Boston Way, Lanham, Maryland 20706
www.rowmanlittlefield.com

PO Box 317, Oxford, OX2 9RU, United Kingdom

Copyright © 2002 by Rowman & Littlefield Publishers, Inc.

British Library Cataloguing in Publication Information Available

Library of Congress Cataloging-in-Publication Data

Splichal, Slavko.
    Principles of publicity and press freedom / Slavko Splichal.
        p. cm. — (Critical media studies)
Includes bibliographical references and index.
    ISBN 0-7425-1614-8 (alk.paper) — ISBN 0-7425-1615-6 (pbk. : alk.
paper)
    1. Freedom of the press.   I. Title.   II. Series.
    PN4735 .S68   2002
    323.44'5—dc21

                                                    2002008930

Printed in the United States of America

♾™ The paper used in this publication meets the minimum requirements of
American National Standard for Information Sciences—Permanence of Paper
for Printed Library Materials, ANSI/NISO Z39.48-1992.

If one cannot prove that a thing is, he may try to prove that it is not. And if he succeeds in doing neither (as often occurs), he may still ask whether it is in his interest to accept one or other of the alternatives hypothetically, from the theoretical or the practical point of view.

—Kant, *Metaphysics of Morals*

Contents

Illustrations

Preface

This book deals with diverse aspects of "publicness." It is not meant to be a comprehensive theoretical and historical account of the concept; rather, it is primarily an attempt at rethinking the relationship between press freedom and personal freedom. It is based on a reexamination and reinterpretation of the major relevant traditions in the history of ideas that relate the theme of press freedom to theories of democracy, public opinion, and the public sphere. The Pantheon of great thinkers in the essay is familiar, but the picture put together from these sources tells a rather different story about press freedom than the usual incantations, and challenges the intellectual foundations that liberal press theory builds on. I started to write this book with the idea of analyzing and confronting the intellectual histories of "freedom of the press" and "the principle of publicity" as the cornerstones of modern democracy, which emerged from earlier ideas of freedom of thought and speech and were first clearly conceptualized by Immanuel Kant as the transcendental formula of public justice and the principle of the "public use of reason," and in Jeremy Bentham's concept of publicity as the basis of a "system of distrust." I find it stunning that the *corporate* freedom of the press was and still is so often considered (essential to) *human* freedom, whereas a *personal* right to communicate is considered tyranny against the real right to *private* property. I believe that this controversy should become central in the contemporary discussions related to what is actually happening with the media and press freedom in the period of neoliberal globalization and media concentration. Eventually, the contradiction between personal and real rights in communication is challenged by new media, which tend to suppress the traditional (technologically driven) division between interpersonal and mass-mediated communication.

The principle of publicity was originally conceived as a critical impulse against injustice based on secrecy of state actions *and* as an enlightening momentum substantiating the "region of human liberty," making private citizens equal in the public use of reason. Early debates on freedom of the press pointed toward the idea of publicity as an extension of *individuals'* freedom of *thought* and *expression*. With the constitutional guarantee for a free press in parliamentary democracies, discussions of freedom of the press were largely reduced to the pursuit of freedom *by* the media, thus neglecting the idea of publicity as the basis of democratic citizenship. The concepts of public service media and, to a lesser extent, the model of social responsibility of the press attempted at recuperating the latter dimension of publicity, but with very limited success. The notion of the press as the Fourth Estate/Power was a valid concept and legitimate form of the institutionalization of the principle of publicity in the period when newspapers emanated from a new (bourgeois) estate or class: they had a different source of legitimacy than the three classic powers, and they developed as a critical impulse against the old ruling estates. Yet the discrimination in favor of the power/control function of the press, which relates to the need for "distrustful surveillance" defended by Bentham, clearly abstracted freedom of the press from the Kantian quest for the public use of reason and personal freedom to express and publish opinions. The conceptual transformation of freedom of the press is closely related to the reconceptualization of publicity clearly reflected in the fact that the very word "publicity," which used to refer to reasoned *debates* has been overshadowed by "the activity of making certain that someone or something attracts a lot of interest or attention from many people" (*Cambridge International Dictionary of English*) or "a type of public relations in the form of a news item or story which conveys information about a product, service, or idea in the media," as advertisers conceive of it. It is my firm belief that in modern democratic societies—where the people rather than different estates legitimize all the powers—the control dimension of publicity embodied in the corporate freedom of the press should be effectively supplemented by actions toward equalizing private citizens in the public use of reason. In other words, reforms of political, economic, and social regulatory practices are needed to open citizens' access to the public sphere and mass media, which can only be based on the legal recognition of the generic human right to communicate.

Several people have read parts of the manuscript in various draft forms and provided helpful comments. In particular, I would like to thank my friend and colleague Hanno Hardt, professor of communications at the University of Iowa and University of Ljubljana, for his advice and comments that contributed to the precision of the final text. I also would like to thank Professor Peter Dahlgren from the University of Lund, Sweden, for his stimulating comments on the final draft. Special thanks are due to the series editor Andrew Calabrese, professor at the University of Colorado at Boulder, and Brenda Hadenfeldt of Rowman & Littlefield. I also thank the production staff of Rowman & Littlefield, Jehanne Schweitzer and Chrisona Schmidt; it was a pleasure for me to work with them. Last but not least, I would like to thank the Slovenian Ministry of Science and Technology for the research grant that enabled me to accomplish the research project that partially informs the present book, the Faculty of Social Sciences, University of Ljubljana, and the Library of the University of Iowa, Iowa City, where most of the research for this book was carried out.

1

In Search of the Roots: Deconstructing the Institution of Freedom of the Press

The main intention of this volume is to explore the intellectual history of the concept "public/ness" (German *Öffentlichkeit*), which has derived from earlier ideas of freedom of thought and speech and has been first strongly conceptualized by Immanuel Kant as transcendental formula of public justice and the principle of the "public use of reason"—in contrast to Jeremy Bentham's understanding of publicity as the basis of a "system of distrust." In the centuries to follow, the latter understanding prevailed in the regulatory practice and sublimed into the legend of the fourth estate or fourth power—the idea of newspapers independent of governmental and party-political control, representing public opinion, and having the power to control the other estates. With the myth of the fourth estate, the broader and more comprehensive idea of public/ness *eclipsed* even before an attempt was made to enact it constitutionally or legally: it was largely reduced to the concept of "freedom of the press" as the fourth power and "the right to publish the truth about the government." In terms of Jürgen Habermas's (1992a, 440, 453–54) differentiation between the three types of actors acting in the public sphere—(1) those who emerge from the public and participate in the reproduction of publicness (essentially, civil society's actors of the late twentieth century); (2) organizations, political parties, interest groups, and similar actors who "occupy an already constituted publicness in order to use it" (they only "appear before the public"); and (3) *publicists*[1] in the media as gatekeepers who set the agenda of public discourse and control the access of contributions and authors to the mass media that control the public discourse—the enactment of freedom of the press marginalized the indigenous group of actors who historically set up the (liberal-bourgeois) public sphere, and whose participation in it is still unavoidably constitutive.

1

The idea of freedom of the press, which was first codified in Virginia's Bill of Rights (1776) and the French revolutionary Declaration of Rights of Men and Citizen (1789), was born in the specific situation of the seventeenth and eighteenth centuries, when newspapers were transformed from mere mediators between democratic conversations taking place in semiprivate clubs and public places, and their readers, into an autonomous "power" that produced themes worthy of public discussion. The newspaper first bore the role of public letter and public conversation, but by the end of the nineteenth century it became a global intellectual power. As the nineteenth-century French sociologist Gabriel Tarde (1969, 318) wrote, it "began as only a prolonged echo of chats and correspondences and ended up as their exclusive source. The newspaper has thus finished the age-old work that conversation began, that correspondence extended, but that always remained in a state of a sparse and scattered outline—the fusion of personal opinions into local opinions, and this into national and *world* opinion, the grandiose unification of public mind."

During the nineteenth century, the notion of the "fourth power," with newspapers as its legitimate corporate agents, gained popularity over Kant's idea of the "public use of reason" emphasizing the personal[2] right of publishing opinions, for it corresponded with the then dominant conception of people's governance as *representative* government, first outlined by Edmund Burke as "government of the people [with their consent], by the people [through their representatives], for the people [for their common and permanent good]," which was expected never to "perish from the earth" (in Hoffman and Levack 1949/1967, xx–xxi). As François Guizot stated in his praise for the representative system of England in the mid-1800s, following Bentham's reasoning, it enables citizens to permanently "seek after reason, justice, and truth" and delegitimizes absolute power "(1) by *discussion*, which compels existing powers to seek after truth in common; (2) by *publicity*, which places these powers when occupied in this search, under the eyes of the citizens; and (3) by the *liberty of the press*, which stimulates the citizens themselves to seek after truth, and to tell it to power" (Guizot 1851/1861, 264; emphasis added). The idea of freedom of the press—in contrast to personal freedom to publish—was perfectly congruent with the conception of *representation*, since it was derived from the principle of public/ness "with the consent of the people," executed by newspapers as "the representatives of the people" with the intention to fulfill people's "common and permanent goal," usually defined in terms of the "right to know." The concept of the press as the fourth power, fourth estate, or watchdog assumes that the press is a *corporate* entity serving collective interests. Consequently freedom of the press is justified by its function of representing the people or the public, or being their agent in materializing their individual rights, such as the right to know. In contrast, the rationalistic and enlightenment conceptualization of freedom of the press conceived of it as a *personal* freedom and right to publish opinions. In fact, the difference between opposing views on the locus of human rights—located either in the press or the individual—is reflected in the definition of freedom of the press as a "great bulwark of liberty" in Virginia's Bill of Rights versus "free communication of thoughts and opinions," which includes "free printing," stipulated in the French Declaration of Rights of Men and Citizen.

Louis E. Ingelhart recently collected in his book *Press Freedoms: A Descriptive Calendar of Concepts, Interpretations, Events, and Court Actions from 4000 BC to the Present* (1987) an immense amount of information about historical events related to freedom of the press in the course of six millennia of human civilization. This book is devoted to "a history and analysis of the emergence and development of the concept of a free press," in which thousands of "facts" related to freedom of speech and press are meticulously compiled. It shows that the entire history of humankind is spread with freethinking beliefs in human reasoning and moral communicative action, though often curbed by oppressiveness of religious and secular authorities. Yet great philosophers such as Benedict (Baruch) de Spinoza, Immanuel Kant, and G. W. F. Hegel, who laid philosophical foundations to freedom of expression and opinion, are not mentioned in it at all; Jeremy Bentham is referred to once; Karl Marx is briefly mentioned four times and a paragraph is quoted from his essay on "Proceedings of the Sixth Rhine Province Assembly" of 1842, and one more paragraph is quoted from John Stuart Mill's essay *On Liberty* (1859)—roughly one page of the whole four-hundred-page book. Of all the six, only Mill's essay *On Liberty* qualified for "the 200 most important references."

These great minds barely (or not at all) mentioned in Ingelhart's *Press Freedoms* are taken as the cornerstones of my project. I am not undertaking an effort to dig out historical details, to picture the lives and works of these great men, and to tell the story of what happened; my interest is neither in the search for the dates when the idea of public/ness first appeared in the Western civilization nor in an exhaustive exploration of the variety of (past) meanings of public/ness, which at the end of the story could prevent us from seeing the forest from the trees. A critical look at history is productive inasmuch as it refers to the present and to the future: the results of a historical inquiry have to be tested—in terms of theory and/or practice—against the existing reality from the point of view of its hypothetical future development and alternatives in the past. It may help us to see what *could* have happened and what *can* happen due to (the lack of) specific circumstances. As Kant suggested in his defense of the "Platonian Republic," we should carefully follow up the ideas past, even if the past thinkers "left us without assistance," and "employ new efforts to place [them] in clearer light, rather than carelessly fling [them] aside as useless" (1781/1952, 174).

The past has not only theoretical relevance for the present, and the present is more than just a point in the linear current of events. The past may reappear empirically in the present, as was typically the case with the revival of the classical period of ancient Greece and Rome during the Renaissance; the latest theories of the present time help reinterpret and better understand the most remote ages; and current social developments may be better illuminated if linked to decisive historical incentives, both theoretical and practical. This of course is not a new method of looking at history and/or interpreting it. It is basically what Hegel named "*reflective* history" and defined as "history whose mode of representation is not really confined by the limits of the time to which it relates, but whose spirit transcends the present." More specifically, it is what he designates as "*critical* history," which is aimed at "a criticism of historical narratives and an investigation of their truth and credibility" (Hegel 1830/2001, 17, 19).

One has to look back in the past time to realize how at a particular point of time the concept of public/ness acquired a specific meaning or radically changed it. New meanings emerge due to substantial changes in social (power) relationship and are later progressively diffused across cultures and become universal, seemingly transcendental—as it happened with the concept of "freedom of the press" by the end of the twentieth century. Nowadays the idea of freedom of the press seems to be self-evident, a matter of fact—as it was centuries ago "self-evident" that freedom of the press was a remedy for a guarded use only, which ought to be entirely in the hands of the State or the King. The genealogy of "freedom of the press" demonstrates that the concept is neither self-evident nor coherent. On the one hand, strong legal and moral convictions favoring severe restrictions on newspapers' publication and distribution prevailed in Europe even after the French Revolution; on the other hand, radically different operationalizations of public/ness existed in the past and continue to exist, such as "freedom to publish," "public use of reason," or "right to communicate." In a remarkable book, *Newspaper's Pleasure and Use* (*Zeitungs Lust und Nutz*), published in Germany as early as 1695—probably the first book ever published—Caspar Stieler argued in favor of state monopoly over the press and censorship in order to prevent newspapers from spreading "false, mocking, and noxious" news that could "mislead, anger, and deceive a simple man" and claimed that

> one should wish that no one is allowed to handle with news or publish them but the one who is liable or swears by his life; on the other hand, his superiors have to protect him and not everybody should be allowed to print news and sell it without their concordance. If this grew into a habit, newspapers would perhaps become a bit more scarce and expensive for the buyer, but also much more reliable and worth of reading. (Stieler 1695/1969, 164–65)

Yet not only the dispute between advocates and adversaries of freedom of the press—so brilliantly analyzed by Karl Marx in *Rheinische Zeitung* in

1842—refers to the distribution of political and economic power in society. Similarly, the belief that "freedom of the press" is a *universal ethical principle* in itself—the peak of a continuous historical progression—may be sapped by demonstrating that the concept of free press and possible alternative or supplementary concepts are interrelated with power struggles. "Universality" of press freedom as a democratic norm may become contestable when set into a historical perspective, which would demonstrate that specific interests are implicated in the concept of "freedom of the press." Different meanings and derivations of the concept "public/ness" cannot be molded into *the* singular historical (democratic) "progression" with *the* beginning and *the* end, or *the* present state. Genealogy reveals that diversity rather than uniformity is the rule of development, and that concepts and meanings *vary* with time and space, rather than *progress* in a linear manner. Analyzing the notion of "the public" in his book on *The Public and Its Problems*, John Dewey argued that "in no two ages or places is there the same public. Conditions make the consequences of associated action and the knowledge of them different. In addition the means by which a public can determine the government to serve its interests vary" (Dewey 1927/1991, 88). Each "age" and "place" creates its specific regime of publicness, and there is no simple better–worse relation between them.

A convincing example of diversification of meanings is another Dewey explanation of how the nature of "the public" depends on the quantitative scope of results of collective behavior. Transactions between individuals and groups may have no indirect consequences for nonparticipants at the beginning, but in the course of time they may begin to produce important consequences for those not directly involved. In other words, a process of transformation from the private to the public may take place. Such changes can be typically observed in the development of *law* that covers different spheres of human actions: in the course of time, different types of transactions become subject to legal regulations. Similar is the case of economy where modes of private business become "affected with a public interest" because of quantitative and qualitative expansion. Opposite is the case of religion in democratic societies: when the consequences of irreligion became irrelevant for the broader community, religion was relegated from public to private domain. In short, as Dewey argued, with the changes in the extent of consequences, the nature and scope of (state) regulation would also change. Yet this does not imply that one regime of publicness is more progressive than the other; in the strict sense, it is not possible to compare them since no independent measure is provided. What is important, however, is the idea that it is virtually impossible to designate any concrete historical form of publicness as a universal functional requirement for the maintenance of publicness in general. If freedom of the press were a functional requirement for the maintenance of democracy and freedom, that would imply that freedom of the press is indeed an irreplaceable "institution" (which history clearly falsi-fies), or that other institutions of freedom—such as freedom of expression or public use of reason—are actually mere appearances of press freedom (which would be basically the same as to claim that freedom of the press it-self is merely an appearance of a transcendental freedom of enterprise).

The point at issue is not whether freedom of the press is a significant dem-ocratic achievement, because it surely is. Rather, the point in question is whether or not freedom of the press is a transcendental concept comparable to Kant's publicity as the transcendental formula of public justice—which it is clearly not. This is why an attempt is needed to deconstruct freedom of the press as an ideal-type concept rather than to accept its functional, ahistori-cal, transcendental supremacy.

"INVENTION OF PRINTING IS NO GREAT MATTER COMPARED WITH THE INVENTION OF LETTERS"

Historically, the idea of press freedom appeared as an "extension" of the free-dom of speech refined in the revolutionary technological, social, and eco-nomic environment of the eighteenth century. The intellectual interest in communication so vividly expressed in writings of great Greek philosophers, such as Plato's *Phaedrus* and Aristotle's *Rhetoric*, sank for long centuries in the darkness of the Middle Ages.[3] The Renaissance and Enlightenment actu-ally represent the perpetuation of intellectual achievements of ancient Greece and Rome after a long historical rupture. The indebtedness of the late Re-naissance authors to the ancient Greek thought is throughout acknowledged and documented, as in John Milton's *Areopagitica*[4] (1644), which begins with the adoption of King Theseus's words from Euripides's tragedy *The Suppli-ants* celebrating the rule of law and freedom of speech: "This is true Liberty, when free-born men,/ Having to advise the public, may speak free,/ Which he who can, and will, deserves high praise;/ Who neither can, nor will, may hold his peace:/ What can be juster in a State than this?"[5]

For more than a millennium of the Middle Ages, freedom of thought and speech was suppressed in Europe, and the development of all sciences and humanities was impeded by the religious dogmatism of the Catholic Church, which postulated subservience to religious and secular authorities as the dominant social value.[6] Johannes Gutenberg's invention of the mechanical printing press with movable type[7] in the mid-1400s represents the milestone in the development of human communication. After Gutenberg's invention and other significant social and technological achievements in Europe in the sixteenth and seventeenth centuries, a favorable wind began to blow in sci-ence and politics, which eventually enabled the mass production of books and newspapers. Freedom of speech, which was of little concern before

Gutenberg's invention, became one of the most vitalizing ideas framing the movement of Enlightenment. Yet the new technology not only stimulated the call for freedom of expression but also enticed those who wanted to exercise a strict control over its use.

Religious schism and wars (with Luther's Protestantism in Germany, secession of the Church of England from the pope, Calvinism in Switzerland and Western Europe, and German religious warfare that ended with the legalization of the religious schism), the establishment of the Utrecht Republic in the Netherlands and parliamentary monarchy in England, together with the discovery of waterways to America and the Far East, the rise of shipping trade, the beginnings of oversea colonization, the growth of capitalism, and the rising economic and political power of bourgeoisie—paved the way for an exceptional swing of spiritual life in Western Europe and, eventually, for the ascent of Enlightenment. A fundamental condition for such revolutionary developments was the struggle for the materialization of personal intellectual freedom and, specifically, "freedom to use reason publicly in all matters," as runs one of the famous Kant's answers to the question, "What is Enlightenment?" (1784), namely, the struggle to legalize freedoms of thought, speech, and publication, which still took place during a considerable part of the nineteenth century. During the late 1800s, however, censorship and even the banning of newspapers were still a common practice in many European countries.[8]

The new printing technology did not revolutionize the kind of convergence of symbolic and material communication tools manifested in the development of writing, but it considerably invigorated intellectual, cultural, political, and economic consequences of the convergence, which are best represented by the rapid spread of new social functions adopted by newspapers. Shortly after Gutenberg printed the first Bible, the Catholic Church implemented a licensing system, followed by strict censorship and the Index Librorum Prohibitorum (Index of Prohibited Books), an official index of prohibited texts that were not allowed to appear in public or to be read in private. The emergence of new intellectual elites—the religious reform movements (e.g., Reformation)—as a reaction against abuses by the Catholic Church and the development of printing technology changed the strategy of religious and lay feudal authorities only in the seventeenth century. Their strategy moved away from exercising restrictive control to more subtle and efficient strategies. The Catholic Church established Sacra Congregatio de Propaganda Fide, its central institution with the main task to consolidate the position of the Church and religion in society through propaganda.

The collapse of the licensing system in Britain caused by the parliamentary revocation of the Printing Act in 1694 was the first sign of emerging libertarian secular policies toward book and newspaper publishing. In 1637, the licensing of all printed works was deputed by a decree of Charles's Star Chamber to the chancellors of Oxford and Cambridge, and to the bishop of London. In 1643, Parliament passed the Regulation of Printing Act providing for preventive licensing of the press, followed by Milton's *Areopagitica* (1644), which attracted little attention and had no immediate impact when it was published but later became a classic defense of freedom of publication. The system of British preventive censorship remained in power until 1694. Shortly after its abolition, in 1702, the first daily newspaper—the *Daily Current*—appeared in Britain. As Karl Bücher noticed, in the early eighteenth century "the press in England acquired the character that was later adopted in all countries: in addition to the task of transmitting news, the one of earnest debate of political issues, thus it became a prop and complement of the parliamentary regime" (Bücher 1926, 19). During the nineteenth and twentieth centuries, political rulers began to discover, similarly to their religious counterparts, the value of popular support for their actions (including wars) and tried to influence public opinion: propaganda, public relations, and massive information subsidies became a far more suitable strategy than censorship for pacifying public opinion.

In his "newspaper study" of 1695, Caspar Stieler argued after monk Bernhard that newspaper readers were swayed by five different kinds of desires: some readers may simply want to know more out of curiosity; "boasters" want to know more in order to become known due to their erudition; "misers" look in the newspapers for proficiency for the sake of profit; some people want to use knowledge from newspapers to stimulate and enrapture others, such as those who express their Christian love; finally, there are those who want to know more in order to educate and improve themselves, which is the goal of the wise. The "necessity of newspapers" derives from the incapacity of human beings to remove, in any other way, barriers of space and time that would prevent them from acquiring knowledge, which Stieler considered a "natural process." Since newspapers developed from writing of letters, according to Stieler, they retained a variety of "functions," as we would say today, of the latter and acquired new ones, for all kinds of newspaper customers and reading situations: tradesmen, lords, wars, churches, high schools, lady salons, at home, on a journey, in accidents, drinking and social gatherings. Despite such a great variety of functions—"uses and gratifications"—newspaper reading always implies *political reasoning* on the part of the reader. Not only was access to the newspaper publishing restricted to competent men of means; reading itself was preclusive of those unable of "political reasoning."

Freedom of speech and freedom of publication, which were simultaneously legitimized as civic liberties during the eighteenth and nineteenth centuries—under the growing influence of the liberal press—constitute one single and indivisible "liberty of expressing and publishing opinions" as a natural right of every individual. Yet freedom of the press as the institutionalized corporate form of personal freedom of speech is not only an "extension" of the latter, but also its negation. Habermas properly differentiates between the fundamental human rights and freedoms that define "the scope for various types of associations and societies"—consisting of freedom of *assembly* and *association*, and freedom of *speech*—and those that safeguard "the media infrastructure of public communication," which include freedom of the *press* and "the right to free *publicistic activity*" (Habermas 1992a, 445).[9] If citizens' freedoms are regarded as a substantial part of "economic and social conditions [giving] everyone an equal chance to meet the criteria for admission" to the public sphere, which is safeguarded only when these conditions are effectively met (Habermas 1962/1995, 86), then "freedom of the press" clearly and progressively reduced the number of citizens who could effectively realize it, as opposed to freedom of thought and speech. The reason is simple: for the realization of freedom of the press it was not enough that one attained the status of property owner in general, but she or he had to dispose of specific communication technology—to own a newspaper or to work for its publisher as editor or journalist. This is not to contradict the general idea that—in Hegel's words—"nature is the element of inequality," but his belief that the "objective right" ought not to "supersede the inequality set up by nature. On the contrary, it produces inequality out of spirit and exalts it to an inequality of talents, wealth, and intellectual and moral education" (Hegel 1821/1971, 164). Whereas personal freedom of thought and expression is realized proportionately to his or her talents and intellectual endowments, and does not directly depend on external sources of inequality, the realization of freedom of the press additionally (or even primarily) depends on the disposal of appropriate means, financial and technical, of printing. Even if we agreed that inequality in wealth is set up by nature, this does not imply the necessity that the realization of one freedom, that of thought and expression, should rightly depend on inequalities of wealth resulting from the realization of another freedom, that of ownership. Incidentally, the difference between the two liberties was also the core of Karl Marx's confrontation with the idea that press freedom is but a kind of commercial freedom suggested by the representative of the "fourth estate" (bourgeoisie) during the debates on freedom of the press in the Rhine Province Assembly in 1842.

Four great communication revolutions broke out in human history: the emergence of writing and alphabet was the first, the invention of printing was the second, the introduction of electric-powered relays in communication was the third, and the convergence of telecommunication, computers, and digitalization is widely considered the fourth revolution in communication technology. *Revolutionary* changes in technology effect, often in controversial ways, changes in the distribution of power in societal structure. Throughout history, new means of communication have been not only *used*, but also *abused*, as Williams (1962/1976, 10) argued—for political control (as in propaganda) or for commercial profit (as in advertising).

Writing denotes the transition from barbarity to civilization; it undermined the locally generated power monopoly of the elders who preserved in oral form the accumulated knowledge, but at the same time introduced class divisions in society. For Tönnies (1922, 220), the difference between *Gemeinschaft* ("community") and *Gesellschaft* ("society") is first and foremost constituted by *writing*; it is also writing that marks the transition from a primeval, classless human community to civilization and class society for Marx and Engels in their *Manifesto*. The transition from the oral tradition to the manuscript age was marked by the struggle between the authoritarian and emancipatory potentials embedded in communication, and this contradiction has persisted until today. The development of writing and human ability not only to speak but also to write made it possible for the communication process to take place without the sender and receiver being physically present: the message can be separated and thus alienated from the sender. Alphabetical codes introduced a radical change in the relationship of an individual to "his" or "her" oral language: the language ceased to exist as a natural relationship as it had been in a primitive collectivity. Learning and education became an essential part of social relations, embedded in the primal social division of labor into manual work versus mental work.

With the development of writing, the idea of human communication as a natural human ability possessed and practiced equally by every member of a collectivity merely because of his or her membership of the collectivity became definitely untenable. The primary civilizational process of enlarging temporal and spatial horizons through communication, that is, surpassing natural existential conditions that determined individual's relations to production as well as his or her relation to community as a form of natural belonging to a collectivity, turned for the first time into its opposite: the rise of alienation. Writing not only made possible the recording of communication but also divided the previously homogeneous collectivity into those capable of the new form of communication and those being short of it. The development of writing made the existence of language and the ability to speak insufficient for an individual's participation in social action. As Marx argued, language that seems to be "a self-evident form of the existence of community" substantially differs from the primary natural conditions of production, which do not result from human production, because it is the result of human production. Consequently, the individual's relation to his or her language is not only directly determined by his or her membership in community (i.e., the relation of a "natural" member of human community), but at the same time it is also a product of community. John Dewey (1927/1991, 154) resumes this idea by saying that "we are born organic beings associated with others, but we are not born members of a community. . . . Everything which is distinctly human is *learned, not native*. . . . To learn to be human is to develop through the *give-and-take communication* an effective sense of being an individually distinctive member of a community" (emphasis added).

Like writing, all other kinds of communication technologies developed through centuries reveal that new forms of communication are part of general changes in human actions on nature and other human beings, and therefore no less significant and/or contradictory as economic and political activities. New means of communication that could enable an expansion of human powers to learn and to exchange ideas and experiences were often (mis)used in the pursuit of particularistic political and commercial interests to the detriment of the community (or the public) at large. The development of *printing* distinctly proved the insufficiency of belonging to human (linguistic) community for human actions since the access to printing facilities is not a question of individual's communication abilities, but a matter of ownership. Thus freedom of publication became a matter of political concern and, eventually, of political revolution. Freedom of thought and verbal expression (uses of symbolic tools) without freedom to print (access to the most advanced material tools for communication) remained a prosthesis for freedom to communicate. The appearance of communication skills as naturally given skills existed only as long as the development of human productive forces did not expose the dependence of communication practice on material conditions of human life and its instrumental nature in social relations. It became apparent that human beings can be as alienated from this seemingly natural ability as they can be in the process of production in general.

Since the early postal networks in ancient Persian, Roman, and Chinese empires, communications effectively performed the function of control, both individual and social. In the most general Western rationalistic sense, control denotes a *purposive influence* toward a predetermined goal. Influence of one agent over another means that the former causes changes in the behavior of the latter. Control is always purposive in the sense that it is directed toward some prior goal of the controlling agent (Beniger 1986, 7). Control includes a range of variance from absolute control to its weakest probabilistic forms, namely, any kind of purposive influence on behavior, however insignificant it may be. For example, television advertising is said to "control specific demands" and direct mail campaigns "control voting on a specific issue"—although in either case only a very narrow segment of the intended audience may be influenced.

Communications simultaneously paved the way for two different forms of control: (1) control as mastery (over things rather than over human beings) based on knowledge and (2) control as coercion and domination. On the one hand, control is a medium through which emancipation and freedom can be achieved. On the other hand, control is oppressive in the sense that it enables an individual or group to control others and force them to act against their will. The idea of benign control was canonized in English utilitarianism with the formula "inquiry, legislation, execution, inspection and report," which Jeremy Bentham's principle of publicity has exquisitely exemplified. A century later, the concept of social control was sensitized by American pragmatists as one of the "foundations of social order" in a (functionally) differentiated society, aiming to "balance warring forces" (Ross 1901/1969, 55).[10]

Technology of printing aggravated the difference between the two forms or directions of control. In early theorizations of the press as a means of social control, the notion of the press as an instrument of searching for truth and happiness preponderated over its repressive power. Later on, when newspapers developed into a foundation of social order, their repressive role became more visible and called for more critical approaches.

Printing, together with changes in transportation, enabled the transition from community to society; it ended the information monopoly of arcane political and ecclesiastical institutions. Tönnies (1922, 91–94) stressed the constitutive role of the new dominant form of (mass) communication in differentiating between community *(Gemeinschaft)* and society *(Gesellschaft)*.[11] Community is identified by opinion heritage *(Überlieferung)*, expressed as passing knowledge from generation to generation (i.e., from older to younger generations) and from higher (predominantly the clergy) to lower strata of community. In contrast, tradition and authority "from upside down" are losing power in society and give way to verifiable reason and critique. Therefore, written communication, and subsequently the press, became historically more important than the formerly dominant forms of oral communication.

In contrast to speech communication—which is always only aimed at, and limited by, those who are present—the press addressed an unknown, unidentified, and physically absent mass of people. It paved the way for the formation of "mass society," which electricity helped create. Digitalization is now believed (hoped) to empower individual citizens and to change the societal power structure in the directions of demassification and democratization of society, as was the case with former progressive innovations in the past—but not without counterprocesses, such as globalization. In all four revolutions changes in personal and mass communication were intertwined, redefining the relationship between the private and the public—although first theorizations of the contrast between the private and the public did not appear before the eighteenth century (Habermas 1962/1995, 2), and clear conceptualization of differences between mass communication and interpersonal communication not earlier than in the 1930s (Peters 1999, 22), following historical and sociological efforts of the late 1800s to conceptualize the rising cultural and economic power of the press.

The progressive rise of newspapers was closely connected with the emergence of a new profession—journalism. They both developed through an increasing degree of *division of labor* and *institutionalization* of communication processes, which of course were contingent on technological innovations. The production and distribution of news as one of the most elementary forms of knowledge is as old as humankind, but it first became routinized in the Middle Ages as an occasional activity performed by messengers, clerical workers, minstrel singers, and traveling bards. In the seventcenth century, newspaper publishing and journalism became supplementary, part-time occupations of otherwise professionally committed individuals in the social communication process, such as printers, postmen, or tradesmen. As a result of industrial and bourgeois revolutions, newspaper production became fully institutionalized in the second half of the nineteenth century, when the press was largely liberated from censorship and party subservience, and the division of labor between the occupations of publisher and journalist completed.

Already in the seventeenth century newspapers were considered "extensions of human organs" improving the limited human capability of information gathering (Stieler 1695/1969). The origin of newspapers was attributed to letters, which every one had the right to write and send, but publication of newspapers was often considered a "special right" or privilege granted to the publisher by the ruler on condition of strict censorship. However, libertarian ideas of the seventeenth century on free expression of opinion mostly conceived of such freedom as philosophic freedom of learned men, which was not directly applicable (and even not meant to apply) to the business of newspapers.

On the one hand, scholars of the nineteenth century acknowledged that the invention of printing introduced substantial changes in the way people (inter)act socially: the press became "the real transmitter in the intellectual exchange between the leading organs of society and the public" (Schäffle 1875, 444), differing from other forms of communication by being "thought-communication between persons who are physically separated" (Knies 1857/1996, 44) and primarily by the fact that it was "a link in the chain of modern commercial machinery" (Bücher 1893/1901, 216). Since the beginning, as Tönnies (1922) argued, newspapers were not only intended to supplement privately mediated news in letters but mostly to spread news that was intended for the public. These early discussions of social consequences of technological achievements, including the rise of dispersed audience or public consisting of physically separated but spiritually connected individuals, remind us that many of the themes these days popularly discussed in association with cyberspace have origins in the emergence of the pre-1900 communication technologies, such as the printing press, telegraph, telephone, and film.

On the other hand, however, the scholars largely agreed, as Thomas Hobbes stressed two centuries after Gutenberg's invention of the printing press with movable type, that "the invention of printing, though ingenious, compared with the invention of letters is no great matter;" a truly "great matter" was the design of letters as a "profitable invention for continuing the memory of time past" (Hobbes 1651/1992, 24). The means of transmissions as "technical-mechanical installations" were considered secondary and external in relation to the mental dimension of the communication process.

The undervaluation of the significance of communication technology is clearly reflected in the original meaning of the German word *Zeitung* (now meaning newspaper) denoting in the late Middle Ages (any) news irrespective of specific means of communication—oral, written, painted, or printed (Bücher 1926, 1).

An intellectual disdain for technological improvements in communication actually began much earlier, in the fifth century before the Christian era, when Plato in *Phaedrus* suggested that writing is not a great matter compared with the spoken word—he believed that writing is inferior to speech. Like a painted picture, it can never answer any question and has no power of adaptation. The same art of suspicion of technological progress can be found much later in Hegel's *Philosophy of Right*, where the press is considered "superior to speech" only because of its "more extended range" but "inferior in vivacity" (Hegel 1821/2001, 254). Print news was believed to have merely "ephemeral existence, its purpose is not to continually satisfy enduring needs, unlike that of the written instruction through the book" (Knies 1857/1996, 47). This obviously conservative conception was later severely criticized by Tönnies, who demonstrated how the development of the press was essential to public opinion, and both the press and the public constitutive of *Gesellschaft*—an ideal-type social structure opposing *Gemeinschaft*, which was based on oral communication.

While newspapers supplemented privately obtained official or business news, their major function was the distribution of those kinds of news, which were intended for the public and/or escaped from being kept secret—a "printed marketplace," as Tönnies (1922, 97) named them. Newspapers were seen as a new way of communication supplementing not only private exchange of news but also *opinions*, and expanding the type of communication initiated by books, pamphlets, and pictures, whose effectiveness was based on repetition. The rising tendency of newspapers to present opinions and influence the public was reflected in the doctrine that—in contrast to "the simple, definite, and open expression of the sense and meaning" characteristic of science—newspapers reside "in the region of opinion and subjective thought," and use specific, somewhat queer methods of presentation, such as "the adroit use of terms, or allusions, or half-uttered, half-concealed opinions" (Hegel 1821/2001, 256). Newspapers' capacities to collect, store, and transmit symbolic material helped maximize the use of symbolic goods by extending personal transactions. Certainly newspapers performed these tasks much more effectively than previously dominant societal institutions, such as museums, schools, and libraries, and they took on new functions important for the worlds of politics and business. Yet the production of symbolic material remained a matter of personal endowment; compared with letters and books, the development of the press was considered more a matter of scale than substance. The greater effectiveness and persuasiveness of newspapers "forced" agents of power—from governments to political parties—to try to take hold of them. They defended themselves against critique in newspaper articles partly with licenses, taxes, closings, censorship, and official correction, and partly with their own newspapers, which they established, purchased, or took unofficially into their service.

The first printed papers in the fifteenth century did not oust immediately the handwritten papers from the market since the latter were better able to evade censorship largely introduced after the invention of the printing press. With the rise of the daily press in the eighteenth century, newspapers paved the way for constitutional provisions of freedom of the press based on the Enlightenment principles of publicity and free speech. Papers of the sixteenth and seventeenth centuries mostly provided readership with news and were named appropriately: "Aviso" and "Relation" in Germany, "Examiner" and "Spectator" in England, "Messenger" in Italy, or just "News," "Novelties," or "Gazette" in different countries and languages. In contrast, newspapers during the Enlightenment often became a "tribune" (even taking on this name), where news intended for the public at large was followed by discussion and opinion was expressed to influence a large number of readers—again continuing the practice of persuasive communication formerly characteristic of dramas, sermons, public speeches, books, and other forms of (re)presenting symbolic material less *massive* than the newspapers. Only the development of the Internet, due to its complete decentralization, enabled the producers of symbolic contents to fully reappropriate technical communication means as "external things" in Kant's terms, thus rendering redundant mediators between the author and his or her public beyond technical manipulation.

Early critics of restraints on free printing saw the press as one of many forms of human communication, arguing that no specific regulation was needed for any of them, including the press. Thus Milton claimed in *Areopagitica* that "If we think to regulate printing, thereby to rectify manners, we must regulate all recreations and pastimes, all that is delightful to man"—including music, dancing, and even day-to-day conversation (Milton 1644/1999, 22). This not only would ask an immense number of "licencers" to examine all the different forms of communication, but would be also meaningless on the ground that "evill manners are as perfectly learnt without books a thousand other ways which cannot be stopt" (p. 20).

Adam Smith and other liberal political economists of the eighteenth century and subsequent generations believe(d) that the market itself offers a powerful system of social coordination matching individual wants with available goods. This idea was largely applied to the "marketplace of ideas" that undervalued the significance of normative issues for democracy in general and specifically for the materialization of freedoms of expression and publication, with no distinction between different kinds of human communication. The idea of a "free marketplace of ideas" effectively vindicated the processes of commercialization and commodificiation of the communication sphere, based on the liberal conception of negative freedom (freedom *from* political authorities). As a consequence, press freedom increasingly became freedom *of the press*—a freedom of those who owned communication means rather than (all) citizens.

In the second half of the nineteenth century, the critique of press censorship went beyond economic liberalism and utilitarianism. It took up the critique of market economics criticizing the normative blindness of the market and focused on the role of restitutive rather than repressive law—on organic rather than mechanical solidarity in Durkheim's terms—to emphasize the right of equity for diverse individuals. Within this context, the legal framework of press freedom, or the notion of its regulation, lost its repressive character and became clearly seen as a core institution of democracy, which brought into the focus of the critique normative issues and social solidarity as key aspects of democratic society. Early writings of Karl Marx (in contrast to his later work, which laid great stress on issues of material interest and power) and John Stuart Mill, and even earlier ideas of Jeremy Bentham represent, in different ways, an explicit break with an idealized picture of the free marketplace of ideas that ought to exist almost without any societal, legal, or governmental intervention.

Within the philosophical discourse of Immanuel Kant, the contradiction between economic market and communication is reflected in his differentiation between the exchange of things and exchange of thought. Kant made clear in his comparison of money and books that both money and books can only be used in the process of *alienation* or *exchange*; yet books represent "the greatest means of carrying on the interchange of *thought*," in contrast to money as "the greatest and most useable of all the means of human intercommunication through *things*" (Kant 1790/1952, 423; emphasis added). The essence of the book (or newspaper, we may add) is not in being a *thing*—another point resumed by Marx in his polemic against the liberal economist understanding of press freedom as freedom of ownership—but a *discourse* of the author with the public. Like books, newspapers and other media that developed in the twentieth century are not natural things one is rightfully allowed to occupy, but a contract is needed to regulate the transactions of *thought* in society, not merely transactions of things in the way of sale and purchase that the marketplace regulates.

Despite the fact that communication technologies are obviously "corporeal things" (material substance) that one can "occupy," such acquisition of things does not entitle us to consider the right to acquire a communication means, for example, a medium such as newspaper, a "real right," which Kant defines as "a right as *against every possessor* of it." Considering it a real right would be as unacceptable as forcing "such men as the savage American Indians, the Hottentots, and the New Hollanders" to enter into a civil union with their occupiers, or to "establish colonies by deceptive purchase, and so become owners of their soil, and, in general, without regard to their first possession, make use at will of our superiority in relation to them" (Kant 1797/1952, 456), which of course both happened in the past. Rather, the right to acquire communication means should be considered a contractual right, as in the case of division of labor and transaction between the author and the publisher, where "the author may be said to speak publicly by means of the publisher" (p. 425). According to Kant, a book represents—and *cum grano salis*, we can extend this to newspapers as long as journalists are considered authors rather than mere (news)workers[12]—a real right only in the sense of "an external product of mechanical art," which can be reproduced by anyone who owns it as a *thing*.

While both are forms of human transaction, exchange through books has a different *function* than exchange through money; it is subjugated to *specific principles* and thus needs *specific regulation*. Early institutional regulations of mass communication limited the autonomy of individuals in the formation and expression of opinions by a free discussion to issues that were not critical of the power elites. Since the very beginning, the institutionalization of communication gave rise to different kinds of distorted communication, which resulted from attempts by private and governmental groups to structure and limit public communication in order to enforce their interests. The intensity of institutional regulation culminated with the rise of print media, first in the form of a strict limitation of freedom of expression and publishing (secrecy and censorship) and later in the form of constitutional and legal enactment of press freedom.

FREEDOM OF SPEECH AS A PRIVILEGE OF LEARNED MEN

The idea of the right to speak freely seems to be a simple one—a "natural right" of individual that is beyond and over any positive legal system—ever since the relativity of the truth and potential erroneousness of individuals' opinions have been acknowledged. The gradual social spread of free opinion formation and expression was an unavoidable consequence of the advances in scientific knowledge, which stimulated the "desire to learn." As John Milton argued in *Areopagitica*, an increase in knowledge is proportional to the spread of free expression and circulation of opinions in society: "Where there is much desire to learn, there of necessity will be much arguing, much writing, many opinions; for opinion in good men is but knowledge in the making" (Milton 1644/1999, 41).

Scientific findings spread faster and deeper across society and stimulated "lay" interest in reading and publishing with the expansion of general *education*, particularly after the invention of *printing*. In contrast to science in antiquity practiced as a solitary, even secret, activity, modern science developing in the Enlightenment became a public activity practiced in academic communities with a growing authoritative power in society (Bensaude-Vincent 2000, 18). During the early 1600s, scientific communities acquired a certain degree of autonomy in thought and action, and by the end of the eighteenth century developed into the "Republic(s) of Letters"—imagined or virtual "empires of thought" whose members could even live in different countries but were connected through letters and literary and scientific journals. The quest for rationality, as a universal norm surpassing cultural, political, and religious cleavages, was not always free of dogmatism in scientific practice and did not directly influence the expansion of freedom of expression and publication. Yet it stimulated individual and social (political) consciousness to comprehend publicness (for Kant both the *right* and *duty* of the individual to use his reason publicly) as an epistemological condition of truth and moral-political condition of justice.

Yet it was not only a political-philosophical question of the nature of truth, and the quest for a free scientific debate, that pervaded the struggle for mental freedom beyond the philosophic principle of freedom of mind. In the progression beyond the sphere of scientific knowledge, the freedom of speech first denoted the privilege of free debate granted to members of political assemblies. Thus Spinoza insisted

> not only that the authority of all the patricians in the decision is equal, and that business is quickly despatched, but also, that everyone has absolute liberty (which is of the first necessity in councils) to give his opinion without danger of unpopularity. (Spinoza 1677/1883, chap. 8, 27)

In some countries, such as Germany, the notion of freedom of speech as a privilege restricted to the aristocratic elite was still prevalent in the mid-1800s. The progressive spread of freedom to broader and lower social classes resulted from the economic and political emancipation of the bourgeoisie which, at the end of the seventeenth century and during the eighteenth century, brought about the first institutions of the public—"those social places that are exceptionally important in everyday life for the formation of an opinion of the public: 'the salon' and 'the pub;' both of them sites for meetings of a reflecting, discussing, cleverly chatting, and politicizing 'world'" (Tönnies 1922, 202). Freedom of thought, speech, and press are liberties that have been enacted by the bourgeois revolutions as expressions of "the fight of the new-bourgeois, the national-bourgeois class that positions itself as a 'public'—and very often as the 'people,' or the 'nation'—for power, i.e., first for participation in the power of old classes and the monarchy which it restrains, and later increasingly for independent power" (Tönnies 1922, 128). By strengthening the power of the bourgeois class, civil liberties also strengthened and became a "universal good" with the Enlightenment idea of the people as the ultimate source of sovereignty, in contrast to former conceptualizations of the people as subjects or servants of the government. The ruling class could not deny the subordinate class those political rights it obtained by fighting for itself "without hitting itself into the face," as Tönnies claimed.

The first powerful ideas of intellectual liberty were created by great philosophers of the seventeenth century. Milton's defense of freedom of publication in the *Areopagitica* (1644), though it evoked little response at the time of its publication in several dozen copies (see Alvis 1999, xii), became, together with the two centuries younger John Stuart Mill's essay *On Liberty* (1859), probably the most often cited justification for freedom of expression and publication in English literature. Milton argued that the press should be freed from authoritarian constraints such as the licensing of book and newspaper printing, which would help attain the "utmost bound of civil liberty," that is, favorable conditions assuring that "complaints are freely heard, deeply considered, and speedily reformed" (1644/1999, 4). He pleaded for an unlicensed printing because licensing, like the Inquisition of the Roman Catholic Church, "hinders and retards the importation of our richest Marchandize, truth; nay it was first establisht and put in practice by Antichristian malice and mystery on set purpose to extinguish, if it were possible, the light of Reformation, and to settle falsehood; little differing from that policie wherewith the Turk upholds his *Alcoran*, by the prohibition of Printing" (1644/1999, 37).

Milton's response to those who believed that reading uncensored books might cause severe harm to the people was that, in order to prevent any harm without fail, "all human learning and controversy" must be removed from the world, including the Bible. To censor all books and pamphlets would not be sufficient, since "evil manners are as perfectly learnt without books a thousand other ways which cannot be stopped, and evil doctrine not with books can propagate" (p. 20). Thus licensing only printing is inconsequential, unless all "recreation and pastimes delightful to man" are licensed as well—music, dancing, lecturing, traveling, or conversing. But even without such an extension beyond printing, the execution of the licensing order in the country would need numerous learned and judicious men "above the common measure" as licensers to avoid any mistakes and injuries. One could hardly imagine that men of such qualities would be willing to lose their time for such tedious and unpleasant work, was Milton's contention; thus "we may easily foresee what kind of licencers we are to expect hereafter, either ignorant, imperious, and remisse, ore basely pecuniary," so that licensing would obviously miss the intention.

Areopagitica, one of the classics of liberal thinking, is a plea for freedom to publish, requiring the revocation of licensing and censorship of printing because they suppress personal freedom to *think* and to *choose*. Milton argued that the reason which God gave to human beings is but *choosing*; thus he would never "praise a fugitive and cloistered virtue, unexercised and unbreathed, that never sallies out and sees her adversary." The virtue of individuals must be freely and continually tested in trials, where contrary experiences and opinions are confronted. "Assuredly we bring not innocence into the world, we bring impurity much rather; that which purifies us is trial, and trial is by what is contrary." Books are most appropriate means "to the trial of virtue and the exercise of truth" (p. 24). The good and the evil, the virtue and sin, truth and error have always coexisted. Truth can only prevail over error if both are put to the proof in a free discourse, and a "pure" human virtue can only develop when different and opposing opinions are tolerated, when freedom to choose exists. We should be allowed to read any books we want and judge them ourselves according to individual conscience. Each and every book may be of different worth to different users; "a wise man will make a better use of an idle pamphlet, than a fool will do of sacred Scripture" (p. 20). And there is no reason, Milton argued, to deprive a wise man of any advantage he might get from a book.

> Since therefore the knowledge and survay of vice is in this world so necessary to the constituting of human vertue, and the scanning of error to the confirmation of truth, how can we more safely, and with less danger scout into the regions of sin and falsity than by reading all manner of tractates, and hearing all manner of reason? And this is the benefit which may be had of books promiscuously read. (p. 18)

This is also Milton's argument against the objections that it would be foolish to allow people to expose themselves without necessity to *temptations* and to *waste their time*: not to *all* men "such books" are temptations or vanities! In conclusion, he compared the power of truth with that of God: "For who knows not that Truth is strong, next to the Almighty? She needs no policies, nor stratagems, nor licensings to make her victorious; those are the shifts and the defences that error uses against her power" (1644/1999, 46). Censorship and licensing only indicate mistrust in the strength of truth, but when truth and falsehood grapple, "who ever knew Truth put to the worse, in a free and open encounter?"

The right to freedom of thought and speech as conceived by Milton was directed against the arbitrary princely power and particularly against religious intolerance (yet not to be granted to Roman Catholics). While Milton accepted the general maxim of the Protestant religion that Scripture is the rule of faith, he emphasized that "no man, no synod, no session of men, though called the church, can judge definitively the sense of scripture to another man's conscience" (1659). Yet he did not declare the need of a *general* "liberty to know, to utter, and to argue freely according to conscience, above all liberties"

(1644/1999, 44); he mainly asked such freedom for himself ("Give *me* the liberty"), and within the boundaries of "neighbouring differences, or rather indifferences . . . whether in some point of doctrine or of discipline, which, though they may be many, yet need not interrupt the unity of Spirit," but not for those tolerating "popery, and open superstition, which, as it extirpates all religions and civil supremacies, so itself should be extirpate" (1644/1999, 47). Milton's enthusiastic idealism was essentially an aristocratic doctrine—full of admiration for ancient Greece and idealization of the aristocratic republic—and not at all a universal affirmation of human rights. In the last instance, his defense in favor of free publication rests on moral and intellectual superiority of the elite, of the *gentlemen.* "For libertie hath a sharp and double edge fitt onelie to be handl'd by just and vertuous men, to bad and dissolute it becomes a mischief unwieldie in thir own hands" (1648/199, 453). In this perspective, Milton's idealism does not seem far from freedom in Hegel's sense, which can only be achieved by the moral individual who aspires to a rational ideal—which according to Hegel cannot be realized in the "state of nature," where "the spiritual is submerged by mere nature," but only within the state (Hegel 1821/1971, 162).

Hegel was influenced by another seventeenth-century thinker, one of the most prominent and pervasive precursors of the Enlightenment, the Dutch philosophical rationalist Benedict de Spinoza (1632–1677). He gained considerable reputation with his *Tractatus Theologico-Politicus* published in 1670. In it he examined the laws contained in the books of Moses. His rationalism and pantheism, in more detail presented in his most important work, *Ethics* (published in 1677 after his death), aroused great resentment among Jewish, Catholic, and Protestant theologians. Anticipating controversy after he had been excommunicated in 1656, he published the *Tractatus* anonymously. In *Tractatus*, Spinoza defended the liberty to philosophize against religious or political interference and argued that no one can or need transfer all his rights to the sovereign power—notably his freedom of expression which, if materialized in rational discussion, fosters human intelligence. He argued against entrusting political authority to ecclesiastics because that presents a permanent danger for religion to be transformed into a dogma. The last five chapters of *Tractatus* also include an exhaustive study of the foundations of the state, and a discussion of the natural and civil rights of individuals, and the rights of the sovereign power.

Spinoza's advocacy for political and religious tolerance in his *Tractatus Theologico-Politicus* (1670/1883) set up the critical direction of thought that prevailed—despite its condemnation by the Reformed Church in 1673—in the following centuries and influenced the thinkers of Enlightenment. From the postulate that "every man is by indefeasible natural right the master of his own thoughts," which implies his freedom of judgment, Spinoza derived the conclusion that "the men thinking in diverse and contradictory fashions" is an unavoidable fact (1670/1883, 258). Thus it is a natural consequence that "in a Free State every man may Think what he Likes, and Say what he Thinks," as he entitled the last chapter of the *Tractatus*. Governments should not be allowed to control human minds, since it would represent an abuse of sovereignty and a usurpation of the rights of subjects. The questions of "what shall be accepted as true, or rejected as false, or what opinions should actuate men in their worship of God . . . fall within a man's natural right, which he cannot abdicate even with his own consent" (p. 257). To impose uniformity of speech and to force men "to speak only according to the dictates of the supreme power" would represent a tyranny against nature and a calamity both for the state and for the individual, which would be perhaps accepted by "the avaricious, the flatterers, and other numskulls, who think supreme salvation consists in filling their stomachs and gloating over their money-bags," but always resisted by those "whom good education, sound morality, and virtue have rendered more free." Spinoza's arguments are clear: laws against freedom of opinion would affect "the generous minded" but not criminals, which would represent a great peril to the state. Moreover, such laws would also be useless because "those who hold that the opinions proscribed are sound, cannot possibly obey the law" (p. 262); thus such a law would be only a privilege for those who reject the opinions as false.

> If formal assent is not to be esteemed above conviction, and if governments are to retain a firm hold of authority and not be compelled to yield to agitators, it is imperative that freedom of judgment should be granted, so that men may live together in harmony, however diverse, or even openly contradictory their opinions may be. We cannot doubt that such is the best system of government and open to the fewest objections, since it is the one most in harmony with human nature. In a democracy (the most natural form of government, as we have shown) everyone submits to the control of authority over his actions, but not over his judgment and reason; that is, seeing that all cannot think alike, the voice of the majority has the force of law, subject to repeal if circumstances bring about a change of opinion. (Spinoza 1670/1883, 263)

While expressing his view on freedom of expression in the strongest possible terms in the title of the last chapter of the *Tractatus* and the text immediately following, Spinoza came down to limitations to the general rule. He admitted the possibility of an abuse of freedom of speech; "but what question was ever settled so wisely that no abuses could possibly spring therefrom?" While he acknowledged the danger of criminal libel, he stressed the significance of "positive law" that should ensure rather than restrain human freedom, as almost two centuries later Karl Marx would say. Not everything can be regulated by law; such unjustified efforts might rather bring about malignance instead of suppressing it. Legal laws have to follow, or derive from, *natural* laws, not annihilate them. Spinoza pragmatically believed that "it is best to grant what cannot be abolished, even though it be in itself harmful." If a number of bad habits and evils are tolerated, he wrote, such as luxury, envy, avarice, and drunkenness, because they cannot be effectively prevented by law, why not freedom of thought and speech—if it were considered a defect. And since it is even not a vice but a virtue "absolutely necessary for progress in science and the liberal arts," so much more it should be legally protected. Such a pragmatic spirit would be later typically manifested by John Locke in his psychological justification of the need to "make us more busy and careful to inform ourselves than constrain others," to be receptive of antithetic ideas and tolerant to the opponents if we want to *maintain peace*, which he considered a "state of nature" rather than war. Since most of the time we cannot be convinced for most of our thoughts whether they are right or wrong, and we cannot expect that others would quit their opinions and accept ours, we simply have to admit a necessary diversity of opinions and accept to leave in "mutual charity and forbearance," Locke claimed in his *Essay Concerning Human Understanding* (1690, 4, 16:6). Similarly to Milton and Spinoza, Locke made a difference between the better educated and the ignorant: the latter must acknowledge that they are incompetent to prescribe their opinions to others, whereas the former "would have a juster pretence to require others to follow them."

According to Spinoza, the true aim of government is liberty—it is not supposed "to rule, or restrain, by fear, nor to exact obedience, but contrariwise, to free every man from fear, that he may live in all possible security; in other words, to strengthen his natural right to exist and work—without injury to himself or others" (1670/1883, 259). As it was commonly the case in the seventeenth and eighteenth centuries, Spinoza believed in the right of any sovereign power to impose "any commands he pleases" because it is very unlikely that a sovereign would impose completely irrational commands. Even if he promotes primarily his own interests, he also has to act according to "the dictates of reason" and consider the public good in order to retain his power. Freedom of speech is not only harmless to the rights of rulers but also necessary for their preservation. In contrast to a slave or a child, a subject obeys the commands of sovereign power willingly because they are not only in the interest of the master but are given for the common interest, which includes interests of all subjects or the whole body politic, regardless of the nature of government. However, Spinoza clearly advocated democracy as "the most natural form of government," which is most consonant with personal freedom. In democracy, according to Spinoza, the individual does not transfer his natural rights to the government "so absolutely that he has no further voice in affairs, he only hands it over to the majority of a society, whereof he is a unit" (p. 206).

Individuals have to abdicate their right to act entirely on their own judgment and transfer their rights (but never *all* individual's rights) to the sovereign power in order to preserve peace in society. Social peace would be
threatened if everyone acted only according to his free judgments—which
may be very diverse and often mutually exclusive, yet everyone would believe only his judgment to be right. Thus individuals have to cede the right
of free action to the sovereign power, but not the right of free thought and
expression if it is grounded in reason. "The individual justly cedes the right
of free action, though not of free reason and judgment; no one can act
against the authorities without danger to the state, though his feelings and
judgment may be at variance therewith; he may even speak against them,
provided that he does so from rational conviction, not from fraud, anger,
or hatred, and provided that he does not attempt to introduce any change
on his private authority" (p. 259). If the power of free judgment is withheld
from individuals, this is a clear deviation from the "natural condition of
mankind" and a dangerous approach to a tyrannical government.

If the rulers have the right to restrain and control "acts" because they are
capable of offending," that is not true of opinions. The authorities may force
people to act in contradiction to what they believe to be best, and bring
them to trial because of their seditious actions, but they should not be allowed to tyrannize over their opinions; they have to allow every person to
think what he likes and to say what he thinks. Although Spinoza believed
in the "natural right" of the individual to speak (but not *act*) even against the
government, such a right should be limited in order to prevent injury to the
authority of the sovereign power and public peace. The fact that no "inconveniences" arise from freedom of speech that cannot easily be checked
represents Spinoza's final argument for the legal protection of the natural
right of free speech. However, an unlimited concession of free expression
would be undesirable on the ground that in some cases "authority may be
as much injured by words as by actions." The line between tolerable and intolerable opinions is defined by the demand of new rights in the state or actions contrary to the existing laws.

> [If a man] submits his opinion to the judgment of the authorities (who, alone,
> have the right of making and repealing laws), and meanwhile acts in nowise
> contrary to that law, he has deserved well of the state, and has behaved as a
> good citizen should; but if he accuses the authorities of injustice, and stirs up the
> people against them, or if he seditiously strives to abrogate the law without their
> consent, he is a mere agitator and rebel. (p. 20:24)

According to Spinoza, all the power of legislation that affects actions
should rest entirely with the sovereign power because "it is the function of the
sovereign only to decide what is necessary for the public welfare and the

safety of the state, and to give orders accordingly" (p. 249). Thus all those opinions which "by their very nature nullify the compact by which the right of free action was ceded" to the sovereign power represent a significant exception to Spinoza's postulate that only acts but not opinions are capable of offending and thus punishable: though they are only opinions, *seditious libel* is liable to punishment. Opinions that do not involve acts violating the contract, such as revenge or anger, may also be seditious, but only if they are in some "corrupt state," by which Spinoza denotes "superstitious and ambitious persons, unable to endure men of learning, [being] so popular with the multitude that their word is more valued than the law." As a general rule, he suggests not seeking to regulate every possible exception to the general freedom by law because that would more likely arouse the corruption than suppress it, while keeping in mind that freedom of thought and speech "is absolutely necessary for *progress in science and the liberal arts.*"

Similarly to Milton and Spinoza, John Locke (1632–1704) published writings immediately after the Revolution of 1688 that had a significant influence on the development of the liberal theory of the press, particularly in the American colonies. Locke, too, zealously propagated a personal right to free expression with the argument that "liberty of conscience is every man's natural right" (1689/1996). He argued against governmental licensing of newspapers, but at the same time, and similarly to Milton and Spinoza, demanded prosecution of expression that might threaten social order.

Like other libertarian writers of the seventeenth century, Locke did not see any contradiction between the principles of freedom of the press and its liability. He opposed press licensing but admitted that "no opinions contrary to human society, or to those moral rules which are necessary to the preservation of civil society, are to be tolerated by the magistrate" (1689/1996). Locke believed that all men had to be freed from all domination over one another, but his principle of toleration—that "every man may enjoy the same rights that are granted to others"—did not imply freedom for atheist expression. He was not a Deist who would allow denunciation of the Christian revelation; he only attempted to rationalize it. While he insisted that not all religions are equally "true," he also demanded that no church and government could judge on this; thus divergence in religious beliefs ought to be tolerated. Nevertheless, he was not particularly broad-minded when defining "opinions contrary to human society," for he only allowed toleration of those "practical opinions, though not absolutely free from all error, if they do not tend to establish domination over others, or civil impunity to the Church in which they are taught," which implied that there should be no toleration for those "who deny the being of a God," nor for the Roman Catholics because of their claim to supremacy in secular matters.

The principle of toleration formulated by Matthew Tindal (1657–1733), the author of the "Deists' Bible," *Christianity as Old as the Creation* (1730), was much more radical. It was based on his Deist conviction, critical of both Roman Catholics and Protestants, that fanaticism was no less an enemy to religion than infidelity was. Tindal, who could be regarded as the founder of the *natural-right* theory of freedom of the press, in essence followed Milton's and Locke's ideas; what was novel, however, was his deep concern for the press, rather than personal freedom of expression. He argued that "a restraint press is inconsistent with the Protestant Religion, and dangerous to the Liberties of Nation"(1698/1974, 3) because it tends to make men blindly subordinate to the religion they have been educated in without choosing it; it prevents them from seeing and examining different opinions and arguments, which is needed to discover truth and to inform one's own judgment; it hinders truth from having any great influence on human minds; or in the case that we nevertheless recognize the truth, it tends to make us feel blameworthy because of that. Tindal concluded that "Whosoever therefore endeavours to hinder Men from communicating their thoughts (as they notoriously do that are for restraining the Press) invade the *natural Rights of Mankind*, and destroy the common Ties of Humanity" (p. 7). He agreed, however, that freedom of the press should not be misused for publishing "atheism, profaneness, immorality, sedition, and treason." Yet the appointment of "licensers," while violating the press freedom, does not solve the problem; instead, as Tindal suggested, the most effective way to prevent publishing such ideas would be "to make the laws against such things severer, and to oblige either the printer or bookseller to set his name to all books whatever" (p. 18).

Libertarian and rationalist ideas propagated by Milton, Locke, and Spinoza inspired generations of critical philosophical and political thinkers of the Enlightenment. Most of them also followed their view of a necessary borderline between tolerable and intolerable opinions, which actually—though neither intentionally nor directly—also legitimized censorship as an instrument to protect the sovereign power of the state. Locke, Milton, Spinoza, and their followers believed that freedom (of speech) was inseparable from responsibility. If peace and security in society would be challenged, for example, then a person's right to express and publish opinions had to be subordinated to "higher values" and restrained accordingly.

Seventeenth-century liberal-rationalist ideas on freedom of expression and publication generated two different intellectual currents in following centuries. On the one hand, the intellectual inheritors fostered the ideas of free press in the framework of *protective democracy* (see Held 1987, 36–71). With utilitarianism the idea of freedom of expression and publication has been instrumentalized in publicity as a means to hold governors accountable to the governed. On the other hand, the idea of freedom of expression and publication, which proceeded from the idea of communication as a generic ability and need and thus natural freedom and right of human beings, remained instrumental in the authentic Spinozean sense—as a right of the individual absolutely necessary for *human progress*. The former stream of thought, which conceived of publicity primarily as a means of surveillance, prevailed in the nineteenth century and has been effectively institutionalized with the press as the "fourth estate" or "watchdog." This conceptualization of freedom of the press served as a powerful means, though not always in the hands of the public, of limiting governmental abuse of power. The alternative stream, which was invigorated by the Enlightenment, focused on human generic freedom to communicate and included political philosophers as different as Rousseau, Kant, Marx, and J. S. Mill among others, but it still lacks an authentic institutionalization of its universal principle of publicity mediating between politics and morals, as first defined by Kant. The opposition between these two currents is crucial. The first rests on functions performed by the public and its immediate instrument, the press. The second is derived from the transformation of natural personal right into civil right to communicate, as a realization of generic human freedom, embedded in the press as the common means of individuals to communicate their spiritual existence and participate in collective (and particularly political) life, which is determinative of everyone's personal and social identity.

IMPOSING "FUNCTIONS" ON THE MEDIA

Constitutive of classical social theory emerging in the nineteenth century were attempts to include *normative* elements. Durkheim emphasized that norms, which represent a framework for human life and social order, form a continuum from uncodified norms such as those of etiquette to the fixed norms of written law. Social norms are internalized through the process of socialization, but also imposed by (the threat of) external sanctions ranging from informal criticism to legal edicts. The norms constituting a complex normative order not only are part of the empirical world that social theorists seek to understand and explain, and perhaps predict, but also inevitably affect the ways social theories conceptualize their objects of study. To use Calhoun's words, "Since to theorize is to open up vistas of understanding, it can never be altogether neutral; it is necessarily *perspectival*" (Calhoun 1996, 437; emphasis added).

Normative principles represent key elements of social theories, but these principles are often tacitly assumed rather than explicitly stated. Such is the case of social functions of the media, which have been in the very heart of theory and research since the earliest communication studies. The idea of "universal functions" of communication and the media is reflected in a number of early media theories. In his famed 1948 essay, Harold D. Lasswell maintained

that three universal functions of communication exist in society—the surveillance of the environment, the correlation of the parts of society, and transmission of social heritage—which supposedly have analogies in every "vital entity." In another celebrated paper published in the same volume, Paul F.
Lazarsfeld and Robert K. Merton differentiated between "social functions" (status conferral, enforcement of social norms) and the narcotizing "dysfunction"
(1948/1971, 560). They considered both types of functions universal: they "can
be ascribed to the mass media by virtue of their 'sheer existence,'" for example, they are not dependent on "varying systems of ownership and control."
Peterson, Jensen, and Rivers (1965) were among the first to recognize that
functions of the media go beyond "natural" existence and are grounded in
"theoretical assumptions." They identified six social functions of the press under "libertarian theory"—public enlightenment, servicing the political system,
safeguarding civil liberties, profit making, servicing the economic system, and
providing entertainment. In contrast, "social responsibility" theory assigns
functions to the mass media as obligations emanating from their constitutionally guaranteed freedom. Thus it accepts the "traditional" functions defined by
the libertarian theory, but it hierarchializes them: the tasks of servicing the economic system, providing entertainment, and making profit should be *subordinated* to higher tasks of public enlightenment and promoting democratic
processes.

The latter example indicates that functions are neither naturally given nor
universal but *externally assigned* to a process or agent, and thus observer
relative; they are held hostage by the conditions under which they were developed at different times in different social settings. The notion of "function" commonly refers to the consequences of a given set of empirical phenomena or their characteristics; it is focused on the relationship between an
element (part) and the whole (society); it implies the existence of a (social)
system, which to some degree is always subjectively determined in terms of
purposes, goals, and values. Since function is (in contrast to the causes of social phenomena) always external to natural processes (or generally to
processes independent from the observer), it has a normative dimension: it
implies a *goal*. The *relative* relevance of specific functions becomes obvious
when the concepts of latent or *unintended* (unconscious) functions are introduced in contrast to manifest or *intended* ones (Merton 1949/1993, 330),
and *dysfunctions* in contrast to functions (Lazarsfeld and Merton 1948/1971).
In both dichotomies, the main principle of differentiation is the normative
desirability and *intentionality* of consequences resulting from communication processes. Desirability and intentionality are *variable* in time and across
cultures on both individual and societal levels, not to mention their dependence on political ideas and norms. In this perspective, "function" may become a deontological category—a *duty* to be carried out by the media: all actions are supposed to be done in accordance with their duties, and the media

are expected to refrain from actions that are recognized as inconsistent with their duties.

A systematic search for the consequences of a given set of social phenomena needs to be complemented with causal and historical analysis. Based on the methodological reasoning first developed in the realm of biology, functional analysis commonly assumes that whatever persists in society is indispensable or utile for its normal working, but it suppresses that this is a valid assumption only inasmuch as an agreed version of "normal working" of society exists. In practice, however, there are always different versions of "normal working" that are in competition with each other. It is too often neglected that the notion of a specific function (e.g., functions of mass communication) result from culturally determined empirical observations and individual or group expectations based on the experiences with a specific media system. While functional analysis is not interested in historical developments, the concept of function itself may be used to redirect attention from the question of whether a certain type of behavior or action attains the purpose of the actor to ranges of consequences not designed or anticipated by the actors, and to "alternative" functions. For example, freedom of the press is largely believed to be a functional prerequisite—a *conditio sine qua non*—to the maintenance of democracy in any society. Yet such a proposition turns attention away from alternative "functional prerequisites" by arguing that only freedom of the press is an indispensable institution to communicatively maintained democracy, whereas other (either complementary or alternative) historical "forms" of publicness are tacitly assumed to be irrelevant if not "dysfunctional." In fact, it tacitly assumes a set of duties without attempting to justify their universal validity.

Through the idea of *dys*function, communication is situated in the world of human values, norms, and principles according to which systems ought to "function." Principles are the "ought" of any human action, from communication to government. If we talk of "dysfunctions" in contrast to "functions," the difference between them we have in mind is purely normative. Thus the idea of dysfunction clearly reveals that the *normative* component is actually fundamental to the notion of function: we can only distinguish between a function and a malfunction if the (actor's or observer's) *goal* is clearly defined. For example, economic functions of the media were "refunctioned" into malfunctions by *some* observers because they saw them incongruent with the general (preferred) *goals* assigned to the media systems in democratic societies. This was perhaps best exemplified by Joseph Pulitzer's defense of freedom of the press in 1904 when he wrote that "commercialism, which is proper in the business office, becomes a degradation and a danger when it invades the editorial rooms. Once let a publisher come to regard the press as exclusively commercial business and there is an end of its moral power" (in Peterson et al. 1965, 111). Despite Pulitzer's warning, later markedly pronounced by Dewey, the "commercial dys/function" outgrew in practice the "functions" of the press. Habermas's critique of the fall of public/ness half a century later (1962/1995) again sets forth the importance of a *normative ideal of publicness* as *the* goal to be reached by the media, and also points to the Kantian principle of publicity *(Öffentlichkeit)* as *the* blind spot in theorizations of media functions in democracy.

Despite conservative biases often inherent to functional analysis, the notion of function still seems useful—in fact, inevitable—for our analysis. As McQuail (1994, 78) argues, a functional analysis "offers a language for discussing the relation between mass media and society and a set of concepts which have proved hard to escape from or to replace." In contrast to McQuail, I don't see the usefulness of functional theorization in specific "main functions" of the media in (for) society, such as those suggested by Lasswell (1948) and Wright (1959). What is more important is how these functions are socially construed. By "function" I mean the performance of a system or its component to attain an effect congruent with the defined goal. Thus functions are not "inbred" characteristics of the media; rather, they depend on, and are defined by, users and observers; they are never intrinsic (they do not exist in an object or "natural fact" irrespective of the human context) but always observer relative (Searle 1995, 14). Whereas a functional analysis mostly focuses on certain *indispensable* functions for the system to survive, my analysis is aimed at "functional equivalents," namely, culturally specific communicative functions alternative or supplementary to such a specific concept as "freedom of the press," and at the historical embeddedness of the system itself in which specific functions are assigned to the media. In contrast to biology, where "functions" are usually taken as if they were natural, no such thing as "natural" function exists in relations among human beings. Searle defines this difference as the difference between "brute facts" and "institutional facts."[13] Essentially, "institutional facts" are always social constructs; they require a system of human institutions for their very existence (Searle 1995, 27) because they are meaningful only within such an institutional setting. As soon as we enter the field of institutional facts, functions may become contested on the ground that questions of goals and purpose are value-laden and thus immanently political and subject to controversy.

Social control is not an intrinsic function of the press. Neither are the "standard" four functions imposed on the media by Lasswell and Wright. In the fourth estate model of the press, the main function attributed to the press is the control of all actions performed by power actors; this normative goal of the press ought to be attained provided that the press is being free. The function has sense only in a specific social context. It is believed that the agents of power have to be controlled since they would use its power in an inappropriate way (e.g., against the common interest) without an external control, and that freedom of the press contributes to a more effective control over the agents of power, thus securing their social accountability. This is not (just) a causal relationship between freedom (of the press) and control (over powers) since it is implied that the latter is a goal that persists even if freedom of the press fails to "induce" control over power agents. Nevertheless, in the long run, a systematic failure of "free press" to enforce responsibility on agents of power may transform its status in a dysfunctional one or contribute to the transformation of the system in which the fourth estate is a functional component.

In general, as Searle (1995, 94–95) indicated, the creation of a status function (the function that, when assigned to an entity, changes it status) is always a matter of conferring some new power. And indeed, by imposition of the function of the fourth estate on the press, the press attained an unprecedented power.

Fundamental in the historical shift from libertarian to social responsibility theory of the press is the substitution (or at least revision) of the guiding principle(s) and aims of media operation. The idea of *autonomy* from any "outside" (nonmarket) interference as the basis of press freedom, which generates media power according to the principles of commodity production, was challenged by the idea of *responsibility*. In the most general sense, responsibility refers to the concern of a human actor with *consequences* of his or her own actions, which should conform to *guiding principles*[14] in society. Whereas the importance of guiding principles is explicitly present in the notion of responsibility, it is hidden in the pure libertarian understanding of media freedom, thus seemingly providing a universal validity to its claims. Paradoxically, both theories evolved around the same central idea(l)—that of *publicness*. However, in the course of history the principle of publicness obtained two (at first glance disparate) meanings: one refers to personal freedom (or right) to form, express, and publish opinions; the other denotes the social need to prevent or hinder abuses of power. In the former sense, publicness refers to "mental, in the exchange of symbols achieved openness between larger or smaller entities of social body"[15] (Schäffle 1875); the principle of publicness is functional as long as it stimulates individuals' participation in a rational public discourse. In the latter sense, the function of publicness is to expose actions that (may) have important consequences for those not taking part in them, to external control. In present-day discussions about democratic potential of the Internet or computer-mediated communication in general, the former concept of publicness refers to the idea of "electronic democracy" with individual rights and freedoms in its center, whereas the latter, much more restrictive meaning is present in the notion of "electronic government" aiming to achieve a (more) responsible "democratic" government.

As with many other social institutions, we usually take the institution of freedom of the press simply for granted, not thinking about how it is (or has been) socially construed. For the present discussion, it is not important whether this institution has been developed on the basis of sheer conscious practice performed by individual journalists and editors, or its evolution has been subsidiary to the awareness of the collective intentionality and/or theorization.[16] It is important, however, to note that theoretical grounding helping the institution of freedom of the press to emerge has not necessarily made it valid.

Since public/ness typically relates to human transactions, it would be a mistake to assume that any historical meaning of it is more than specific. Freedom of the press in eighteenth-century England does not mean the same as freedom of the press in the twenty-first-century United States. The notion of the press as the fourth estate/power was a valid concept and legitimate form of the institutionalization of the principle of publicity in the period when newspapers emanated from a new (bourgeois) estate or class: the press had a different source of legitimacy than the three classic powers, and it developed as a critical impulse against the old ruling estates. Yet later on, with the growth of the press into a branch of industry and commerce, the power/control function of the press that relates to the need of "distrustful surveillance" defended by Bentham, definitely abstracted freedom of the press from the Kantian quest for the public use of reason as an individual's personal right. As a consequence, "the absence of publicly relevant mind has come to mean that powerful decisions and important policies are not made in such a way as to be justified or attacked; in short, debated in any intellectual form. Moreover, the attempt to so justify them is often not even made" (Mills 1956/2000, 355). As I will argue in chapter 4, in democratic societies where the people rather than different estates should legitimize all the powers, the control dimension of publicness embodied in the corporate freedom of the press should be effectively supplemented by actions toward equalizing private citizens in the public use of reason.

Early debates on freedom of the press pointed toward the idea of publicness as a *moral* principle and an extension of *personal* freedom of *thought* and *expression*, which ought to restrain self-interest of individuals, rather than a mere pursuit of self-interest based on a sort of contractual exchange. With the constitutional guarantee for a free press in parliamentary democracies, discussions of freedom of the press were largely reduced to the pursuit of freedom *by* the media, thus neglecting the idea of publicness as the basis of democratic citizenship. Such an unjustified slide from the universal principle of publicity and citizens' freedom to express and publish opinions to the right of the media to access to information and freedom to print it, however, brings a danger of transforming the media into an autonomous power on their own merits and jeopardizes their task to serve the public.

NOTES

1. The verb *publicirn* (in this form) first appeared in German in 1472, from the Latin verb *publicare,* and meant "to publish." The "publicist" is a person who is engaged in public issues, particularly those related to public law, and as an author presents his or her political beliefs (Noelle-Neumann and Schulz 1971, 11).

2. Throughout this book, the adjective "personal" refers to the individual human being or natural person; it does not include corporate "legal persons."

3. The Western history of communication ideas is still extremely Eurocentric and completely neglects all "non-Western" history. For example, part of the "Dark Age" of the seventh to the eleventh centuries in Western history was the "Golden Age" in the Islamic community. The Umayyad (661–750) and Abbasid (750–861) regimes marked the most prosperous and most productive periods in the entire Islamic history of the Middle East, when rulers supported arts and sciences and protected and sustained scholars and artists of all kinds. Perhaps the greatest contribution that the early Abbasid caliphs made to Islamic humanities and scholarship was their encouragement of the translation of several important Greek books into Arabic. See Ayish 1998.

4. Milton entitled his pamphlet after Areos Pagos, a court in ancient Athens composed of about three hundred members elected by the citizens of Athens who met on a hill named after the god Ares, next to Parthenon. Although the pamphlet was subtitled as "A Speech of Mr. John Milton for the Liberty of Unlicenc'd Printing, to the Parliament of England," it was actually never delivered before Parliament.

5. In E. P. Coleridge's translation the passage is worded differently: "Freedom's mark is also seen in this: 'Who hath wholesome counsel to declare unto the state?' And he who chooses to do so gains renown, while he, who hath no wish, remains silent. What greater equality can there be in a city?" The Internet Classics Archive, classics.mit.edu/Euripides/suppliants.html

6. In contrast, for example, the Islamic legal system based on the Qur'an (seventh century) included from the very beginning the principle of freedoms and rights recognized in the Western world only much later, such as the rights to know, to choose belief and behavior, to read and write, the right to power, and even the right to choose government. The Qur'an also proclaims that news and knowledge have important consequences, which may be injurious to individuals, groups, or societies; thus freedom of expression is counterbalanced with responsibility. According to the Qur'an, news has to be verified: "O ye who believe! If a wicked person comes to you with any news, ascertain the truth, lest ye harm people unwittingly, and afterwards become full of repentance for what ye have done" (Qur'an 49:006)—and not damaging to any one's reputation (Qur'an 49:011,012). News must also provide benefit (*Nafa'*) to the people (Qur'an 13:017). See Hamada 2001 for more details.

7. Strictly speaking, Gutenberg's invention of the printing press was not an "invention," since the first movable type appeared in China four centuries before Gutenberg.

8. In Germany, for example, freedom of the press was constitutionally guaranteed as late as 1919, but in practice it was considerably limited. Even in the Weimar Republic, laws enacted to protect the republic actually limited freedom of the press.

9. Even normatively, however, such a "right" has never existed; in empirical terms, it would be even difficult to speak of "freedom of publicistic activity" as individual freedom. As Habermas writes a few pages later (1992a, 455), what actually exists in modern democracies is constitutional regulation of the "fourth power," which only determines whether the media depend more on one kind of agents of power or another; basically, they are controlled either by political or commercial actors.

10. Ross emphasized the difference between *social* and *class* control, the latter being "the exercise of power by a parasitic class in its own interest" (1901/1969, 376).

11. Tönnies's term *Gesellschaft* is usually translated as "society," but I agree with Turner that "association" would be more appropriate, or at least less confusing. See Turner 1996, 17.

12. In contrast to the rather technical meaning of journalism referring to the workforce in institutionalized forms of (*mass*) *communication*, the Greek concept of journalism, δημοσιογραφία (*demosiografia*), means "writing about/for the people" and is focused on the social substance of journalism by emphasizing people rather than a particular class, or nature. Since *demos* means more than population but *citizenship*, journalism implies political relevance, which indeed was its most significant common trait until very recently.

13. "Brute facts exist independently of any human institution; institutional facts can exist only within human institutions. Brute facts require the institution of language in order that we can *state* the facts, but the brute facts *themselves* exist quite independently of language or of any other institution. . . . Institutional facts, on the other hand, require special human institutions for their very existence. Language is one such institution" (Searle 1995, 27).

14. In a general conceptualization of media responsibility, sources of information, subjects of media discourse, and audiences (publics) represent three main categories of social actors to be respected by the media, and to whom the media are responsible.

15. Schäffle equated publicness *(Öffentlichkeit)* with the unity of consciousness *(Bewusstseinseinheit)*.

16. As in many other cases, the imposition of functions on objects may proceed from false beliefs. "As long as people continue to recognize the X as having the Y status function, the institutional fact is created and maintained. They do not in addition have to recognize that they are so recognizing, and they may hold all sorts of other false beliefs about what they are doing and why they are doing it" (Searle 1995, 48–49). As Searle points out, this may imply beliefs such as that "money is backed by gold," or that "marriage is sanctified by God," or that "the Constitution is divinely inspired." Whereas the maintenance of the institution does not depend on whether the assumptions on which the imposition of functions is based were/are true or false, the question of validity of assumptions is fundamental in "deconstructing" the concept of an institution. An instance of great significance is ideology, which can have a major role in the evolution of an institution. It is precisely the question of validity of assumptions that enables us to look at alternative institutions, which could possibly develop because of changed assumptions.

2

Free Press for Social Control: From Bentham to American Pragmatists

THE IDEA OF SEPARATION OF POWERS AND THE PRESS

The terms *fourth estate, fourth power,* and *watchdog,* often used as *cognomina* or nicknames for the mass media, suggest that social functions of the media refer to the exercise of power and control in society and reflect the general significance of the relationship between (political) power and the media. In *The Fourth Estate,* one of the earliest English books on the press, Frederick Knight Hunt came to the conclusion that

> the power and value of the Press have made it a fourth estate. . . . By the value and fidelity of these various services . . . the Newspaper has earned its power and its position; has grown with increasing years, and strengthened with increasing rectitude, until it has received the cognomen, and wields the power of a FOURTH ESTATE. (Hunt 1850, vii, 8)

The notion most closely connected with the doctrine of Charles Montesquieu's *The Spirit of the Laws* (1748), that freedom is not possible where the powers of the state are not kept strictly separated, is that of the media themselves as another, the fourth power. The concept of the fourth power aligns the media with the executive, legislative, and judiciary powers of the state. Thus Hunt could have argued for England that "he who, speculating on the British Constitution, should omit from his enumeration the mighty power of public opinion, embodied in a free press, which pervades and checks, and perhaps, in the last resort, nearly governs the whole, would give but an imperfect view of Government of England" (Hunt 1850, 6). Hunt also argued that "it is the Newspaper that secures that publicity to the administration of the laws which is the main source of its purity and wisdom."

From the theoretical point of view, the idea of the press as the fourth power partly reduced the paradox in the idea of the separation of powers, which to some theoreticians appears incompatible with the democratic principle. It was seriously criticized by Hegel, who believed that the idea of separation of powers "contains the fundamental error that they should check one another. But this independence is apt to usurp the unity of the state, and unity is above all things to be desired" (Hegel 1821/2001, 242). Similarly, though for more practical reasons, Bentham (1776) regarded the idea as inefficient and nonviable; he trusted parliament with the omnipotent legal sovereignty and the people with the ultimate political sovereignty. Bentham's critique may be seen as well founded in Montesquieu's own ideas about the foundations of political freedom in individual safety and the absence of fear: "The political liberty of the subject is a tranquillity of mind arising from the opinion each person has of his safety. In order to have this liberty, it is requisite the government be so constituted as one man need not be afraid of another" (Montesquieu 1748/1966, bk. 11, 6).

In the eighteenth-century Britain that Montesquieu chose as the model for his doctrine of the separation of powers, the powers had *different sources of political and social legitimacy*: the legislative legitimacy was founded on the people's will, the executive fostered by the legitimacy of the dynasty, and the judges were connected with the tradition of the nobility incorporated in the House of Lords and the judiciary. Since the equilibrium established through the "separation of powers" was based on conflicting interests of three different estates, and the press as a capitalist nonstate enterprise and an "organ of public opinion" differed from them in terms of sources of legitimacy, it actually represented an important and effective form of control over the three prebourgeois branches of power. This was not the case with later republican governments, such as those in France and the United States, since all the branches of government had the same source of legitimacy—the people. In a system of "equipoise . . . between three powers, the ministry, the House of Commons, and the people" the press remained the only power that was not "in touch with people, who sit as arbiters" (Bryce 1888/1995, 254)—a power not responsible to the people.

Whereas the concept of the separation of *powers* refers to the institutional level, the triad of *estates* refers to the sociological level (see table 2.1). An alternative sociological account of the eighteenth-century "estates" in France is much more centered around the rising bourgeoisie, based on the analysis of social structure. In the eighteenth-century sense of the French term, *bourgeois* primarily means simply "citizen of a city," but special uses of the adjective (e.g., a bourgeois house) and examples of the adverb also "evoked a certain way of life: 'He lives, he speaks, he reasons *bourgeoisement*. At noon, he dines *bourgeoisement*, with his family, but well and with good appetite.'"[1] Bourgeoisie represented *l'état second*, the second estate, following the first

Table 2.1. Mass Media as the Fourth Power and Fourth Estate

Power/ Estate	Institutional Level of Power (Sources of Social and Political Legitimacy)	Sociological Level of Estates (Classes)
1. Legislative	People's will	Commons
2. Executive	Legitimacy of dynasty	The king
3. Judicial	Tradition of nobility	Lords
4. Mass media	Capital	Middle class

estate, which consisted of the clergy. While the traditional typology differentiated between the clergy of first estate, the nobility of second estate, and the remaining majority of population in third estate, the bourgeois-centered typology excluded the former first estate altogether. The nobility—consisting primarily of those who acquired nobility as owners of state offices rather than feudal nobles—was elevated to the rank of "first estate." "Second estate" consisted of the bourgeoisie—magistrates, professionals, merchants, and those who lived from their revenues (rents and annuities) without having any particular profession, and was usually considered "the most useful, the most important, and the wealthiest in all kinds of countries. It supports the first [estate] and manipulates the last according to its will."[2] Finally, the "third estate" included the common people—workers or labor force, as we would call them today. In contrast to France, in Germany of the early nineteenth century, the "fourth estate" *(der vierte Stand)* denoted peasants (see Marx 1842a/1974), who in provincial assemblies joined heads of princely families and representatives of nobility and towns.

William A. MacKinnon was perhaps the first who "deduced" the idea of the public entirely and directly from the bourgeois class defined primarily in terms of wealth. Like Bentham, MacKinnon drew a distinction between three social classes which, in his case, were entirely based on wealth because "where freedom and civilization exist, wealth is so entirely the only power either to individuals or to government, that no other means or choice is left of distinguishing the several classes of society, than by the property of the individuals of which they are formed" (MacKinnon 1828/1971, 2). Using statistical criteria, MacKinnon divides society into (1) the upper class, consisting of those who "have the means of constantly supporting one hundred, or any greater number of men, fit for labour," (2) the middle class, consisting of those individuals who are able to "support" from two to one hundred working men, and (3) the lower class, which consists of all others. Historically, public opinion was seen to be created only when the following five fundamental conditions are met: (1) the increase of the power of machinery, (2) communication (transportation) facilities, (3) proper religious feeling, (4) the spread of information through society (e.g., improved systems of education, the press), and (5) the amount of capital. All of these conditions were linked to the development and relative growth of the middle class and, to a lesser degree, of the upper class, the size of which was strictly limited in "free countries" by the growing middle class.

MacKinnon was the first to attempt to formulate certain sociological "rules" of the formation of the public and public opinion. He emphasized that the power of public opinion primarily depends on the proportion that the *upper* and *middle* classes of society bear to the *lower class*. The size of the middle and upper class population relative to a smaller lower class matches "the quantity of intelligence and wealth that exists in the community" (p. 15), which is essential for public opinion to develop. Following Burke's distinction between "the people" and "the public," MacKinnon differentiated between "popular clamour" and "public opinion." The former is powerful in proportion as the lower class is ignorant and numerous and relies on the ignorance and prejudice of the uneducated, whereas the fundamental characteristic of the latter is that it is well-informed and intelligent, and formed by "the best informed, most intelligent, and most moral persons in the community, which is gradually spread and adopted by nearly all persons of any education or proper feeling in a civilized state" (MacKinnon 1828/1971, 15). Theories of public/ness from Burke to MacKinnon attributed sovereignty to the public as the materialized form of the principle of publicity,[3] yet the public has always been limited by the competence of individuals and thus to the minority of competent individuals, and efficiently institutionalized into the political system of the bourgeois legal state.

In the "power" perspective, the idea of the press as the fourth power refers to the notion of different sources of legitimacy. As the fourth power, the press pertains to the totality of legislative processes; in addition, it corresponds, perhaps more accidentally than intentionally, to a new momentum, radically different from all the earlier sources of legitimacy—to the *power of capital*. In the "estate" perspective, the traditional Anglo-Saxon notion of the fourth estate might point to the fact that newspapers emanated from a new— the "middle," predominantly bourgeois—class. Yet the bourgeoisie-centered categorization of estates in English and French did not leave any room for a "fourth estate," as distinguished from the three primary estates, that would dispose of any power.

Such a metaphor would only become sensible with Marx's and Engels's typology of social classes, centered around the *proletariat*, "recruited from all classes of the population" and gradually empowered. Once "slaves of the bourgeois class, and of the bourgeois state," proletarians were increasingly seen as the true revolutionary power: "The other classes decay and finally disappear in the face of modern industry; the proletariat is its special and essential product" (Marx and Engels 1848/1998, 45–47). Marx used the term "fourth estate" to denote the "non-bourgeois urban estate" (1842a/1974). However, the fourth estate metaphor referring to the press had been coined already at that time, with no reference whatsoever to the working class/estate. More importantly, Marx's vision of the press was quite the opposite: he praised the mental "power" of the press against material—political and economic—powers.

In comparison with the concept of the fourth estate/power, the watchdog concept of the press is the most generalized idealization of a (possible) *function* of the press in society—its acting on behalf of the public to bring to its attention any political, economic, or administrative *abuses* of power. Hunt (1850, 7) praised the newspaper as "a daily and sleepless *watchman that reports* to you every danger which menaces the institutions of your country, and its interests at home and abroad" (emphasis added). Such an understanding of a "unique social role" of the press was particularly in the interest of publishers, who "argued that newspapers required special protections under the freedom of the press because the institution of the press had a duty to gather and report information about the operation of the government and other matters of public interest. They claimed that the press held unique newsgathering and news disseminating abilities" and, consequently, they expected the law to recognize an "institutional right to freedom of the press" and special protection for the press in libel law (Gleason 1990, 4).

The main difference between the "power" and "watchdog" concept of the press refers to the relation between the institutional press and the government. While both concepts are structurally embedded in a polyarchal environment, their functions in relation to other "estates" or "powers" and audiences differ. The "watchdog" concept assumes nonpartisanship of newspapers, which ought to gather news and report it objectively to their readers, thus making the public believe it has access to government information through the press—an idea sharply in contrast to the practice of the press in the eighteenth and nineteenth centuries, which published not only news but also opinions and commentaries. The notion of the "fourth power/estate" does not imply such an idealized (tacit) assumption; it primarily stresses trustworthiness of the press as the basis on which its "power" is generated regardless of whether the press is partisan or not.

If the terms fourth estate, fourth power, and watchdog (or watchman) do not have exactly the same meaning, they still have at least two significant traits in common.

First, they give preference to the concept of *press freedom* as a corporate or institutional right over personal *freedom to publish* as declared, for example, in the French revolutionary Declaration des droits de l'homme et du citoyen of 1789.[4] Even if the media are not understood as part of the elite, a clear distinction is made between the media and the public, or the general population. Since exercising and controlling power at the same time was seen as contradictory and even impossible, the people seemed to be the natural control on authority (Burke), but in practice that function was "delegated" to the public as the "representative of the people," and eventually—since the late nineteenth century—to newspapers as its generalized "organ." Burke computed that in England and Scotland

> those of adult age, not declining in life, of tolerable leisure for such discussions, and of some means of information, more or less, and who are above menial dependence (or what virtually is such), may amount to about four hundred thousands. There is such a thing as a natural representative of the people. This body is that representative; and on this body, more than on the legal constituent, the artificial representative depends. This is the British public; and it is a public very numerous. The rest, when feeble, are the objects of protection; when strong, the means of force. (Burke, *Selections*)

In some propositions of the press as the fourth estate/power, public opinion was considered to be *embodied in a free press* (Hunt). The "embodiment" of the surveillance function—which originally pertained to the public (or public opinion)—in the press represents a further step closer to devaluation of the principle of publicity. A Benthamian idea of a "watchdog" *public*, with the public as the agent of control over the state powers, is quite an insignificant departure from the individual-based right of expression and publication compared with the idea of "watchdog" *press*, which institutionalized the transfer of controlling power from the individual, or the collectivity of individuals (the public), to the press.

Second, all three concepts refer to autonomy of the media from control, and their power to control other (state) powers, but ignore the question of who controls the controllers. As a matter of fact, the press is given more freedom than is granted to individuals by the freedom of expression principle. None of the three concepts is related to *responsibility* or accountability of the press, which assumes that "the motive for these beneficial acts [of the media] is located either with the civic virtue of the journalists or in the commercial value of such journalism" (Sparks 1995, 52). Yet the press is supposed to be legally protected in performing its (assumed) *functions for society*, such as *newsgathering*, which are considered obligations and responsibilities (e.g., to *provide news* to the public) of the press emanating from its constitutionally guaranteed freedom.

It is not only that with the concept of freedom of the press as the fourth estate, more freedom is granted to the corporate entity than to the individual. An obvious symptom of the one-sidedness of the fourth power/estate concept is also hidden in the fact that it "makes" the press (or mass media in general) as an agent of power comparable (and to some degree competitive) to the forms or branches of *state* (political) power only.[5] Yet mass communication obviously involves wider areas of competing interests and powers. In addition to the three classic branches of power, which represent the center of political system connected with the "rest of society" through complex networks of communication, including mass media, at least five distinct *classes of interest* in the mass media can be identified: (1) media owners' interest in using their media as a means of self-expression and profit maximization; (2) the general interest of capital to advertise commodities on an ever larger scale; (3) demand from audiences for media uses; recipients' interest in receiving information and opinions; (4) various civil society groups' interest in having access to the media to publish their opinions; (5) a general (ethical) interest of citizens in maintaining the citizen rights and in the media performing their public service functions. At least the first two categories of "nonstate powers" are able to materialize their interests, which they historically did very effectively—*through* the press. Justice Potter Stewart stated that "the free press guarantee is, in essence, a structural provision of the Constitution . . . The publishing business is, in short, the only organized private business that is given explicit constitutional protection" (quoted in Gleason 1990, 10). It is easy to understand that Justice Stewart's thesis has never been sustained by the U.S. Supreme Court.

The questions of "separation of power(s)" between the economic sphere and the state, as well as within the economic sphere itself, are no less relevant for freedom of expression and publication than the separation of "classic" ruling powers. Commercial impediments to citizen freedom of expression and publication of opinions are no less critical than political obstacles. It is commonly justified that a "free marketplace of ideas" or a "media marketplace" can, although they are not perfect, best serve the variety of interests among audiences, but it is hardly ever pointed to the fact that the idea of the free marketplace rests on a number of false assumptions (Splichal 1999, 291–92). Despite the popularity of the idea, particularly in the U.S. Supreme Court, the "marketplace of ideas" lacks of any sound definition; it basically means the "free flow of ideas" but alludes to economic forces behind the "free flow"—a generalized idea of laissez-faire economics. Early dissertations on freedom of expression and freedom of the press either did not refer to economic conditions of a free press or considered economic interference functionally equivalent to the political one. In the age of Enlightenment, the principle of publicity and the public use of reason were not subordinate but *opposed* to the economic sphere and its dominant right of private ownership, which led Marx to conclude that "the primary freedom of the press is in not being a business" (1842a/1974, 71).

With the expansion and convergence of the media fostered by new communication technologies, and the rise of critical understanding of the relationship between media and society, the fourth power/estate concept has run into severe difficulties related to the social and political implications of power and responsibility. A central issue in contemporary debates surrounding the notion of the fourth power/estate is the problem of (the absence of) *accountability*, which raises questions of the functions of the media in relation to the public, whose interests the media should ideally serve and act as its "organ," the relationship between the media and other branches of power, and relations of power within the media themselves. The fourth estate/power model "emancipates" power of the media from responsibility and reduces audiences to passive consumers. The press not only became an independent participant in the political process; it is also given more freedom and less responsibility than individual citizens are. In contrast to the public's right to know, "the right of the press" to have access to information—which is supposedly justified by the people's right to know (Gauthier 1999, 197)—has no counterpart in *legal* obligations; the press is only *morally* obligated to be responsible to the public, and therefore it is *privileged*.[6] Its legal responsibility is restricted to the *mode of dissemination* of information (and primarily opinion) which of course also applies to citizens. However, in contrast to the media, personal responsibility to know is at least partly *legally enacted* in all democratic systems. For example, citizens have the duty to be informed about all legal matters relevant for their personal *civil* obligations. A legal responsibility to know also applies to the gathering of information that individuals need to carry out their *professional* obligations.

PUBLICITY, PUBLIC OPINION TRIBUNAL, AND THE FOURTH ESTATE

From its first appearances during the Enlightenment, the notion of public/ness had a critical sting; it was directed against the social and political structures of the traditional, premodern, or prebourgeois society and hereditary authoritarian power that, in Tönnies's terms, could be denoted as *Gemeinschaft*. Contemporary meaning/s of the concept/s "public/ness" are controversial on a number of accounts. Most generally, there is a rather obvious contradiction between the normative meaning of "the Public" (Ger. *Öffentlichkeit*) and the empirical meaning of "the Public" (Ger. *Publikum*). The latter concept denotes a specific, empirically measurable social group, usually a "mass," which acts as audience in relation, or consists of a set of individuals exposed to, a communication source or a medium. The normative concept, however, is primarily understood as a sort of "imagined community" of individuals and social groupings concerned with social or political—*public*—issues, resulting from the public nature of their actions. The normativeness of the concept of the public is best presented in the Deweyan understanding of the public/ness as involvement in the regulation of long-term consequences of transactions in which individuals are directly not involved yet seriously affected—to such a degree that a systematic regulation of the consequences is believed necessary (Dewey 1927/1991).

Earlier uses of the two concepts were not (or certainly less) contradictory. In the eighteenth century, the concept of the public as *Publikum* denoted groups of erudite individuals critically discussing primarily literature and art, reading, and occasionally contributing to newspapers. The concept of critique was central to the idea of public/ness and to the ideas of Enlightenment in general, which is clearly expressed in Kant's essay "Beantwortung der Frage: Was ist Aufklärung?" and the series of his books set as "*Critique of . . .*" This critical orientation dominated theoretical and political discourse in Germany at least until the publication of Tönnies's voluminous book entitled *Critique of Public Opinion* (1922).

However, conceptualizations of publicness in *English liberalism* of the eighteenth and nineteenth centuries, which was elaborated by the utilitarian school and its main representative, Jeremy Bentham, did not completely follow the Continental line of thought on publicness. Bentham is the most notable harbinger of the idea of publicness as a form of democratic curtailment of improper behavior of individuals and groups in power. He authored the first systematic discussion of public opinion, which he considered a form of social control, a "system of distrust" constituted as the space of the visible, where primarily political actions and events are (should be) made available to "the public," thus preventing the abuse of power by the legislators and executives. It is largely to Bentham's merit that by the mid-1800s the concept of public opinion gained entry into democratic theories, and at least indirectly Bentham substantially contributed to the construction of the concept of the fourth estate.

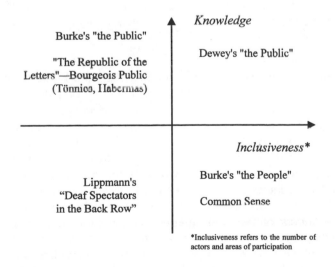

Figure 2.1.   Two Dimensions in the Principle of Publicity Historically Materialized in Different Forms of "the Public/s"

It had been long wrongly believed that Edmund Burke, the principal British interpreter of Montesquieu's ideas of division of power, suggested—as part of his conservative reforms to prevent the British Empire from injustice, disorder, and "political imbecility"—that the press constituted the "fourth estate" in addition to the three political estates—"an inheritable crown; an inheritable peerage; and a House of Commons." The invention of the new concept that dominated the discussions on freedom of the press throughout the nineteenth and twentieth centuries was attributed to Edmund Burke by Thomas Carlyle, who suggested that "Burke said there were Three Estates in the Parliament; but, in the reporters' Gallery yonder, there sat a *fourth estate* more important far than they all" and emphasized that the idea of the fourth estate "is not a figure of speech, or a witty saying; it is a literal fact" (Carlyle 1840/1966, 164).[7] But in fact, Burke never said what Carlyle attributed to him. As Brucker (1951, 30) suggests, the term "fourth estate" was actually first used by Thomas B. Macaulay, who became intensely interested in the ideas of Jeremy Bentham during his studies in the Trinity College in Cambridge in the early 1800s and later turned into the harshest Whig critic of utilitarianism.[8] Carlyle probably cursorily read Macaulay's essay on Hallam's book on the constitutional history of England and misascribed his idea on the fourth estate to Burke. In this essay, Macaulay praised in a rather Benthamian way publication of the parliamentary debates:

> The gallery in which the reporters sit has become a fourth estate of the realm. The publication of the debates, a practice which seemed to the most liberal statesmen of the old school full of danger to the great safeguards of public liberty, is now regarded by many persons as a safeguard tantamount, and more than tantamount, to all the rest together. (Macaulay 1827/1999, 105; emphasis added)

Since in the next sentence Macaulay refers to Edmund Burke's speech on parliamentary reform, Carlyle probably mistakenly ascribed Macaulay's own ideas to Burke. Regardless of this misattributed quotation, the idea of the press as a fourth power would not have been strenuously supported by Burke. Indeed, he was convinced that "to follow, not to force, the public *inclination*; to give a direction, a form, a technical dress, and a specific sanction to the *general sense of the community* is the true end of legislature" (p. 106; emphasis added). But this is not to say that Burke would have supported an idea of the elected political representatives to follow demands and particularistic interest of their constituents: "Statesmen are placed on an eminence, that they may have a larger horizon than we can possibly command. They have a whole before them, which we can contemplate only in the parts, and often without the necessary relations. Ministers are not only our natural rulers but our natural guides" (Burke, *Selections*). When discussing the ministerial responsibility, Burke suggested that those "who have not the whole cause before them, call them politicians, call them people, call them what you will, are no judges." He insisted that the representative had to be accountable to his or her conscience rather than loyal to his or her constituents. Representative democracy excludes "the people" from direct influence on national power. Those in power, once elected, had to be trusted by the people to act in the best interest of the whole and not abuse those trusts; after all, that was the reason they have been elected. This was not to say, Burke argued, that the people would be "degraded" or "enslaved." They must have the right to demand information because "he that is bound to act in the dark cannot be said to act freely," but it is up to governors to decide if people's desires are not at variance with their true interests.

If it was by oversight that Edmund Burke was credited for naming the press as the fourth estate, the ideas of his twenty-year younger contemporary and critic Jeremy Bentham about publicity may be indubitably considered the intellectual foundation of the concept.[9] In a way this may sound paradoxical, as he regarded the idea of the separation of powers as completely inappropriate,[10] and he actually never used the term "fourth estate." Rather, he believed that the Supreme Legislative had to be omnicompetent on the whole territory of the state and in all fields of human action, with the executive (administrative and judiciary) authorities as its *immediate instrument*. "To its power, there are no limits. In place of limits, it has checks. These checks are applied, by the securities, provided for good conduct on the part of the several members, individually operated upon" (Bentham 1830/1983, 41–42). Nevertheless, Bentham (1791/1994) was the first to conceptualize the rule of publicity as the foundation of the doctrine of the sovereignty of the people and public opinion. In contrast to Locke's "laws of the commonwealth" or the "laws of opinion or reputation" (1690) as a sort of mutual social control—the "power of thinking well or ill"—which "by a secret and tacit consent, establishes itself in the several societies, tribes, and clubs of men in the world,"[11] Bentham's *Public* Opinion Tribunal is "enacted" as the supreme *control over government*.

In one of his earliest essays on parliamentary democracy, Bentham defined publicity as "the fittest law for securing the public confidence" and a necessary precondition "for putting the tribunal of the public in a condition for forming an enlightened judgment," and argued that political institutions had to be founded upon the principle of publicity as the basis of a "system of distrust" (1791/1994, 590). Central to Bentham's idea of surveillance of all the actions of the legislature was *public opinion* or, as he named it in the *Constitutional Code*, the Public Opinion Tribunal rather than the press alone. He saw publicity as the "central characteristic and indispensable instrument" of the Public Opinion Tribunal (1822/1990, 28), and the press an "instrument of publicity and public instruction." More specifically, he considered "*Newspaper* . . . not only an appropriate organ of the Public Opinion

Tribunal, but the only constantly acting visible one" (p. 45), whose editor is, however, "but one member amongst millions" (p. 57).

Bentham's idea of surveillance in his writings on parliamentary democracy differs from his ideas of surveillance in *Panopticon* (1787/1995). In the design of inspection house, his interest was focused on how to bring *large numbers of people* under permanent surveillance of the few by making them "not only suspect, but be assured, that whatever they do is known, even though it should not be the case." Publicity, however, does not need to *assure* anyone of surveillance since it is clearly visible and those who are exposed to surveillance take an active part in publicity.

Bentham's conceptualization of publicity was part of his defense of representative democracy as the only form of government that would serve the public interest and not misuse its power—a danger that comes from the fact that governors do not deal with their own affairs, but with the affairs of others, and their personal interests may be in opposition to the interests confided to them. Bentham treated the government as constantly exploiting opportunities to promote "sinister," partial interests. As he argued, "such is the nature of man when clothed with power—in that part of the field of government which is here in question, whatever mischief has not yet been actually done by him to-day, he is sure to be meditating to-day, and unless restrained by the fear of what the public may think and do, it may actually be done by him to-morrow" (1820, Letter I).

Like John Stuart Mill after him, Bentham rejected any conception of the separation or balancing of powers as the means to attain good government. The fundamental principle in Bentham's democratic theory was that liberal government could not be a weak government. Rather, he believed that the legislative function must exercise *absolute, all-comprehensive,* and *unlimited* power. He endorsed the complete legislative sovereignty of the political assembly (parliament) and the ultimate political sovereignty of the people; only in this way could the interest of government be in accord with the public or general interest. An enlightened public opinion ought to ensure government's responsibility. Instead of limitations to the legislature, Bentham prescribed "checks" consisting of institutions that would force the representatives in the assembly to promote the public interest. Since public opinion was the only "power" not included in government, it was "the only force therefore from which the force of government when operating in a sinister direction can experience any the least impediment to its course" (Bentham 1822/1990, 121).

Bentham's idea of society was that of community composed of individuals pursuing each his separate interest—he considered driving forces of human behavior only personal interests and motives—which together with the prevention of the conflict between legitimate interests ought to be secured by the legislator. Public (or popular) opinion represents in his early theory one of the three powers influencing human behavior, in addition to the law and religion, as sources of pleasure and pain of the individual in any society. These three powers—by which alone a man can ultimately be forced to do what is to be done—he named "sanctions" or "obligatory powers"—"the political sanction, operating by the rewards and penalties of the law; the religious sanction, by those expected from the Ruler of the Universe; and the popular which he characteristically calls also the moral sanction, operating through the pains and pleasures arising from the favour or disfavour of our fellow-creatures" (Bentham 1781; see Mill 1838/1859). The notion of sanctions as the "means of control" was later resumed by Edward A. Ross, who differentiated between "the sanctions of *opinion*, the sanctions of *intercourse*, and the sanctions of *violence*," which all are used by "Public Opinion" (Ross 1901/1969, 89), but primarily not in the direction suggested by Bentham, which I will discuss in the next section.

Bentham's main concern in his public opinion theory was in securing that all transactions in the political assembly would be subject to the surveillance by the public. He saw the main benefit brought about by publicity in providing information about public issues, primarily those discussed by authorities to the public, rather than in its contribution to enlightened judgments formed in a rational *discussion* by members of the public. His principle of publicity is primarily related to a *system of distrust* because he believed that "every good political institution is founded upon this base." John Stuart Mill (1838/1859) argued that of the three great questions Bentham has posed about government—"to what authority is it for the good of the people that they should be subject? . . . how are they to be induced to obey that authority? . . . by what means are the abuses of this authority to be checked?"—he was really interested only in the third one.[12] That is why a Foucaultian reading of Bentham focusing on distrustful surveillance is at least as accurate as a Habermasian emphasis on rational discourse. Habermas's suggestions that Bentham "conceived of the parliament's public deliberations as nothing but a part of public deliberations of the public in general," and of publicity as securing "critical political debate" (Habermas 1962/1995, 100) do not truly reflect Bentham's conceptualization of publicity and public opinion. As Gaonkar and McCarthy (1994, 559) suggest, Bentham's ideas on publicity and disciplinary technology for regulating legislators are "remarkably similar to the disciplinary technology elaborated in *Panopticon* for regulating the body of the prisoner,"[13] which Bentham compared in his letter to Brissot with a "mill for grinding rogues honest, and idle men industrious" (Stephen 1900). Although the similarity of surveillance *methods* (aimed at visibility of the object under surveillance) in two different spheres—politics and disciplinary institutions—is "remarkably similar," there exists a fundamental difference in terms of the source and direction of control. In the political sphere the method of surveillance is used to enable control of the majority of the population over the

minority of elected representatives; in the case of *Panopticon* it is aimed
at controlling large numbers of people in an institution by a limited number
of professional keepers. Besides, Bentham did not consider publicity only
as a means of control, nor did he reduce the role of public opinion to the
function of surveillance. We should not ignore Bentham's discussion of the
functions of the Public Opinion Tribunal: his list included not only "statistic" ("evidence-furnishing") and "censorial" (referring to judgments of dis/
approbation)[14] functions of public opinion, but also "executive" and, notably,
"melioration-suggestive" functions (1830/1983, 36–37), which suggest that
new ideas about what could be done, "a conception of something better,"
should be notified to "those whom it may concern," with the aim to bring the
idea into practice. Thus, public opinion not only has the function of surveillance but also that of *innovation*.

Compared with later theories of public opinion, Bentham's idea of Public
Opinion Tribunal as a sort of generalized social context of individual members of society could be identified in Robert Park's theory. According to Park
(1904/1972, 81), public opinion is the shared insight individuals gain
through criticism and the resulting explanation of the "collective drive" that
to some degree always retroactively influences the public. As in Bentham's
tribunal, public opinion has no existence outside reciprocally communicating individual members of Park's public. Public opinion is generated by individuals and it only exists in the mind of individuals, and as such it is able
to influence an individual opinion.

> It is a mistake to view public opinion as one which is acceptable to each indi-
> vidual member of the public to the same degree. It is much more an opinion or
> an attitude which is external to every individual and which is viewed as some-
> thing objective. Precisely because public opinion is seen as the product of indi-
> vidual critical attitudes, *it expresses itself variously in different individuals.*
> (Park 1904/1972, 59; emphasis added)

The *panoptical* perspective could be more accurately attributed to Bentham's notion of *publicity* than to *public opinion,* since the former comprise
dimensions of general visibility and accessibility, with indeed the primary
function to enable an efficient control over authorities and prevent them
from (temptation to) abuse of their power. The universality of the rule of
publicity is clearly stated in *Panopticon*, where Bentham indicated that the
"inspection principle" is not only applicable to limited physical spaces in
which a number of individuals can be kept under inspection, but also to
what nowadays would be named "virtual" communities or "imagined"
spaces, where everyone, including inspectors themselves, could be in-
spected by "the tribunal of the world." In fact, an effective application of the
inspection principle extends from penitentiary houses to society as a whole,
and "publicity" may be seen as one of its instruments:

I take for granted as a matter of course, that under the necessary regulations for preventing interruption and disturbance, the doors of these establishments will be, as, without very special reasons to the contrary, the doors of all public establishments ought to be, thrown wide open to the body of the curious at large—the great *open committee* of the tribunal of the world.[15] And who ever objects to such publicity, where it is practicable, but those whose motives for objection afford the strongest reason for it? (Bentham 1787/1995, 47–48)

Similarly, publicity of actions and discussions in political assembly should enable an efficient control by a "great open committee"—later named the Public Opinion Tribunal—over elected representatives to prevent them from the misrule, together with the four other political reforms he proposed: annual parliaments, virtually universal suffrage, equal suffrage, and secrecy of suffrage. The secrecy of suffrage serves the same purpose as publicity of political institutions—to promote the public interest against private ones. In contrast to open voting, where electors could be threatened or bribed by the candidates, the secret ballot makes such threats impossible. Consequently, electors would express their own will instead of being misused by the will of others. As Bentham argued, the voter's natural tendency would be to vote in a way that advanced his particular interest. However, he believed that the candidate for a political assembly who promised to advance particular interests would certainly not get electoral support. Only the candidate's promise to represent common interests of the electorate would potentially attract electors.

As *secrecy of suffrage* is a fundamental condition for the promotion of the public interest by the representatives, *publicity of actions of public functionaries* is a necessary condition to the same goal. Representatives in a political assembly have a *moral* obligation to keep their promise to promote the public interest, and the *legal* system enables electors to "punish" the representatives who would fail to do it with dismissal from office at the next elections—provided that the public obtained information about their misconduct. Bentham believed that this should be "a sufficiently hard punishment to prevent the assembly, under normal conditions, from conspiring to promote its own sinister interest" (cited in James 1981, 55).

Publicity Should Prevent Misrule and Ensure People's Happiness

Bentham's notion of publicity as the "public eye" is essentially a *regulatory* one: it ought to be implemented as a mechanism of distrustful surveillance. His idea that publicity itself should be regulated comes as a matter of course; in a sense, then, while publicity is a means to regulate human actions that exist independently of publicity, regulatory rules are constitutive for the publicity itself. Consequently, Bentham designed an efficient system of control over the parliament, which included four methods to make all actions of the parliament public, and specified the cases that ought to represent exceptions to the rule of publicity. The public workings of the parliament ought to be guaranteed through four methods: (1) authentic publication of the transactions of the assembly, (2) keeping the minutes of all speeches, questions, and answers, (3) toleration of "non-authentic publications" (e.g., unofficial journals), and (4) admission of strangers—but not women[16]—to attend the meetings of the assembly. His claim that all decisions by authorities ought to be made public includes the publication of "the number of votes on each side," (i.e., a clear indication of the strength of the *opposition)*, as well as "the name of the voters." The latter is not just a matter of control—in order to prevent the members of the assembly from absenting from sessions—but also helps the public determine "the quality of votes." It is not only the number of votes but also their quality that influences opinions at large. Bentham's conception of publicity also provided a defense of selective administrative intervention to minimize potential detriments. Publicity ought to be suspended if it favored enemies, injured innocent persons, or indicted "too severe a punishment upon the guilty" (Bentham 1791/1994, 591).

Fundamental to Bentham's idea of publicity is its function to assure *the greatest happiness of the greatest number of people*, which is Bentham's principal axiom for measuring the right and the wrong. As a utilitarian, Bentham reduced all human experiences to pleasure and pain, maintaining that the only function of the state was to increase pleasure and reduce pain; publicity should be completely subordinate to those aims. Specifically, publicity should (1) help constrain the members of the assembly to perform their duty, (2) secure the confidence of the people and their assent to the measures of the legislature, (3) enable the assembly and the governors to know the wishes of the governed, (4) enable the electors to act from knowledge (e.g., in choosing their representatives in the assembly), (5) provide the assembly with the means of profiting by the information of the public, and (6) generate the amusement that by itself increases the happiness of the people (1791/1994, 581–86). The first two reasons listed by Bentham instituted his striking idea of establishing a social system in which "the whole nation has been spectators" into the sphere of politics.

The principal organ or outlet to secure control over those in power was *the public*. Newspapers (e.g., the publication of parliamentary debates in them) were considered only an element in the "surveillance system," and only in Bentham's later works were they operationalized as an autonomous and the most important organ of the Public Opinion Tribunal—the idea fully and enthusiastically adopted by the prophets of freedom of the press as the fourth estate after Bentham's death. Bentham considered the public "a sort of imaginary tribunal" that, however, "is more powerful than all the other tribunals together" (1791/1994, 581). Its power results from its incorruptibility, its permanent tendency to become enlightened, its wisdom and justice, which make its punishments unavoidable. These are not the qualities any (political) assembly can have, because the parties included cannot be impartial to exercise the true function of judges. The internal "censure" secured by the opposition in the assembly cannot prevent from dishonesty, but only the "external censure"—the public. Wise and honest men would never try to escape from it because they have nothing to fear; yet those who have immoral intentions are righteously afraid of the Public Opinion Tribunal. On the other hand, publicity assures an assembly of public confidence:

> Suspicion always attaches to mystery. It thinks it sees a crime where it beholds an affectation of secresy; and it is rarely deceived. For why should we hide ourselves if we do not dread being seen? . . . The best project prepared in darkness, would excite more alarm than the worst, undertaken under the auspices of publicity. (Bentham 1791/1994, 582)[17]

Bentham compared publication of parliamentary debates with memoirs, which represented the most "profound" books; yet publication of debates in newspapers far exceeds the usefulness of books, because it is *immediate* and *available* to a great number of those interested in the debates. He found publicity so favorable in many respects that he concluded: "One of the Roman emperors proposed a reward for the individual who should invent a new pleasure: no one has more richly deserved it, than the individual who first laid the transactions of a legislative assembly before the eyes of the public" (Bentham 1791/1994, 586).

Indeed, as Bentham believed, publicity was the remedy for misrule and the means to achieve people's pleasure and happiness. Publicity, or as Bentham put it in a more operational way, "the number of the persons to whom on each occasion the appropriate information is notified," determines the "power of public opinion," which Bentham considered in his later works as "the only check that can be applied to the power of arbitrary government" and, at the same time, an "indispensable supplement" to the beneficial government (1822/1990, 129; 1830/1983, 36). In contrast to later critics of a "tyranny of unthinking majority," such as Tocqueville, J. S. Mill, and Bryce, Bentham believed that the maximization of public distrust and suspicion of legislative and executive (administrative and judiciary) authorities would definitively prevent any misrule by the governors. In the *Constitutional Code* he claimed:

> Public Opinion may be considered as a system of law, emanating from the body of the people. . . . Even at the present stage in the career of civilization, its dictates coincide, on most points, with those of the *greatest happiness principle*; on some, however, it still deviates from them: but, as its deviations have all along been less and less numerous, and less wide, sooner or later they will cease to

be discernible; abberation will finish, coincidence will be complete. (Bentham 1830/1983, 36)

The Public Opinion Tribunal was designed to be a public court but also a sort of legislative body creating *moral* obligations. Although Bentham saw the Public Opinion Tribunal in the same relation to the "Supreme Constitutive" as was the relation of the judiciary toward the Supreme Legislative—as the main check of its power, he did not consider this relationship a simple control of the majority over the rulers. Rather, the effectuation of control is an interactive process that primarily depends on the will of the rulers: "Able rulers lead [public opinion]; prudent rulers lead or follow it; foolish rulers disregard it" (p. 36). Bentham's attitude is remarkably similar to what Edmund Burke wrote half a century earlier, that "to follow, not to force, the public inclination; to give a direction, a form, a technical dress, and a specific sanction to the general sense of the community is the true end of legislature" (Burke 1967, 106), and to MacKinnon's (1828/1971) maxim that in a "civilised country,"[18] the government has to be governed by public opinion and must follow its dictates because it would be an error to imagine that the government can command public opinion, apart from shorter periods of despotic governments.

Bentham's position was not as paternalistic toward the people as Burke's, but he would basically agree that, "as to the detail of particular measures, or to any general schemes of policy [the people] have neither enough of speculation in the closet nor of experience in business to decide upon it" (Burke 1967, 219). We can easily see Bentham to be agreeable to Burke's belief that there ought to be some influence from the elected to the electors, but certainly not with the idea that the elected "should not dutifully serve, but [they] should basely and scandalously betray the people, who are not capable of this service by nature, nor in any instance called to it by the constitution," which Burke "deduced" from what only those "who are very ignorant of the state of every popular interest" would not know, namely that there is always "some leading man . . . who is followed by the whole flock" (pp. 219–20).

Unlike Burke, Bentham argued that not only the people's happiness increased with publicity, but also the elite, the minority consisting of upper and middle classes—the realm entirely dominated by men, especially men of property—was directly gaining from publicity. The question of whether publicity is beneficial or injurious primarily pertains to the elite—to those (elite) members of society who judge and direct public opinion.

[I]f this class judge ill, it is because it is ignorant of the facts—because it does not possess the necessary particulars for forming a good judgment. This, then, is the reasoning of the partisans of mystery: "You are incapable of judging because you are ignorant; and you shall remain ignorant, that you may be incapable of judging." (Bentham 1791/1994, 587)

Consequently, more informed opinions of the elite would also direct opinions of the less learned segments of the public and make them "more correct." In this way, "the order which reigns in the discussion of a political assembly, will form by imitation the national spirit" (p. 583). Keeping the public separate from information about parliamentary debates would represent a vicious circle, which would perpetually prevent the public (and the people) from reasoning. Therefore Bentham believed that even if "I should concede, that in the mass of the public there may not be one individual in a hundred who is capable of forming an enlightened judgment . . . it would not appear to me to have any force against publicity" (p. 586).

In his critique of William Blackstone's *Commentaries on the Laws of England*, Bentham conceded that in the majority, while "there is likely to be a want of wisdom," this could not disavow the fact that "The greater part being poor, are, when they begin to take upon them the management of affairs, uneducated: being uneducated, they are illiterate: being illiterate, they are ignorant . . . they have no leisure to reflect. Ignorant therefore they continue" (1776). He admitted that the largest part of the public consisted of those who can hardly occupy themselves with public affairs because they have no time to read and reason (1822/1990, 58). On the other hand, it may well be that members of the aristocracy, the minority, "are at leisure to reflect, as well as act. They may therefore naturally be expected to become more knowing, that is more wise." However, it would be important to know what is the reason for such a difference, and Bentham argues that it is "greater opportunities of acquiring the qualification of experience" in aristocracy, which is not a consequence of a "characteristic nature" of its members, but purely accidental.

In his later works Bentham maintained that, while the majority of people were not as skilled and competent to reason as aristocracy, they were wise enough at least to choose those for their representatives who would best look after the interests of the electors. Moreover, he suggested that all the four functions he ascribed to the Public Opinion Tribunal—statistic, censorial, executive, and meliorative-suggestive—might be exercised by "every person, elector, inhabitant, or foreigner." Nevertheless, Bentham did not equate the Public Opinion Tribunal with the people at large, but only with those who were able to "take the cognizance of the question" under discussion—which was mainly the middle or bourgeois class. In the *Constitutional Code* Bentham even criticized "the stupid ignorant patience of the people" who tolerated the misrule.

As a matter of principle, Bentham believed that the people as the supreme rulers would not select their representatives or "agents" from their own kind, but from the relatively higher social classes, because they would realize (for the reasons discussed above) that in this way their interests would be better cared for. Their political representatives would discuss issues and propose decisions with the best intention to promote the fundamental utilitarian principle—to achieve the greatest happiness of the greatest number of the people. In these actions, the representatives would not act as mere representatives of the electorate, but according to their own understanding of what is right and good for the people, thus also as a sort of educators. Bentham was clearly aware that there might be, at least occasionally, a substantial difference between what would be considered the right solution or decision by the representatives, and the will of their constituents. On such occasions, the duty of the representatives would be to try to convince the constituents and to change their opinion in the first place. If this failed, the representative should publicly argue for his proposal; and

> after *speaking* in *support* of an arrangement, which in the opinion of his Constituents, is contrary to their particular interest, he gives his vote *against* that same arrangement,—in such conduct there is not any real inconsistency. By his *speech*, his duty to the *public* is fulfilled; by his *vote*, his duty to his Constituents. (Bentham 1830/1983)

Bentham argued that his pragmatic solution of the conflict between the reasoned opinion and national interests defended by the representative, and the partial opinion and particularistic interest of the constituents was both ethical and congruent with the majority principle. Since the national interest is for Bentham nothing but an "aggregate of several particular interests," his calculation was simple. If the representative voted for the national interest against the particular interest of his constituents, that would not change the outcome, since the national (= majority) opinion would prevail anyway. If, however, he voted against the national interest in favor of his constituents, that again would not change the outcome if there was a true national interest supported by the majority. Thus in either case his *vote* could not change the outcome. Consequently, as Bentham believed, the action taken by the representative is only a matter of *sincerity*, and he saw his solution as perfectly sincere.

Bentham's pragmatic (almost naive) reasoning about moral questions is not at stake here. What this piece of Bentham's discussion clearly indicates is his distinction between *the public* (or the Public Opinion Tribunal) and the *constituency*: the former is an imagined intellectual community consisting of those individuals communicating on a relevant issue; the latter is merely a physical aggregate of passively coexisting individuals (citizens). Despite his democratic trust in the power and reason of citizens, Bentham's conceptual difference between the public and the people reminds us of the widespread belief at that time, which attributed the rise of the public to the bloom of the middle class. Similarly to Edmund Burke, Bentham did not proclaim the view that all individuals have an (equal) ability to use reason. Burke argued that among 8 million people in Great Britain in the last quarter of the eighteenth century—"those of adult age, not declining in life, of tolerable leisure for such discussions, and of some means of information, more or less, and who are above menial dependence"—only 400,000 citizens constituted a "natural representative of the people," which was the "British public" (Burke, *Selections*). In the same way Bentham distinguished three segments of the public: (1) the most numerous class is formed by those who can hardly occupy themselves with public affairs because they "have not time to read, nor leisure for reasoning,"[19] (2) those who borrow judgments from others because they are not able to form opinions on their own, and (3) the elite—those who are able to judge for themselves (Bentham 1822/1990, 58). The latter—those "by whom actual cognizance is taken of the matter in question in the first instance"—represent the "Committee" of the Public Opinion Tribunal; those who join their publicly expressed opinions form "the body of public opinion at large," which may consist of any number of members up to the total number of members of society (p. 121).

This comparison of Burke and Bentham indicates that Bentham saw the composition of the public and the capability of the people to reason in a rather Burkean way, but not so its relationship to government and its educational openness to lower classes. The belief that legislators ought to act as a sort of "elected educators of the people" (Steintrager 1977, 109), as this was part of their role to act in the people's best interest, was commonly shared in Bentham's times both in Britain and in Continental Europe (e.g., Kant, Hegel). It was also commonly believed that an unequal distribution of wealth and property was necessary for economic development, and the rise of the public was seen as intrinsically rooted in that process.

In Bentham's view, the Public Opinion Tribunal consisted of all "auditories" at meetings and assemblies dealing with political questions, and all individuals "taking, for the subject of their speeches, writings, or reflections, any act or discourse of any public functionary, or body of public functionaries belonging to this state" (1830/1983, 36). Although Bentham did not directly relate the formation of "enlightened judgement" to a general rational (critical) discussion in the public, such an idea is to some degree implied by his polemics against those who tried to invalidate the "régime of publicity." He argued against the belief that the public could never become a competent judge in the matters of politics because it depended too much on the ignorance and passions of the majority of those who compose it, and pointed to the fact that incompetence is the consequence of the *lack* of publicity.

Bentham identified several reasons for objections and prejudices against publicity. First, the governors may wish to act without responsibility and to withdraw their actions from public inspection; even more, they may want to keep the people in subjection by their ignorance. Nevertheless, such clearly immoral motives (which nobody would defend in public) could be ascribed only to a minority of those in power, and there was no need for Bentham to polemize with them. Thus he concentrated on "specious objections" that tried to justify delegitimization of publication of the proceedings of a political assembly by arguing that (1) the public is an incompetent judge, (2) publicity may expose members of the assembly to hatred, (3) the desire of popularity may lead to the abuse of publicity with the intention of seduction rather than "the eloquence of reason," and (4) the exposure of the members of the assembly to the monarch may obstruct the freedom of their decisions.

All four objections, as Bentham made clear, derive from the presumption of the incompetence of the people to form reasoned judgments, to distinguish between its friends and enemies, and to judge of their true interests. Bentham's key argument against any opposing belief about the publicity was that "the public do judge and will always judge," thus publicity could only help those who make "ill judgments" to make "more correct opinions" on the basis of accurate information. As he later argued in his essays on the liberty of the press and "public discussion in free meetings," it should not be difficult to see that the benefits ensured by any freedom far exceed its potential weaknesses: "In all liberty there is more or less of danger: and so there is in all power. The question is—in which there is most danger—in power limited by this check, or in power without this check to limit it" (Bentham 1820, Letter I). His answer is congruent with Kant's principle of publicity: "Without publicity, no good is permanent: under the auspices of publicity, no evil can continue" (Bentham 1791/1994, 589).

The Press: The Unique Organ of Public Opinion

In his later works, Bentham focused more on the role of newspapers as the most important instrument of the Public Opinion Tribunal. Whereas in his earlier essays the role of the check to be applied to the power of government was attributed to public opinion in general and, specifically, to its "Committee" consisting of the most educated and knowledgeable men, the rise of the (daily) press obviously inspired Bentham with a greater confidence in newspapers. In the essay "On the Liberty of the Press" (1820), Bentham operationalized the rule of publicity with "the *liberty of the press* [which] operates as a check upon the conduct of the ruling few; and in that character constitutes a controlling power, indispensably necessary to the maintenance of good government." Being one of the "checks" Bentham prescribed for rendering the representative dependent on his constituents, the "free press" actually attained in his later theory the status of a separate power—comparable to that of the Public Opinion Tribunal. As thirty years earlier in the defense of the rule of publicity, Bentham later argued against the belief that freedom of the press might be "dangerous."

Inspired by the success of democracy and free press in the United States, which he greatly admired, he was convinced that all possible evils to any individual or group resulting from the press freedom were always greatly outweighed by its wholesome social consequences, in the first place "the security for good government" which a free press may provide. Although he initially emphasized in "Securities against Misrule" that a newspaper editor is but one among a million members of the Public Opinion Tribunal (1822/1990, 57), he continued with a much stronger inclination toward the specific position of the editor, describing him as one of the "leading members" or "Presidents," but at the same time as "the President of the Presidents" in the Committee of the Public Opinion Tribunal, thus as a sort of judge arbitrating on behalf of the Public Opinion Tribunal (pp. 61–64). The great importance Bentham attributed to the role of the press in democratic society is evident from his belief that only the political function of prime minister is more important than that of newspaper editors (1822/1990, 45, 57). It is the task of the press to collect, select, and publish information in an accessible form to the readers, or the public. To the newspaper function of reporting on government activities and proceedings of the legislature (which is important for the public in the first place), Bentham added the task of presenting "suffrages" (opinions) of the people. All these functions of the press can only be performed if freedom of the press exists. In such circumstances, the press may be said to be "an appropriate organ of the Public Opinion Tribunal," and "the only constantly acting" organ of public opinion (1822/1990, 45).

Bentham did not conceive of liberty of the press as a "natural" one in the sense of an activity one can perform according to his own wishes and without any external (i.e., societal) restriction. Rather, it is liberty in the sense of "security"—based on law and the principle of noninterference, securing freedom from any form of oppression or misrule. Bentham claimed that individuals' pleasure and security that make up their happiness are "the sole end which the legislator ought to have in view" (1781/1996). In "Letter to Spanish People" (1820) he argued on the basis of the practice of the Anglo-American United States—where "there is no more restriction upon men's speaking together in public, than upon their eating together in private"—that the *absence* of any restriction on public meetings or prosecution "for anything written against the government" is indispensably necessary to good government.

Since the liberty of the press "operates as a check upon the conduct of the ruling few," Bentham's belief was that nobody should be punished for defamation of the public functionary unless it is consciously based on false assertions, and not at all for vituperation. He strongly opposed the idea that an offence in the case where the party offended is a public functionary should be considered more mischievous. On the contrary, his argument went, it should be considered *less* harmful because public functionaries certainly have much more, and more effective means of, defense than private individuals. A functionary's position itself is a "compensation for all the evil" caused by such unjust imputation, and the higher is his position, the more abundant is the "antecedent compensation" he receives from it.

> The military functionary is paid for being shot at. The civil functionary is paid for being spoken and written at. The soldier, who will not face musquetry, is one sort of coward. The civilian who will not endure obloquy, is another. Better he be defamed, though it be ever unjustly, than that, by a breach of official duty, any sinister profit sought should be reaped. (Bentham 1830/1983, 40)

Bentham considered two arguments usually pointed against the liberty of the press at that time: its *dangerousness*—"it may lead to insurrection, and thus to civil war"—and *needlessness*—"other remedies that government itself affords are adequate to the prevention of misgovernment." His arguments in favor of freedom of the press in 1820 were essentially the same as those in favor of publication of the proceedings of a political assembly in 1791. His answer to the first objection regarding "dangerousness" of press freedom was that each freedom implies more or less danger; but the same holds true for power. The true question then is, when more danger arises— if power is limited by freedom of the press, or if no such limit exists. Similarly to John Milton (1644/1999, 20), who believed that "evil manners are as perfectly learnt without books a thousand other ways which cannot be stopt," Bentham concluded: "Take away this check, there remains no other but the exercise of this same liberty by speech in public meetings: and in that shape, besides that it is not applicable with nearly equal advantage, it is much more dangerous."

The question of whether freedom of the press is needed or not relates to the essence of Bentham's *utilitarian* theory. The main argument *against* press freedom as identified by Bentham was that the rulers "have nothing so much at heart as the happiness of all over whom they rule," certainly much more than any of their subjects (1820, Letter I). The latter, in addition, possess appropriate means against the incompetence of the rulers or their misuse of power—from removal from the office to prosecution and punishment; thus freedom of the press could only be detrimental, the argument against freedom of the press went.

Bentham's main objection to this misconception of press freedom was that the rulers are primarily human beings like everybody else and thus "have their own happiness more at heart than that of all over whom they rule put together." They may be wiser than the general population, but their wisdom is still far from perfection, which can only be achieved through the press freedom as the "all-comprehensive means of information." More than that, Bentham believed that those in higher positions do not strive to acquire appropriate information because they would not be exposed to sanctions even in the case of obvious inaptitude—in contrast to those in lower "situations." Again, he followed the arguments he has enumerated in favor of publication of parliamentary discussions in 1791: without the public eye to which the rulers are exposed through the press, they would have more sympathy for their incompetent colleagues than for the people's interest.

Freedom of the press is presented as particularly important from a disciplinary perspective, in order to make the formal lawsuit efficient. "For the establishment of the truth or falsity of the imputation—for the establishment of the guilt or innocence of the party suspected of delinquency—the utmost stock of relevant and applicable facts and arguments that can be secured by prosecution, is very imperfect without the addition of those which *this liberty and nothing else is capable of supplying*" (Bentham 1820, Letter I; emphasis added). As Bentham believed, the press would supply "informal informations" and thus assist, and to some degree substitute, judicial prosecution. Although Bentham's general interest was primarily in happiness of the individual, he did not see freedom of publication as a personal motive or interest, but rather as an institutional means for social reforms that would eventually bring about individuals' happiness.

Bentham takes for granted that publicity serves some utilitarian ends, and that the "interaction" between the assembly and the public mediated through newspapers would increase the satisfaction on either side. The main task of publicity ought to be the publication of parliamentary discussions, rather than pursue personal rights and freedoms. The idea of publicity with the main task of providing control over the parliament through the "fourth power" of "unauthorized," independent newspapers reduces the power relations to the actors (institutions) directly involved in the legislative process, but it neglects other agents of power in society and, particularly, the people. The aspect of *rational* debate has only secondary importance; the *critical* character of publicity (e.g., in the sense of an opposition to the government) is almost absent; and the rationalist idea of human freedom is lacking completely.

Nevertheless, Bentham pointed to the importance of recognition that different opinions existed on all public matters. Thus in the first six articles of the "Constitutional Securities of the Tripolitan Nation" he declared that every person has (1) freedom to express and publish "whatsoever in his judgment it will be contributory to the greatest happiness of the greatest number to be informed of: and this, although disapprobation be thereby expressed toward persons in authority;" (2) to converse with one another, at all times and in any number, on all subjects, including the conduct of persons in power; and (3) to speak, write, and publish freely about religion (1822/1990, 79–83).

Custodians Exempt from Custody?

While the press ought to represent a "controlling power" limiting the power of the ruling elites, it became one power among other powers. Yet Bentham never considered the possibility that the free press itself would become vulnerable to the influence of "sinister interests"—including those of the "omnicompetent legislature"—and promote the organization of group interests, so that the domination of particular interests in the press would eventually even lead to the degeneration of democratic system into an authoritarian one. Thus he did not see any need to limit the power of the press. Neither he nor his immediate followers had any idea about resources needed for a newspaper to become a "constantly acting" organ of control—the financial or business side of the action seemed marginal in relation to its utilitarian ends. The "grand metaphor" of the "free marketplace of ideas," which became an even more persuasive argument for a commercial concept of freedom of the press than the idea of the fourth estate, was invented much later, often—what an irony again!—used erroneously in reference to John Stuart Mill's defense of freedom of expression.

The reason for Bentham's disregard of the danger that the press, like any other power, may be used as an instrument of misrule, was rather simple. At the beginning, newspapers were still characterized by an intimate association between author/editor and specific reader, and by an honorable status of the author of literary and scientific texts alike, reflected in readers' trust and admiration. Essentially, the attitude of the public toward newspapers did not significantly differ from that toward books. Gradually newspapers increased their circulation and they were intended for a much larger readership or public; the influence of the press was less and less based on an individual point of view presented in the newspaper or respect for the author. Rather, as Tönnies put it, the newspaper became "a thing that speaks to the unknown about unknown" and persuades most effectively by "periodic repetition." The most significant changes in the development of the press from an intimate "companion" to an industrial corporation took place in the nineteenth century—after Bentham codified his ideas on the press as the organ of the Public Opinion Tribunal in the *Constitutional Code.*

Yet the changes that took place afterward radically challenged Bentham's unconditional trust in the press. In his study of public opinion a century later, Tönnies described the empirical relationship between the publicity and the public inversely to Bentham's principle of publicity: publicity was not the principle enabling the public to control authorities, but practical activity aimed at influencing the public. The role he attributed to the press was to "set the public into motion and to draw it to its side." The public appeared as a latent condition that needs some external stimulus to revive—a process that regularly happens during turbulent times. In order to achieve this condition, the press presented its contents as "public opinion." Following Bauer, Tönnies differentiated between two kinds of publicity, based on the "kind of relation the publicist has toward his own products": a publicist may either present his views out of an *internal* need created by his own conviction or follow entirely *external* motives and impulses. By the end of the nineteenth century the type of journalism motivated by "internal needs" of the author slowly but surely yielded the dominant role to the money-making journalism. A decisive point in the development of the press was soon recognized by German *Zeitungswissenschaft*:

> The modern newspaper is a capitalistic enterprise, a sort of news factory in which a great number of people . . . are employed on wage, under a single administration, at very specialized work. This paper produces wares for an unknown circle of readers. . . . The simple needs of the reader or of the circle of patrons no longer determine the quality of these wares; it is now the very complicated conditions of competition in the publication market . . . [in which] the newspaper readers take no direct part. (Bücher 1893/1901, 242)

Tönnies came to the same point in his analysis of the relationship between the press and public opinion. He criticized Bauer's differentiation between writing and the press, in which he argued that various media were mere *instances of the same*. Bauer failed to recognize that a newspaper was "a large capitalist business whose direct and main goal is to create profit in management" and even journalists must conform to this objective (Tönnies 1922, 179–80). Corruption and corporate control were causing a rather evident bias of newspapers, so that independent newspapers became a complete illusion. Tönnies therefore considered newspapers to be merely (potential) *mediators*, and by no means autonomous subjects of public opinion. The inner circles of public opinion ("the Committee of the Public Opinion Tribunal," as named by Bentham) were thus in close relation with a "more *reliable* literature" than newspapers—books.

After the rise of the mass ("penny") press in the second half of the nineteenth century, the notion of the marketplace was becoming less and less alien to conceptualizations of the press in general, and the free press in particular. The metaphor "free marketplace of ideas" became a reference to an ideal situation in which people could speak and exchange opinions freely, assuming that since market forces act toward the highest and best use of *all* resources and maximize the individual's autonomy from the state and society, they ought to be also the best form of regulation for the press. In fact, the market economy decisively influenced the press once all forms of censorship were abolished. Walter Lippmann made bold to say that printing and circulating news is *business*. Civil liberties themselves do not guarantee circulation of (public) opinions because the truth is neither spontaneous nor "the means of securing truth exist when there is no external interference" (Lippmann 1922/1991, 319). Yet political science, Lippmann argued, simply missed coming to grips with the problem of "how to make the invisible world visible to the citizens," in order to enable them to participate in political processes; it did not consider newspapers relevant to the political process.

> This insistent and ancient belief that truth is not earned, but inspired, revealed, supplied gratis, comes out very plainly in our economic prejudices as readers of newspapers. We expect the newspaper to serve us with truth however unprofitable the truth may be. . . . [T]he community applies one ethical measure to the press and another to trade or manufacture. Ethically a newspaper is judged as if it were a church or a school. . . . A free press, if you judge by the attitude of the readers, means newspapers that are virtually given away. (1922/1991, 320–2)

Advertising as an "indirect taxation of the reader" that kept the direct newspaper price low, was the most effective way to increase the circulation of newspapers, which was needed to cover the expenses of "earning the truth" (providing news). The economic transformation of newspaper into capitalist enterprise had the immediate consequence of transforming "the public" into "the *buying* public." As Lippmann argued, "it is for this buying public that newspapers are edited and published" (p. 324). Consequently, the dominant function of the press changed: it was not any more to provide *truth*, but only *news*; it only has to "signalize an event," not "bring to light the hidden facts, to set them into relation with each other, and make a picture of reality on which man acts" (p. 358). Similarly, Tönnies (1922) believed that in contrast to science the essence of publicity is not a pursuit of *truth* but rather *influence*, although occasionally some products of publicity can be even closer to the truth than a scientific statement. Publicity usually involves prejudice and bias dealing with state-legislative, political, and economic problems and struggles, and it tends to achieve immediate, short-term effects. Being much more critical toward the idea of the press as the organ of public opinion than Bentham's followers to Tönnies, Lippmann concluded that it was neither "workable" nor "thinkable" that the press would act as an organ of the court of public opinion because that would be beyond the power of the press and the capacity of citizens.

Lippmann's critique of the ideas of the "omnicompetent" citizen being unable to participate in political process and "omnipotent" press unable to serve as the organ of public opinion denotes the end of the period of unlimited trust in the power of the press to control other powers, whether that was considered a grandiose task, as by Bentham, or mischief, as by Tocqueville. But the two pretentious metaphors referring to the press as "the fourth estate" and enthroning it into "the free marketplace of ideas" already began to lead their independent ideological life. They effectively hide the fact that the "fourth power" is not an autonomous power and "the free marketplace of ideas" does not give equal opportunity to everyone to present his or her opinion. To say that the "fourth estate becomes the property of the new power elite" expresses the transformation of media industry bringing about a new set of media barons.[20] Those who, according to Bentham, ought to provide opportunities to the members of the Public Opinion Tribunal mind primarily their own business. According to Article 3 of the Constitution of the International Federation of Journalists, the main aims of this confederation of national journalists' trade unions are (1) to protect and strengthen the rights and freedoms of *journalists* and (2) to respect and defend freedom of *information, media* freedom, and the independence of *journalism*, which are followed by a number of specific professional and trade union tasks. Apart from themselves, journalism, information, and the media, there are no other interests journalists would believe they have to heed.

The fourth estate doctrine of journalism became in the twentieth century an aristocratic ideology of the "professionals" following Milton's example: "*Give me* the liberty to know, to utter, and to argue freely according to conscience, above all liberties" (1644/1999, 44; emphasis added). It firmly supports Bentham's ideas of indispensability of the press for democratic process, the utility of its power status (as the fourth power) to perform its functions, and the requirement that nobody is punished for defamation of the public functionary unless it is consciously based on false assertions, and not at all for vituperation. Yet there is much less enthusiasm (if any) over the necessity of the separation of powers, public control over power(s) and potentially corrupt interests, moral superiority of those who act on behalf of the public, and everybody's right to publish freely without any external restriction (such as restricted access to the media).

The professionalism of the twentieth century is clearly reflected in the dominant paradigm of communication theory and research, which legitimize professional ideology by specifying "universal" functions of mass media in society: surveillance of the environment, correlation of the parts of the society in responding to its environment, transmission of cultural heritage, and entertainment (Wright 1959). Social-psychological and sociological reconceptualizations of "power to control" carried out by public opinion partly followed the functionalist approach by considering questions of social integration and order, but significantly departed from it by stressing the creative, interactive nature of human communication in which meanings are not simply "packed," "sent," or "distributed" in messages, but culturally "shared" and "coproduced"[21] (particularly American pragmatists J. Dewey, G. H. Mead, R. E. Park, and C. H. Cooley).

PUBLIC OPINION AND THE PRESS
AS MEANS TO CONTROL MASS BEHAVIOR

Even if Bentham's ideas of publicity in the nineteenth and twentieth centuries attracted ardent followers approaching the press as the "fourth power," his justification of publicity and freedom of the press did not fit in with the ideas of a number of his contemporaries and later normative theorizations of public/ness. Of course, his liberal-utilitarian attitudes toward freedom of the press were bitterly attacked by many of his conservative contemporaries, but those political "critiques" are of no theoretical relevance. What is much more important, however, is how Bentham's ideas relate to those of his followers and theoretical adversaries. One of them, John S. Mill (1838/1859), sharply criticized Bentham's lack of "Imagination," characteristic of great writers, which enables them "to conceive the absent as if it were present, the imaginary as if it were real, and to cloth it in the feelings which, if it were indeed real, it would bring along with it." Mill saw Bentham's work as "wholly empirical." To make it worse, Bentham had little knowledge about human behavior and feelings, and what influences them internally and externally; his work was superficial and partial, primarily because he disregarded diversities and singularities. Thus Mill concluded that—due to his limited knowledge of agencies which (should) influence human actions and beliefs—Bentham was far too ambitious in his attempt to "give a rule to all human conduct." His aim to regulate men's "outward actions" is flawed by the absence of any insight in inter- and intrapersonal relations in family and primary group, and "self-education; the training, by the human being himself, of his affections and will"—on which an actual social regulation always depends.

Nevertheless, Mill simultaneously expressed great admiration for Bentham's seminal work in his essay on Bentham: "Who, before Bentham (whatever controversies might exist on points of detail) dared to speak disrespectfully, in express terms, of the British Constitution, or the English Law? He did so; and his arguments and his example together encouraged others" (Mill 1838/1859). Bentham's principle of publicity based on the ideas to minimize naive public confidence and maximize distrust in government, and to provide the Public Opinion Tribunal with a free press as its powerful organ, certainly represents one of the grandiose contributions to democratization of both politics and (political) communication. Mill was justified in proclaiming Bentham "the great subversive, or, in the language of continental philosophers, the great critical, thinker of his age and country" and "the father of English innovation both in doctrines and in institutions."

Resurgence of the Power to Persuade and Discipline in Mass Society

Only half a century later Bentham's innovative or even subversive, as Mill might put it, concept of publicity has come to a critical point. While it has become widespread even among some critical theorists (e.g., in the Chicago School), it has reached a radical redirection that became dominant in the twentieth century. Whereas Bentham primarily saw the function of publicity in enabling the public tribunal to sanction political representatives who would fail to promote the public interest, a version of the rule of publicity developed in the field of social psychology has been redirected to "how public opinion bears on a man as member of society, rather than as its agent or spokesman" (Ross 1901/1969, 97 n.). The new conceptualization did not stress the impelling power of public opinion to control the rulers but rather its power to discipline the people liberated of their critical function and active part in forming public opinion.

The theories of the rule of public opinion from Burke to Bentham attributed sovereignty to public opinion and to the public itself, but the public, as the materialized form of the principle of publicity, has always been limited, either implicitly or explicitly, by the competence of individuals, thus excluding lower classes of society. This restriction helped the public become efficiently institutionalized into the political system of the bourgeois legal state, which according to Habermas represented the beginning of a gradual disintegration of the classical bourgeois public, or its "refeudalization:"

> The principle of publicity based on the public of educated people who reason and enjoy art and the medium of bourgeois press—which, at the beginning, undoubtedly had a critical function against the secret practice of the absolutist state and was consolidated in the methods of organs of the legal state—has been refunctioned for demonstrative and manipulative purposes. (Habermas 1965/1980, 10)

The fall of the ideal of the reasoned public began just a few years after Bentham designed the *Constitutional Code*, in which sovereignty was conferred on the Public Opinion Tribunal and its "organ," the press. Bentham's trust in the impartiality of public opinion and the press was immoderate. As soon as newspapers, under the new political circumstances characterized by the abolition of censorship, were able to develop as free commercial enterprises, they became interested primarily in the kind of services they could provide to their readers and new powerful actors in the field—advertisers. It turned out that the power of the press as an "organ of public opinion" could be put to a more effective and *profitable* use if not aimed to control other ruling powers but to act on its readers by flattering them.

In a complete contradiction to liberal ideas of the free press, the persuasive capacity of the press developed more fully in democratic countries than in authoritarian societies. Relatively early on, Lippmann issued the warning: "The creation of consent is not a new art. It is a very old one which was supposed to have died out with the appearance of democracy. But it has not died out. It has, in fact, improved enormously in technic. . . . Persuasion has become a self-conscious art and a regular organ of popular government" (Lippmann 1922/1991, 248). As Tönnies (1922) claimed, newspapers were transformed from organs of public opinion into organs of political parties and commercial corporations.

In *Democracy in America,* Alexis de Tocqueville demonstrated that *all* powers had a tendency to endanger individual freedoms. His reconceptualization of the power and disciplinary function of public opinion originated from the critique of the "tyranny of majority." Tocqueville was perhaps the first to discover that public opinion is not only a powerful weapon against the misrule of those in power but also a means of permanent coercion in the hands of the majority, which may be used effectively against any minority of those who do not think like the majority. As Tocqueville suggested just a couple of years after Bentham's death, the disciplinary power of public opinion may far exceed the power of law—not by forcing the rulers to maximize people's happiness, but by driving into despair those who would try, hopelessly, to oppose the majority and forcing them to conform. In contrast to Bentham's civil functionaries, who are paid for being exposed to public surveillance and criticism, negative sanctions against ordinary people by public opinion are compensated with no reward.

> Whenever social conditions are equal, public opinion presses with enormous weight upon the minds of each individual; it surrounds, directs, and oppresses him; and this arises from the very constitution of society much more than from its political laws. As men grow more alike, each man feels himself weaker in regard to all the rest; as he discerns nothing by which he is considerably raised above them or distinguished from them, he mistrusts himself as soon as they assail him. Not only does he mistrust his strength, but he even doubts of his right; and he is very near acknowledging that he is in the wrong, when the greater number of his countrymen assert that he is so. The majority do not need to force him; they convince him. (Tocqueville 1840, sec. 3, chap. 21)

What Tocqueville had in mind was not an intentionally designed system of control over citizens to make them, for example, less corruptible, and was not based on their moral obligation to obey. Rather—in Edmund Burke's words—the sort of control observed by Tocqueville is a kind of "style of all free countries." For Burke "*the* style" common in free countries was a system of leaders and their followers, "the minority of leaders followed by the whole flock," which made a system of surveillance by the public over the elected absurd to him. In contrast, "*the* style" identified by Tocqueville was "despotism of the majority," where the majority had absolute power both to make the laws and to control their execution; and authority both over those in power and the community at large.

Tocqueville was aware that the difference in "style" was not a matter of attitude or theoretical perspective, but the consequence of practical developments. Only in the beginning of the American Revolution did public opinion not tyrannize individuals. "Those celebrated men, sharing the agitation of mind common at that period, had a grandeur *peculiar* to themselves, which was *reflected* back upon the nation, but was by no means *borrowed* from it"

(1835, chap. 15; emphasis added). Yet he believed this was essentially "the style" of aristocracies, which gradually disappeared in democracies, where "public favor seems as necessary as the air we breathe, and to live at variance with the multitude is, as it were, not to live" (1840, sec. 3, chap. 21).

A substantial element in the "despotism of majority" was represented by the free press, whose pressure toward homogenization of the people and loss of individuality Tocqueville again related to social equality: "A newspaper . . . address[es] each of its readers in the name of all the others and . . . exert[s] its influence over them in proportion to their individual weakness. The power of the newspaper press must therefore increase as the social conditions of men become more equal" (chap. 6). Tocqueville attributed the existence of the large number of newspapers in the United States to a kind of conspiracy: "the only way to neutralize the effect of the public journals is to multiply their number," with the aim of maintaining public order in which the mediocrity of the majority dominated the minority and dissenting individuals (chap. 11). Thus the importance of an independent press for democracy is not, according to Tocqueville, primarily in that it secures a permanent surveillance over political elites, but rather in limiting the power of the *intolerant majority* and breaking its *pressure toward conformity*.

This conservative doctrine of public opinion emerged as a critique of early liberal democratic ideas not because of the intrinsic invalidity of the idea of public opinion governance, but because in "democratic" practice the arbitrary power of public opinion (and the press) assumed the position of the power(s) it was supposed to control. The kind of intolerance criticized by Tocqueville in the mid-1800s is not uncommon 150 years later. In praise for the "broadcasting marketplace" as supposedly the best regulator of rational use of key resources, Fowler and Brenner (1983, 667) argue that such regulation is perfectly in accord with the principles of free inquiry and expression. "Those who deliver popular, acceptable speech have little reason to fear the rebuke of the majority. Only words and ideas that trouble or confound need the special aid of constitutional protection." In other words, the "free" marketplace effectively eliminates troublesome and annoying ideas. The persistence of the "free marketplace of ideas" argument indicates that Habermas's criticism of the "reactionary liberalist" response to the growing power of public opinion was superficial. Habermas's argument that it appeared "as soon as this public was subverted by the propertyless and uneducated masses" (1962/1995, 136) may well correspond to the historical fact that the two processes paralleled each other; yet it does not follow from the historical coincidence that the liberalist reinterpretation of public opinion was a *consequence* of the enlargement of the public with lower social classes.

A trenchant impetus to the transformation of the press from controlling the ruling powers into influencing public opinion—still, in both cases the press could also (re)present public opinion—was given by the rise of media monopolies (which Tocqueville believed to be the most effective remedy against intolerance) and interpenetration of political and economic powers. Following the critique of rationalist reliance on the self-evidence of truth, studies of public opinion and the press adopted new rules of "scientific method" in sociology and psychology stressing experience as the main source of knowledge. The more public opinion was becoming a topic in social psychology,[22] the more the whole field of public opinion studies was turned toward its immediate manifestations and away from the normative components dominating the eighteenth and nineteenth centuries. In his comparative dissertation on the crowd and the public (1904/1972), bearing mostly on the French and German thoughts of the turn of the centuries, Park emphasized the fundamental epistemological problem related to the shift from the substance of public opinion, the general will, to its empirical manifestations. The psychological turn brought to the forefront common actions in the inward domain of (sub)consciousness typically arousing in any situation where different interests confront, yet the interest of the whole (or just majority) has to prevail over the interest of any of its parts to maintain social order. Public opinion as an instrument of "social control" and "social organization," as suggested by Ross, Cooley, and Park in the beginning of the twentieth century, was freed of any normative-political relevance.

"Social control is the central fact and the central problem of society," Park conclusively stated (Park 1921, 20). In the famed book *Introduction to the Science of Sociology* (1921), which he has edited with Ernest Burgess, Park classified public opinion among two other forms of social control—elementary or spontaneous forms of social control in the crowd, ceremony, prestige and taboo, and institutions. Park (and notably Dewey later) still emphasized the difference between the crowd and the public, arguing that in the public "there will be no such complete rapport and no such complete domination of the individual by the group as exists in a herd or a crowd . . . but there will be sufficient community of interest to insure a common understanding" (Park 1921/1967, 216). He considered the public a "universe of discourse" within a "circle of mutual influence." The former is the basis to ensure a common understanding, the latter to reach consensus needed for the formation of public opinion.

> In the final judgment of the public upon a conflict or an issue, we expect, to be sure, some sort of unanimity of judgment, but in the general consensus there will be some individual differences of opinion still unmediated, or only partially so, and final agreement of the public will be more or less qualified by all the different opinions that co-operate to form its judgment. (Park 1921/1967, 220)

Dewey later defined the public as a large body of persons (citizens) having a *common interest in controlling the consequences of social transactions* in which they do not participate directly (1927/1991, 137, 126). Like Bentham, Dewey endorsed two fundamental constituents of the classic theory of democracy: (1) that each individual is of himself equipped with the intelligence needed to participate in political affairs and (2) that general suffrage, frequent elections of officials, and majority rule reliably secure the accountability of elected officers. Dewey's conceptualization of the public strengthened the centrality of interaction and rational discussion in public opinion process, and unrestricted publicity as its fundamental precondition (see Splichal 1999).

Yet the more empirical stream of pragmatism abandoned the normative concept of Bentham's "Public Opinion Tribunal" on account of empirical counterevidence supplied by a number of studies, such as those by Tocqueville (1840) and Bryce (1888/1995), and more novel sociological analyzes of social *organization* and social *control*. While stressing the broad organizational power of publicity, Charles Horton Cooley did not yet lose trust in the "enlightened public" to control the government, but his trust was flawed by an idealized and controversial notion of the public. In almost the same way as Bentham, Cooley conceived of publicity as the remedy for malfunction of government.

> The rule of public opinion, then, means for the most part a latent authority which the public will exercise when sufficiently dissatisfied with the specialist who is in immediate charge of a particular function. It cannot extend to the immediate participation of the group as a whole in the details of public business. (Cooley 1909/1983, 131)

Cooley realized that it was actually not the "general public" but the opinion of specific powerful groups that ruled over specialists, including politicians—except on the "day of reckoning," such as general elections. The publication of facts should unleash the general moral sentiment, which would find "organs" through which it could act effectively—particular individuals or groups who would organize and effectuate such sentiment. The press is an organ that "has a motive to exploit and increase [such sentiment] by vivid exposition of the state of affairs; enthusiasm, seeking for an outlet, finds it in this direction; ambition and even pecuniary interest are enlisted to gratify the demand" (Cooley 1909/1983, 133).[23]

The weakness in Cooley's argument lies in his assumption of the existence of a unity of "moral sentiment" among the people, which is presupposed in his concept of public opinion. Yet no such moral unity ever existed in society that could be simply unleashed by the publication of facts. The ideal of "a moral whole or community wherein individual minds are merged and the higher capacities of the members find total and adequate expression" (p. 33) may fit in with Cooley's definition of primary group, but not with the modern industrialized society of his time. As he recognized himself, "modern industry . . . has

attained a marvellous organization . . . while the social and moral side of it remains in confusion" (p. 384); he criticized anarchy and corruption in commerce
and finance, as well as the state; he saw the people confused and "morally isolated by the very magnitude of the system, the whole does not commonly live
in their thought" (p. 385). Cooley became aware that moral unity, or society as
a "moral organism," is not given but should be actively and constantly produced "through endless elaboration of means," such as institutions, communication, public opinion, or classes, but he failed to critically analyze controversial consequences of such means in full operation.

He also failed to observe that there was a conflict of interests, or at least competition in terms of relation to public opinion, between the political elite and
the press, for they both take aim at influencing public opinion and express it as
its effective organs. With much regret Cooley estimated that the bulk of the contents of newspapers was of the nature of gossip, which tended "through the
fear of publicity, to enforce a popular, somewhat vulgar, but sound and human
standard of morality" (p. 85). Since defining and organizing "confused tendencies of the public mind" is also the function of leaders (p. 135), the specificity
of the controlling function of the press as a separate power disappears.

From Communication to Domination

Stimulated by the work of Scipio Sighele, Gustave Le Bon, and Edward A.
Ross who introduced them to American readers, Cooley supplemented the
notion of publicity as a means to control authorities with a radical idea of the
press as not only a medium of communication but also (class) *domination*.
The controlling function of the press is not unidirectional since the control of
government is only one possible function of publicity and part of broader social organization. On the one hand, as an extension of interpersonal communication in primary group, newspapers are generally—and idealistically—
seen by Cooley as contributing to a general "we-feeling," being a "reservoir
of common-place thought of which every one partakes," promoting "democracy and breaking down caste." On the other hand, however, his analysis of
the ascendancy of the capitalist class in America is marked by a devastating,
concise political-economic critique of capitalist press subordinated to commercial rather than moral aims:

> Newspapers are generally owned by men of wealth, which has no doubt an im-
> portant influence upon the sentiments expressed in them; but a weightier con-
> sideration is the fact that they depend for profit chiefly upon advertisements, the
> most lucrative of which come from rich merchants who naturally resent doctrines
> that threaten their interest. Of course the papers must reach the people, in order
> to have a value for advertising or any other purpose, and this requires adaptation
> to public opinion; but the public of what are known as the better class of papers
> are chiefly the comparatively well-to-do. And even that portion of the press

which aims to please the hard-working class is usually more willing to carry on a loud but vague agitation, not intended to accomplish anything but increase circulation, than to push real and definite reform. (Cooley 1909/1983, 270)

Cooley shows that "public opinion" is largely molded by capitalists, either through education or the press. In the newspapers, journalists "live unconsciously in an atmosphere of upper-class ideas from which they do not free themselves by thorough inquiry." Yet Cooley was afraid to accept the consequences of his own analysis, which would bring him close to Gramsci's idea of "hegemony," that is, the ability of the dominant class to maintain its power through "ideological apparatuses" rather than by direct (material or physical) coercion. Thus he merely concluded that the dominant class in the States had less influence on the "inner life of the time" than in any older society, believing in spite of his own criticism that "whatever the state undertakes should be something likely to be watched by public opinion; not necessarily by the whole public, but at least by some powerful group steadfastly interested in efficiency and capable of judging whether it is attained" (p. 406).

In contrast to Cooley, his fellow Progressive and convert from economy to sociology, Edward A. Ross, abandoned the idea of the public's control of the government through publicity altogether. Quite the contrary, publicity became a common disciplinary instrument coercing the general population to conformity beyond any class division. Ross saw in the state "an organization that puts the wise minority in the saddle" and aims at "a rational safeguarding of the collective welfare" (Ross 1901/1969, 74). The same sort of "regular organs of the public" once designed (theoretically at least) to control the mightiest are now primarily considered instruments of mutual control in "the all-inclusive association" or "union of civilized men"—which is modern society. In contrast to its broader meaning in Cooley's theory, where the concept of social control was used to link empirical sociology to the value of social *progress* in the attempt to explain "irrational" behavior in society and to identify methods of society's self-regulation, Ross's conceptualization already indicated the trend of narrowing its meaning to the processes of producing conformity through socialization.

> We are come to a time when ordinary men are scarcely aware of the coercion of public opinion, so used are they to follow it. They cannot dream of aught but acquiescence in an unmistakable edict of the mass. It is not so much the dread of what an angry public may do that disarms the modern American, as it is sheer inability to stand unmoved in the rush of totally hostile comment, to endure a life perpetually at variance with the conscience and feeling of those about him. (Ross 1901/1969, 105)[24]

Ross's ideas that social control should limit deviant behavior and ensure social order remind us unequivocally of the order in Bentham's "Inspection House" designed to bring large numbers of people under permanent surveillance and make them "not only suspect, but be assured, that whatever they do is known, even though should not be the case" (Bentham 1787/1995, 94)—a permanent object but never the subject of information which, according to Foucault (1977, 201), "assures the automatic functioning of power." Ross actually "anticipated" Poster's much later criticism of Foucault's appropriation of the Panopticon concept, arguing that Foucault did not realize how information and communication technologies *extended* Panopticon monitoring considerably, "not simply to massed groups but to *the isolated individual*. The normalized individual is not only the one at work, in an asylum, in jail, in school, in the military, as Foucault observes, but also the individual in his or her home, at play, in all the mundane activities of *everyday life*" (Poster 1984, 103; emphasis added). This was essentially what Ross already suggested in his *Social Control*, looking for specific levers operating in community and, primarily, society.[25] The fundamental principle on which social control should be based is to give "the most welfare for the least abridgment of liberty" (p. 427), which may be seen as an attempt to "modernize" Bentham's *maximization of happiness* principle.

Like George Herbert Mead, Ross emphasized the importance of being able to participate on a footing of equality in social interaction in democratic community because it is fundamental to the defense of common prosperity from the destructiveness of egoism manifested in extreme differences between social classes. Ross saw a major peril in the domination of minority over majority, which by necessity leads to a violent, authoritarian social control. In contrast, social interaction helps individuals internalize the rules and thus prevents violent actions. However, Ross's discussion of interaction remained mostly on a descriptive level; Cooley and Mead contributed a much more important insight into the social-psychological nature of interaction.

Unveiled of any normative component, Ross's publicity helps maintain the interest of the whole over the interest of its parts and the domination of society over the individual (which Ross termed "Social Ascendency"), which should coerce the individual to "avoid the resentful action of others" (Ross 1901/1969, 104). Such control became indispensable as soon as groups smaller than the social whole began to exist, which competed with one another and sought to monopolize benefits and privileges. Social control could effectively legitimate or baffle such efforts with the task to "preserve that indispensable condition of common life, social order" (p. 395). Society is differentiated in terms of sources of control. Ross adopted Tarde's idea that social power is concentrated or dispersed in proportion to the degree people "feel themselves in need of guidance or protection." If the majority feel secure, the monopoly of social power by the few is terminated; society differentiates and power is "displaced" to different groups that become "radiant points of social control." Similarly to Tönnies (1922, 107), Ross specifically mentions the elders, the military, the priesthood, the officials, the capitalists, the learned, the elite of ideas and talents, and the geniuses (1901/1969, 80–84). But in a primordial "natural community" as a compact social whole, the undifferentiated mass (the "Crowd") was the sole seat of social power. "Artificial society" developed as a consequence of the division of labor and social differentiation, in which

> men of superior character, sagacity, or disinterestedness come to influence their fellows more than they are influenced by them. The seat of the common will, then, is no longer the crowd, but *the Public*. In this *organization of minds* every man counts for something, but one man does not always count for as much as another. (p. 80; emphasis added)

Ross believed that the progress of humanity and social democratization would replace external pressures or repressive surveillance of individuals with internal discipline internalized in social interaction. Like other Progressives, Ross trusted in popular education and enlightenment to help the people apperceive social foundations of moral actions and the obligations they had as members of a democratic community. He was very critical of capitalist monopolies, greed, profit mentality, and egoism as main impediments to the development of democratic community. For example, he criticized "the newspaper-owner [who] manufactures the impressions that breed opinion and, if he controls a chain of important newspapers, he may virtually make public opinion without the public knowing it" (1917–1918, 630). Simultaneously, however, Ross came near to racism by emphasizing that the development from community to society was largely due to remarkable talents of a smaller number of individuals, which also brought about the differences in capabilities between groups, peoples, and races, of which the Teutonic race seemed to Ross the most capable and civilized (p. 16). The civilization of white men in America was unproblematic to him despite expropriation of Native Americans and slavery, since he saw these groups as uncivilized and socially deviant, which was a rather typical view of just domination at that time.

In Ross's conceptualization of social control the press does not pursue any specific function, and it is not considered a specific "means" through which society disciplines its members; rather, it is a "pontiff" carrying out massive "social suggestion"—a process in which "the stubborn individual will is bent to the social purpose" without the use of immediate punishments or rewards. The press is seen only as an important *source* of suggestion, like any other form of the social use of language. Of course, Ross admitted that suggestion was actually part of any "devise of social control" as "secondary service," but he was specifically interested in social suggestion in the sense of the direct shaping of volition and conduct of individuals (p. 146), namely, persuasive communication as "the art of introducing into a man's mind unwelcome ideas so neatly as not to arouse the will to expel them" (p. 147), which would ultimately lead to a situation of a perfect censorship "when unwholesome news will be edited in the interest of public morality" (p. 157). In a similar

manner, public opinion is no more considered a process of opinion formation over public issues that ought to ensure government's responsibility, but
a means of domination of society over the individual.[26] Ross relates public
opinion closely to (mass) suggestion: "In public opinion there is something
which is not praise or blame, and this residuum is mass suggestion. From this
comes its power to reduce men to uniformity as a steam roller reduces bits
of stone to smooth macadam" (pp. 148–49).

When looking ahead, however, Ross's conception of control was somehow irresolute—favorable toward some forms of social control, particularly
those to be introduced by the state to restrict economic individualism and
promote social welfare, and adverse to the others. He considered any form
of class control immoral, hostile to citizens' freedom, and actually ineffective.
He also anticipated, quixotically, the rise of autonomous sources of power
that would counteract the growing state power, taking its rise—as it has been
commonly believed by the Progressives[27]—from the development of social
sciences rather than natural sciences:

> The chief security for spiritual freedom in this educating modern state seems to lie
> in the vigor of other spiritual associations lying over *against the state to check it
> and redress the balance*. The "free church in the free state," *the press*, the organi-
> zation of science, the republic of letter, the voluntary cultural associations—these
> forbid the undue ascendency of the control organization of society. (pp. 178–79;
> emphasis added)

Yet Ross expected a growing necessity of social control and the growth
of more pervasive means of control in the future, and publicity would play
a central role in their development: "Suggestion, education, and *publicity*
. . . will be used, perhaps, even more freely and *consciously* than they now
are" (p. 432; emphasis added). Ross believed in the progressive role of the
state as "an organization that puts the wise minority in the saddle," which
aims, despite all weaknesses, "more steadily at a rational safeguarding of
the collective welfare than any organ society has yet employed" (p. 74).
An unreserved trust in the progressive organizational role of the state was
a common trait of the Progressives, notably John Dewey, who defined the
state as "the organization of the public effected through officials for the
protection of the interests shared by its members" (Dewey 1927/1991,
33).[28] Social control was believed to direct the behavior of members of society according to consensually accepted core system values. Louis Wirth
conceptualized societal organization as depending on consensus as "the
only reasonable equivalent of 'mind' in the individual organism that we
can think of as an essential in the social organism" (Wirth 1948, 4). Consensus is produced particularly through the mass media and commands
people's loyalty but also implies that "partial or complete understanding

has been reached on a number of issues confronting the members of . . . a society."[29]

Apart from their common trust in the progressive role of the state, Progressives differed in their theorizations of the public and public opinion, as well as the press. Park, Cooley, and Dewey emphasized the democratic (political) significance of public opinion, and Dewey considered the press in modern society functionally equivalent to genuine interpersonal discussions in a small community, recreated on a larger scale. He also saw dissemination of scientific information as a major function of the press. Formation of ideas and judgments concerning the public depends on an effective collection and dissemination of information from social inquiry. Systematic social inquiry has to be followed by the spread of its results through the press to stimulate, and extend the scope of, dialogue. Dewey believed that "a genuine social science would manifest its reality in the daily press, while learned books and articles supply and polish tools of inquiry." Social sciences will remain impotent as long as "they are remote from application in the daily and unremitting assembly and interpretation of 'news'" (Dewey 1927/1991, 180–81). Only if the principle of publicity is enacted, and freedom of expression ensured in both scientific inquiry and the press, can the press perform such a function. In contrast to social inquiry, which is a matter of *scientific* merit, dissemination and presentation of news in press is considered by Dewey also as a matter of *art,* since a "scientific" presentation could not attract the attention and stimulate action of members of the public, with the exception of a few intellectuals.

Dewey's "scientific vision" of the press, with the emphasis on freedom of inquiry and dissemination of facts and opinions, is the radiant of pragmatism most clearly *dissociated* from the control paradigm. Ross, however, reconceptualized public opinion and the press in exactly the opposite way of universalized societal control over individuals—in two mutually exclusive ways: as *rational* means of societal control in the last part of the book, in contrast to his earlier understanding of public opinion (whose organ is the press) as a device of *irrational* social influence.

The reconceptualization of publicity into a generalized form of social control would later be found in the foundations of the functional theory of (mass) communication, which paradoxically coexisted with the fourth estate model of the press, although the former extended the idea of surveillance to such a range that the latter remained only a tiny, insignificant element in it. Harold Lasswell identified three functions of communication and the media "when we examine the process of communication of any state in the world community": *surveillance* of the environment, disclosing threats and opportunities affecting the community and its parts; *correlation* of the parts of society in responding to the environment; and *transmission* of the social heritage from one generation to the next (Lasswell 1948/1971). Charles R.

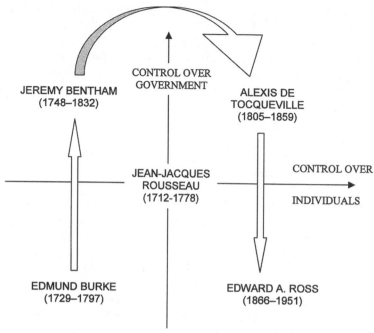

Figure 2.2. Transformation of Disciplinary Conceptualizations of Public Opinion in the Eighteenth and Nineteenth Centuries

Wright (1959, 16) added "popular identifications" for the three functions: surveillance corresponds to "news," correlation to "editorial or propaganda," and transmission of social inheritance to "educational activity." The latter two functions were named by Wilbur Schramm (1971, 19) *consensus* and *socialization*, respectively. The three major functions of the media are clearly related to the maintenance of social order through social control (external and internal, intra- and intergenerational), similarly to kinship, rituals, religion, law, or social networks. None of the three functions is focused on the processes of social transformation and change, and all the three assume a passive user of the media. There are no such "functions" of the media as "to secure public confidence" or "to check the abuses of authorities," which would correspond to the concept of the press as the fourth estate, in the sense in which Bentham defined the role of the press to make his principle of publicity instrumental.

Perhaps Lasswell and his inheritors missed that function because it is not of the sort of "*specializations* that carry on certain functions." But it is more than that. The *direction* of social control specified with the three functions of the media is *opposite* to what Bentham expected from publicity: it is aimed at integration and organization of society at large. Problems of control maintenance are seen primarily in the perspective of a centrally controlled system at the societal, group, or individual level, which is close to Bentham's idea of *Panopticon* yet without "the great *open committee* of the tribunal of the world," namely, "liberated" of the rule of publicity. In practice, the power of publicity devalued in proportion to the intensity of connections and interdependence between economic and political powers, and the media that have been transformed into large (transnational) commercial corporations. In practice the "fourth estate" of the twentieth century more *resembled* the power it ought to control than it actually controlled it. Thus one could certainly not expect that a function of "public use of reason" be discerned within the Laswellian horizon of "viewing the [communication] act as a whole in relation to the entire social process."

The functional media theory of the mid-1900s reflected two general problems of the concept of "social control" as developed in early 1900s (Sumner 1997, 5): (1) the nature of *control* (e.g., integrative versus conflict-generating forces; local versus global control) and (2) the nature of the *social* (e.g., consensual and collaborative versus hegemonic control; progressive versus conservative). While the foundational value of Bentham's societal order that was supposed to be maintained by social control (surveillance of the power) was clearly defined with the principle of *the greatest happiness of the greatest number of people*, in the 1900s it was much less explicit. It was also less a radical conception (as was the concept of publicity in Bentham) and much more related to practical reformist social policies of capitalism. The idea of three common functions of mass media seems perfectly congruent with the general observation that the notion of social control as developed in American sociology of the early 1900s has inbred bias against social "deviations" as recognized already by Tocqueville. "The social character of 'control' was put on the political agenda by people in territories where the means of production, the means of 'legitimate' violence, and the means of mass communication were in the hands of elites and specialists . . . whose power derived in one way or another from the violent suppression of alternative claims on those resources" (Sumner 1997, 8). By the end of the nineteenth century, the increase in mutual influence between the elites transformed once open and diversified liberal press markets into mass media systems, which are highly concentrated in terms of capital, markets, and firms, and highly diversified or segmented in terms of products, formats, and audiences, whereas audiences are narcotized—highly attentive to the media but lost in the exuberance of information snapshots that media provide, and consequently diverted from the real actions they are supposed to control, impede, and/or sanction, as Bentham would have suggested. According to Dewey's trenchant criticism, newspapers succeeded so perfectly in isolating sensational news from their connections with the broader course of events that "only the date of the newspaper could inform us whether they happened last year or this" (1927/1991, 180).

In the beginning of the twentieth century, the Progressive ideas of social control were reflected both in Europe and the United States in the vision of radio as a public utility that should be used for cultural and intellectual purposes and thus regulated and controlled by the state in the public interest (Kellner 1990, 30). However, the power of the biggest monopoly corporations that wanted to develop commercial, entertainment oriented broadcasting prevailed over the noncommercial uses of broadcasting. The public service model[30] was soon marginalized in the United States, but it continued for decades in many European countries as an important part of the media systems and a counterweight to the commercial model. The decline of Progressive ideas of social control in the twentieth century may have contributed to the absence of legal regulatory efforts, so that not only the press but also broadcasting remained regulated by the market forces. The emergence of a consumer society after World War II further stimulated the growth of commercial media to advertise a large variety of consumption goods. The introduction of television represented a new momentum in the development of media systems. In the beginning, television performed important democratic functions even in the United States, where it has been established as a part of the capitalist economic system and dominated by the imperative of profit maximization. In the European public service broadcasting model(s) the priority has been given to content diversity and services to the audiences. In contrast, the Benthamian "responsibility" of the media to expose abuses of power was more in the forefront in the United States.

In the late 1900s, however, broadcast media were largely "deregulated" everywhere: democratic moments of the media diminished while commercial interests augmented. At the time of "deregulation," two hundred years after Bentham's design of "the system of distrust" in which the public and the press ought to control the political power in order to prevent its abuse, the term social control largely lost any specific meaning—denoting simply all the different ways (yet all under the dominant influence of the marketplace) in which society responds to (the threat of) deviant behavior.

I will return to the relationship between the media and the public after the discussion of the historical alternative(s) to the utilitarian fourth estate concept of the press, which pursue the idea of the press and mass media as vital components of a democratic system from different perspectives—those of human liberty, equality, reason, and ethics.

NOTES

1. The examples are taken from the *Dictionnaire universel françois et latin, vulgairement appelé Dictionnaire de Trévoux* (Paris 1771), quoted in Darnton 1984, 114.

2. The quotation is from a book written by an anonymous French author, published by Joseph Berthelé as *Montpellier en 1768 d'après manuscrit anonyme inedit* (1909), as cited in Darnton (1984, 125).

3. MacKinnon shared Burke's belief (1769/1967, 106) that "to follow, not to force, the public inclination; to give a direction, a form, a technical dress, and a specific sanction to the general sense of the community is the true end of legislature," and suggested that in a "civilized country" the government is governed by public opinion and must follow its dictates. The government cannot command public opinion except but in shorter periods of despotic governments (MacKinnon 1828/1971, 9).

4. Paragraph 11 of the Declaration stipulates: "La libre communication des pensées et des opinions est une des droits les plus précieux de l'homme: tout citoyen peut donc parler, écrire, imprimer librement," in contrast to the 1776 Virginia Bill of Rights, which protects freedom of the press rather than *citizens'* freedom of publishing: "Freedom of the press is one of the great bulwarks of liberty, and can never be restrained but by despotic governments." This might be a Euro-centric reading of the Bill. As Anderson argues, the generation of the Framers of the First Amendment has regarded freedom of the press in line with the spirit of the French Declaration, as "the freedom of the people to publish their views, rather than the freedom of journalists to pursue their craft" (2002, 447). However, a significant difference between the two conceptualizations of freedom was perceived already by Tocqueville (1835, chap. 11), who attributed it to the difference between the *commercialized* American and *opinioned* French press: "In America political life is active, varied, even agitated, but is rarely affected by those deep passions which are excited only when material interests are impaired; and in the United States these interests are prosperous. A glance at a French and an American newspaper is sufficient to show the difference that exists in this respect between the two nations. In France the space allotted to commercial advertisements is very limited, and the news intelligence is not considerable, but the essential part of the journal is the discussion of the politics of the day. In America three quarters of the enormous sheet are filled with advertisements, and the remainder is frequently occupied by political intelligence or trivial anecdotes; it is only from time to time that one finds a corner devoted to passionate discussions like those which the journalists of France every day give to their readers."

The European Convention on Human Rights of 1950 still does not speak of "freedom of the press." It guarantees that "everyone has the right to freedom of expression. This right shall include freedom to hold opinions and to receive and impart information an ideas without interference by public authority and regardless of frontiers" (Art. 10 of Convention). However, the Charter of Fundamental Rights of the European Union (2000) also includes "freedom and pluralism of the media," which "shall be respected" (Art. 11 of the Charter).

5. An understanding of the business side of the press as a fourth estate is reflected in the editorial positions of trade publications. For instance, *The Fourth Estate* ("A Newspaper for the Makers of Newspapers and Investors in Advertising"), established in 1894, carried in its masthead a quote, mistakenly attributed to Carlyle, which read, "Edmund Burke said there were Three Estates in Parliament, but in the Reporters' Gallery yonder there sat a Fourth estate more important far than they all." See Hardt 1996.

6. Powe (1991, 233) identifies two "models" deriving from the right-to-know principle: One (which is the biased interpretation of the principle as I am suggesting) "would grant the press preferred status among all communicators, complete with the special legal privileges that entails. This right-to-know model elevates the press as the public's surrogate in vindicating the public's rights." The other is closer to a specific concept of the public as "political state" developed by Dewey (1927/1991, 35), suggesting that "the government is a surrogate for the public" and thus "regulates the press in those ways essential to seeing that the public's right to know receives vindication in fact as well as rhetoric." The bias of the second Powe model lies in the suggestion that the government is "a *surrogate* for the public," which should of course immediately disqualify the model as a nondemocratic solution. But if Powe followed Dewey's ideas, he would have come to a very different conclusion, namely, that the state is truly servicing the public: "This public is organized and made effective by means of representatives who as guardians of custom, as legislators, as executives, judges, etc., care for its especial interests by methods intended to regulate the conjoint actions of individuals and groups. Then and in so far as, association adds to itself political organization, and something which may be government comes into being: the public is a political state" (Dewey 1927/1954, 35).

7. This falsification is still largely accepted as a matter of fact. See, for example, Powe 1991, 233–34, 261.

8. See Macaulay's critique of James Mill's *Essay on Government*, published in 1829 in the *Edinburgh Review* (Macaulay 1828/1992).

9. As J. S. Mill suggested, Bentham's intellectual influence goes far beyond his own writings; it was often indirect, through the minds and pens of his contemporaries and followers. The idea of the fourth estate is a rather typical example.

10. See chapter 3 of Bentham's *Fragment on Government* (1776).

11. As we shall see later, this very idea of *pre*-public opinion—as the "power of thinking well or ill" rather than "using one's reason in public"—reappeared after two centuries as the idea of a kind of *post*-public opinion, which indicates that the concept of "public opinion" *in the strict sense* only pertains historically to the (liberal) bourgeois public in the period of its struggle for power, as Habermas has suggested.

12. Mill was very critical of Bentham's disciplinary approach centered around the idea that the majority of population should exercise the control over the political representatives: "We cannot think that Bentham made the most useful employment which might have been made of his great powers, when, not content with enthroning the majority as sovereign, by means of universal suffrage without king or house of lords, he exhausted all the resources of ingenuity in devising means for riveting the yoke of public opinion closer and closer round the necks of all public functionaries, and excluding every possibility of the exercise of the slightest or most temporary influence either by a minority, or by the functionary's own notions of right."

13. Gaonkar and McCarthy (1994, 555) argue that Habermas actually misread Bentham's argument in favor of his partial interpretation that "the public is well-placed to make an informed judgment or informed opinion on matters of public policy and interest under deliberation in the assembly." Yet their argument is deficient. By arguing that "only a privileged few can benefit from this interaction among publicity, the habit

of reasoning, discussing and forming enlightened opinion" in Bentham's "regime of publicity," they suggest that Habermas's concept of the liberal bourgeois public is much wider and all-embracing, which it is not.

14. Compare with Rousseau's "censorial tribunal" discussed later (pp. 85–90).

15. In his later works, Bentham replaced the term "tribunal of the world" with "Public Opinion Tribunal." "Committee" represents in his theory the central, most active and wise but slim fraction of public opinion.

16. The male character is clearly a characteristic only of Bentham's early theorization of the public. In his later work, however, Bentham emphasized just the opposite: "Not excluded from this judicatory [Public Opinion Tribunal] are, as such, any persons of the female sex. From the exercise of a share in the Constitutive power by means of votes in the election of the possessors of the supreme operative power or a share in it, they the gentler half of the species stand as yet excluded by tyranny and prejudice. But from a share in the power of this judicatory or judicatories, *not even the united force of tyranny and prejudice ever have altogether excluded them any where, much less will henceforward ever exclude them*" (1822/1990, 58; emphasis added).

17. Again, Gaonkar and McCarthy are perhaps hasty in concluding that Bentham has "an awkward position" in the "ideal synthesis in Kant" as interpreted by Habermas. Kant's idea of the principle of publicity is different, but not opposed to Bentham's "rule of publicity," since both stress that if an action is public, it means that there is no distrust in the underlying intentions.

18. In MacKinnon's work, Great Britain is most often cited as an example of a "civilised country" while Turkey is usually referred to as a typical noncivilized, barbaric country.

19. As many as half a million of people from this sector of society would be held in Bentham's proposed *Panopticon* against their will and deprived of all freedoms.

20. This was the title of a recent analysis of the transformation of the media landscape in South Africa. Retrieved December 2001 from the World Wide Web: www. btimes.co.za/96/1124/news/news10.htm.

21. Robert Park answered the question "What does communication do?" in the following way: "Communication creates, or makes possible at least, that consensus and understanding among the individual components of a social group which eventually gives it and them the character not merely of society but of a cultural unit. It spins a web of custom and mutual expectation which binds together social entities as diverse as the family group, a labor organization, or the haggling participants in a village market. Communication maintains the concert necessary to enable them to function, each in its several ways" (1938, 192–92).

22. Writings by two French authors, Gustave LeBon (*Psychologie des foules*, 1895) and Gabriel Tarde (*L'opinion et la foule*, 1901), focusing on mass behavior were—though in different ways—most influential in swerving the interest from the rational discourse forming public opinion to the behavior of common people directed by public opinion.

23. Cooley was a keen opponent of the "average theory" of public opinion. He compared the idea that public opinion ought to express an "average or commonplace mind" with the idea that "the capacity of the body for seeing is found by taking an average of the visual power of the hand, nose, liver, etc., along with that of

the eye" (Cooley 1909/1983, 125). As an organism always uses its most appropriate organ for an effective action, so each group, if it is appropriately organized, "seeks definite and effectual expression through individuals specially competent to give it such expression" (p. 124).

24. Ross's argument is almost a replica of Locke's persuasive discussion of "the punishments due from the laws of the commonwealth" (or the "laws of opinion or reputation"), suggesting that "no man escapes the punishment of their censure and dislike, who offends against the fashion and opinion of the company he keeps, and would recommend himself to. Nor is there one of ten thousand, who is stiff and insensible enough, to bear up under the constant dislike and condemnation of his own club. He must be of a strange and unusual constitution, who can content himself to live in constant disgrace and disrepute with his own particular society. Solitude many men have sought, and been reconciled to: but nobody that has the least thought or sense of a man about him, can live in society under the constant dislike and ill opinion of his familiars, and those he converses with. This is a burden too heavy for human sufferance: and he must be made up of irreconcilable contradictions, who can take pleasure in company, and yet be insensible of contempt and disgrace from his companions" (Locke 1690, bk. 2, chap. 28, p. 12).

25. Like Durkheim and Tönnies, Ross differentiated between "natural" community and society; it is only the latter in which processes of social control and maintaining social order are constitutive.

26. Ross does not explain why in the preface to the book he included public opinion among the means of an unintentional and nonpurposeful *social influence*, along with "mob mind, fashion, convention, custom . . . and the like" (p. viii, in contrast to intentional *social control*), but then discussed it as a specific means in the part of the book devoted to purposeful social control.

27. Weinberg and the Hinkles (1969, xxxvii) comment on his Progressivism: "Unlike the patrician Easterners who became Progressives to stave off revolution from below, the former Marion [where the young Ross lived after the death of his mother] farmboy was alarmed at the prospect of 'parasitism' and reaction from above."

28. On the other hand, Dewey emphasized (in contrast to Ross and Cooley) the importance of a "constant watchfulness and criticism of public officials by citizens," which ought to enable the maintenance of the state "in integrity and usefulness" (Dewey 1927/1991, 69).

29. Wirth emphasized the difference between a true consensus and "pseudoconsensus": if a seeming unanimity is obtained by coercion, it "does not truly give us consensus"; rather, it is "pseudoconsensus," or *Gleichschaltung*, as it was called by the Nazis (Wirth 1948, 8). In contrast to consensus, the pseudoconsensus is forcefully imposed. It is the result of coercion, which forces individuals to accept and follow a norm of behavior or decision because they fear possible reprisal. See Splichal 1999.

30. The *public service* model is distinguished from other models of media operation by its specific definition of goals and duties, rather than mere legal form of ownership.

3

Freedom to Reason, Right to Communicate

Much of the "control paradigm" substantiating the need and utility of freedom of the press is focused on the role newspapers (may) play in order to contribute to "happiness" and "pleasure" of the people, to "check the government," or to "organize people's minds." In earlier rationalist studies, freedom of speech had been considered primarily a privilege of men of letters to express their *opinions* in public—yet based on the premise, as Benedict de Spinoza argued, that no human being can ever be deprived of the right to *reason* and *judge* under democratic government; only his *actions* have to be submitted to the control of authority. In contrast, theorizations of social control established through institutionalized forms of communication were concerned with the flow of *information*. As Edmund Burke stated, the people must have the right to demand information from the government because "he that is bound to act in the dark cannot be said to act freely." Consistent with these ideas, the press and public opinion were perceived as a means to control the deeds and behavior of either the privileged few or the population at large, but not their minds. The idea of the publicity of all government actions in Jeremy Bentham's theory was closely connected with the "public's right to know"—an idea justifying the fourth estate function of the media, which after World War II became almost synonymous with "freedom of the press" in the United States. Specifically, according to Bentham, the task of the press ought to be to disseminate *information* between the governors and the governed in both ways, thus contributing to knowledge "for forming an enlightened judgment" on both sides.

The surveillance paradigm of publicity shaded the *creative* dimension of publicness and degraded the idea of freedom of the press to freedom of *distribution* rather than *expression*. Its focal point is the press (or "public opinion" in general) as a mediator between the governors and the governed, as a "transportation" means to deliver information to those who (should) need it. Like the radiation of a beam of light, information dissemination would throw light on the government (or any other entity from the individual to the population at large) and make it visible far and wide. Publicity may be a perfect "system of distrust," as Bentham wanted to design it in practice, in which each one sees in other persons a constraint to his own freedom and must constantly survey the environment to protect his or her own interests. Less likely, however, such a publicity could provide "the greatest happiness of the greatest number of people," and it certainly cannot enable the realization of human *freedom*. As John Stuart Mill claimed, the utilitarians of Bentham's generation desired liberal government because they believed it would bring about an *efficient* system, and not for the sake of *freedom* as a moral value in its own right. Unlike individual freedom of expression, freedom of the press became seen—particularly by professionals in the media and communication—as freedom of journalists, editors, or publishing corporations, based on the argument that the press pursues important functions for society and/or citizens, thus being an "instrument" for the realization of *other* citizen rights and freedoms. I shall argue that an instrumental justification of press freedom, which presents freedom of the press as absolutely different from freedom of expression, is not justified in the intellectual history of the concept, but rather in a partial interpretation of that history.

The age of Enlightenment, brought about by new scientific and geographic discoveries and rationalist thinkers of the seventeenth century, engendered an almost unrestrained faith and confidence in the capacity of human reason. It was a "Western" (European and North American) philosophic and broader intellectual movement of the eighteenth century that prepared the terrain for democratic revolutions. The word itself suggested a radical departure from the previous "dark ages" in which ignorance, immaturity, and dependency prevailed, with people subordinated to religious authorities. The age of Enlightenment is popularly considered to have died with the French Revolution of 1789, but in fact it profoundly influenced also the ideas of the nineteenth and twentieth centuries. With its adoration of personal freedom, citizens' equality, human right to reason freely on matters of religion and politics, and respect for human reason as the supreme arbiter and the historical motive power, the Enlightenment stimulated humanitarian reforms and progress throughout the nineteenth century. A significant part of those reforms pertained to the press, which became a powerful tool for spreading ideas of Enlightenment and liberating human mind and action.

The discourses opposing autocratic censorship and favoring freedom of the press that flourished during the eighteenth and nineteenth centuries were derived from the assumed necessity of personal freedom to think—or, as Kant would say, to "use reason in public"—and the emergence of reasoned individuals in "public opinion" aimed against absolutist authority. In the period when governments' claim to sovereignty was not yet legitimized by the people's consent, press freedom was considered a guarantee against illegitimate exercise of power by the State and other authoritative institutions such as the Church over the individual. A free press did not represent an end in itself, but a means of the personal freedom to express and publish opinions.

Conceptualizations of freedom of the press that in the nineteenth and twentieth centuries pursued Bentham's "tribunal" concept of publicity and the idea of the press as the fourth estate sharply deviated from the rationalist[1] democratic ideas of personal freedom of expression and publication of opinions. The latter approaches to publicity—arising since the seventeenth century—emphasized the "power" of knowledge and individual's *reason*, and the need to use it in public discourse, which would eventually give rise to *public opinion*, as well as the autonomy of moral will. In these considerations the press was normatively conceived of as a means of expression of public or general will, rather than of any particular interest group or estate. Yet freedom and moral obligation of publication must belong to individuals or they will be seriously endangered.

LIBERTY IN EQUALITY: CONTROVERSIES ON ROUSSEAU'S CENSORIAL TRIBUNAL

At first glance, ideas professed by Jean-Jacques Rousseau (1712–1778) have no relevance for freedom of expression and publication, and even less for freedom of the press. A more thorough analysis of his ideas, however, reveals a great deal of connection. In fact, Rousseau was among the first to realize the importance of publicity and public opinion. He added public opinion, together with morality and custom, to the three conventional categories of law—political law constituting a state, civil law regulating relations between citizens, and penal law regulating relations between the individual and law—as the fourth one. He considered public opinion the *fourth power* "graven . . . on the hearts of the citizens," which "forms the real constitution of the State, takes on every day new powers, when other laws decay or die out, restores them or takes their place, keeps a people in the ways in which it was meant to go, and insensibly replaces authority by the force of habit" (1762a). In *The Social Contract*, he saw public opinion as an assurance of the execution of all other laws rather than a special type of law; for that reason, and since *everybody* participates in its formation and execution, it is believed to be the most important of all forms of general will. Together with morality and custom, public opinion represents "a power unknown to political thinkers, on which none the less success in everything else depends" (1762a/1952, 406); but it may also controvert the general will, since it "confines the course of life within the limits of the most miserable uniformity," as Rousseau claimed in *Emile* (1762b, 1235).

Very much in contrast to his contemporaries, Rousseau did not see any connection between public opinion and the press, but this is certainly not the only uniqueness of his conception of public opinion.

Contrary to Kant or modern neo-Kantians (see Hutchings 1996), Rousseau's public opinion tends to be opinion *about* public matters, but it is clearly not opinion formed in or by the public (through public discourse). In his writings it is not even always clear that it is indeed opinion about *public* matters. According to Rousseau, public opinion is based (and here he resembles Montaigne) on a moral authority and therefore comes close to the role of moral arbiter (Tönnies 1922, 291). In contrast to his contemporaries in France and elsewhere, Rousseau did not consider public opinion a new form of institutionalization of rationality to legitimize political decisions, but a customary, controversial, and even irrational collective opinion. In the fifth book of *Emile*, where Sophie is to become Emile's companion, Rousseau—while discussing her education—relates public opinion to both *sentiment* and *reason*:

> Sentiment without respect for public opinion will not give [to women] that delicacy of soul which lends to right conduct the charm of social approval, while respect for public opinion without sentiment will only make false and wicked women who put appearances in the place of virtue.
>
> It is, therefore, important to cultivate a faculty which serves as judge between the two guides, which does not permit conscience to go astray and corrects the errors of prejudice. That faculty is reason. (1762b, 1339, 1340)

Rousseau does not see any need for deliberation over public matters among citizens at large. As he argued in *Emile* and *The Social Contract*, public deliberation is only competent to bind private persons to the "public person" or "sovereign" when individuals make a contract with themselves, by which they are bound to the sovereign—the body politic consisting of all citizens. As Rousseau states, "no one is bound by any engagement to which he was not himself a party" (1762b, 1651), and that is only the case in relation to all the others constituting the body politic of the Sovereign. Otherwise, such deliberation could lead to the formation of "cliques" and "groups" based on their private interests, and acting to the detriment of the community and general will. It usually happens in public deliberation, according to Rousseau, that "particular wills are substituted for the general will," as a consequence of the fact that "the best advice is not taken without question." "Contradictory views and debates" and the absence of "unanimous opinion," which are characteristic of public deliberation, are considered by Rousseau signs of "the broken social bond . . . in every heart," and of a growing influence of particular interests over the general will.

Public opinion ought to ideally result, without any intermediary, from small differences between opinions of citizens who would not interact. Rousseau assumed that differences would remain small if people would not interact, whereas interaction would produce factions and increase the differences. Instead, the only form of citizen deliberation needed is *intra-personal*; internal cognition of public good based on adequate information is the basis of the formation of the general will. In such cases decision would always be right, since it would tend to the general good and public advantage, the "greatest good" and "the end of every system" being *liberty* and *equality*—"liberty, because all particular dependence means so much force taken from the body of the State and equality, because liberty cannot exist without it" (1762a; emphasis added). In an ideal situation, public debate is altogether *superfluous*, public opinion is a consensus of hearts and needs no arguments presented in a public discussion; in fact, according to Rousseau it needs no communication at all.

Rousseau's conception of public opinion as a moral force is embedded in his theory of the general will developed in his best known work *The Social Contract or Principles of Political Right* (1762a). In it he elucidates the relationship between the individual and society, which is also essential for his concept of public opinion. Contrary to his earlier support for the state of nature, Rousseau in the *Contract* suggests that the human race had reached the point where the preservation of the state of nature cannot subsist any longer. Thus he was seeking to solve the problem of how "to find a form of association which will defend and protect with the whole common force the person and goods of each associate, and in which each, while uniting himself with all, may still obey himself alone, and remain as free as before." His solution was the "compact" agreed to among individuals that sets the conditions for membership in society, thus establishing a *"moral* and *collective* body"* (the republic or community of citizens) in which all individual rights, including that of property,[2] are rights within the community defined in relation to others and not against them. Rousseau argued that the main goal of government—which should only be the "minister of the sovereign," a sort of commission, "an employment," in which officials appointed by citizens exercise in their own name the power entrusted to them by citizens—should be to secure freedom, equality, and justice for all members of society, regardless of the will of the majority.[3]

One of the primary principles of Rousseau's contemplation is that politics and morality must not be separated. He followed David Hume,[4] who challenged the view that morality involves a rational judgment, arguing instead that the role of reason in moral decisions is very limited. Thus, for Rousseau, the question of liberty is essentially a moral question: "To renounce liberty is to renounce being a man, to surrender the rights of humanity and even its duties. . . . Such a renunciation is incompatible with man's nature; to remove all liberty from his will is to remove all morality from his acts" (Rousseau 1762a).

In contrast to natural liberty as an "unlimited right to everything" a person tries and/or succeeds to get, restricted only by the strength of the individual,

Rousseau introduced the concept of *civil liberty* that is based on morality. Contrary to the lawlessness of natural liberty, civil liberty is "obedience to a law which we prescribe to ourselves" and thus limited by the general will: "when the voice of duty takes the place of physical impulses and right of appetite, does man, who so far had considered only himself, find that he is forced to act on different principles, and to consult his reason before listening to his inclinations" (1762a). Only with civil liberty, which a person acquires in the "civil state," does he or she develop from "a stupid and unimaginative animal" into an intelligent and moral human being. As Rousseau romantically argued in *Emile*, "Liberty is not to be found in any form of government. It is in the heart of the free man" (1762b, 1719).

The moral foundation of liberty is specifically reflected in Rousseau's conviction that true liberty is based on *equality*. While he conceded that equality does not imply that "the degrees of power and riches are to be absolutely identical for everybody," he rejected the idea that liberty is by nature inegalitarian. Without equality, no liberty can really exist. For Rousseau, equality—like liberty—is both moral and legal category; equality is constitutive of liberty not only in the sense of equality of opportunity and before the law. He emphasized that by "equality" we should understand

> that power shall never be great enough for violence, and shall always be exercised by virtue of rank and law; and that, in respect of riches, no citizen shall ever be wealthy enough to buy another, and none poor enough to be forced to sell himself: which implies, on the part of the great, moderation in goods[5] and position, and, on the side of the common sort, moderation in avarice and covetousness. (Rousseau 1762a)

He admitted that an ideal-type equality would be difficult to attain in practice, but precisely because circumstances continually tend to destroy it, legal regulation should be designed to maintain it. According to Rousseau, the fundamental part of social contract and social system is the establishment of "an equality that is moral and legitimate, and that men, who may be unequal in strength or intelligence, become every one equal by convention and legal right."

Like J. S. Mill after him, Rousseau's concept of democracy followed the example of the ancient direct democracy of Athens, although he was critical of it (e.g., of the lack of division between legislative and executive functions) and more often took examples from ancient Rome. Rousseau's ideal of democracy, though on the national scale, was modeled on antique Greek city-state meetings, celebrating citizens actively involved in political processes. Hence it is not difficult to understand why he so firmly believed that "the larger the State, the less the liberty" (1762a). Nor it is difficult to understand that Rousseau's warning against an extensive increase in the size of the state was not popular in the era of the growth of nation-states and world powers, eventually brutally crushed down in the two World Wars. At present, however, processes of globalization, the rise of transnational corporations, integration of national markets, and (inter)national politics on a worldwide scale gave rise to the reexamination of how participation relates to complexity; computer-mediated communication, such as the Internet, may help solve the problems, but it is not *the* solution in itself. This also raises a more specific question of how globalization relates to freedom of the press—a question I will address in chapter 4.

Rousseau was convinced that the people on their own would always *want* the good (liberty and equality in the last instance), but they would not always *see* the good and may need to be directed. Even if deliberations of the people are wrong, which may happen, it is not on account of corrupted will, but because of deception and their limited capacity for judgment that guides deliberation. Thus it is very important that citizens receive appropriate information and, in particular, that they are properly educated. Education plays the central role in Rousseau's conceptualization of democracy and freedom. Only education can prevent the people from deception and enable them to see what is good; and only then the general will tending to the public advantage would be right. Rousseau's ideas about education—suggesting that a child's emotions should be educated before his reason, limiting the importance of book learning, and emphasizing learning by experience—have profoundly influenced modern educational theory.

A serious problem in Rousseau's theory is that he left the concept of "general will" very abstract, most of the time identified with "the constant will of all the members of the State," and expressed in (abstract) law as its only "authentic acts." Yet laws are only authentic if ratified in person by the people as the sovereign. In *The Social Contract*, he postulates two fundamental conditions for the formation of the general will: that every citizen reasons with his or her own reason and that no special interest groups exist in society because they would concern themselves with their own instead of the general interests. (If these groups already exist, it is necessary to ensure that there are as many of them as possible and to prevent inequality among them.) A discussion of public issues among citizens would be needed only in the case that partial associations were formed: the will of each of these associations then becomes *general* in relation to its members and *particular* in relation to the state, which would make it more difficult to form the general will. In such cases, "the will of all" would prevail over "the general will." The former includes private interests, thus being merely a sum of particular wills, whereas the latter only considers the common interest. Potentially, then, the press—which was never a serious subject in Rousseau's writings[6]—would be needed only for disseminating information and not exchanging opinions.

Notwithstanding, some public discourse is needed to reach decisions; in such cases, publicity is reduced to a discussion of public issues in public assemblies rather than among citizens in general. Thus the general will is based on the debate and decisions of enlightened and appropriately educated people only, and it is expressed as general opinion—as, for example, by voting in a political assembly[7]—whereas special opinion (the opinion of special groups) prevails at times when the general will does not exist. There is no specific "organ" needed to form the general will because the sovereign (citizenry) cannot be represented by any other body than itself (themselves). Rousseau celebrated active and enlightened citizens who would ideally meet together to decide what is best for the community and make appropriate laws. Ideally, decisions would rest on publicly reached agreement on the public good; if opinions on the public good differ, majority rule would be an acceptable approximation of agreement.

Rousseau postulated the sovereignty of people more strictly than any of his predecessors: he did not see the government, and even not people's deputies, as their representatives but only as their agents, who could be even chosen randomly—provided that an adequate (but not absolute) level of social equality of citizens would be achieved. He favored direct democracy where the government should be merely an administrative committee taking the burden of implementing the general will. However, it has to act in a moral fashion or else it ceases to exert genuine authority over the individual and preserve his or her freedom.

The idea of direct democracy is also clearly reflected in his conceptualization of public opinion. In both instances Rousseau supposed that the executive "committees" (the government and censorial tribunal) would merely "execute" general will and public opinion vested in the citizens. But of course he could not explain how that could really be done—and many "experiments" with revolutionary committees in history from the French Revolution to East European or East Asian socialism of the twentieth century falsified the idea.

Two Faces of Public Opinion

A further complication with Rousseau's concept of "public opinion" originates from his significant distinction between the "general will" and the "will of all." The former represents a *consensus* on the common good and the latter only the aggregate of different individual, *partial* desires. Apart from the distinction between "public opinion" and the three other kinds of laws in *The Social Contract*, Rousseau did not consistently differentiate between the general will and public opinion. His notion of public opinion is contradictory, entirely congruent with neither the concept of "general will" nor "the will of all." The general will is expressed through laws, whereas public opinion is the judgment of the people specifically institutionalized as a "form of law which the censor administers, and, like the prince, only applies to particular cases. The censorial tribunal, so far from being the arbiter of the people's opinion, only declares it, and, as soon as the two part company, its decisions are null and void" (Rousseau 1762a). Following the example of the magistrates of ancient Rome who took a register of the number and property of citizens for taxation and also exercised the office of inspectors of morals and conduct, Rousseau conceived the institute of "censor" or "censorial tribunal," whose task should not be to judge "the opinion of the people" but just to make it public. The demarcation between public opinion and censorial tribunal is clearly in analogy with Rousseau's strict separation of the executive function of the government from the legislative function appertaining to the sovereign citizenry; yet the institute of censorship as a separate "commission" remains rather obscure. Its function is contributing to the *preservation* of customs and morals but not *changing* them; the task of the censorial tribunal is to "apply" public opinion but not judge it. A possible interpretation would be that Rousseau saw in public opinion de facto, and in all other kinds of law de jure general will.

However, his alternative conceptualization of public opinion as a corruptive force, particularly in *Emile* (1762b), suggests that public opinion is closer to the aggregate "will of all" formed by "subjects" than to the "general will" formed by "citizens." In any event, it remains unclear how individual desires and opinions make public opinion "the most important type of law" that also ensures the implementation of all other laws. Indeed, Rousseau was very controversial on this issue. If public opinion shares its nature with morals and manners, but the latter are "particular wills" in relation to the "general will" represented in law, as Rousseau claimed, it is a logical confusion to claim that public opinion is a form of general will. Rousseau also emphasized that "opinions of a people are *derived* from its constitution; although the law does not regulate morality, it is legislation that gives it birth," which would imply that public opinion is secondary to (at least political) law (1762a). In either case, however, the necessity of some form of *institutionalization* would be constitutive of public opinion, although Rousseau obviously rejected the idea that newspapers could perform that function, as one can infer from his negative attitude toward "horrid disorders which the press has already caused in Europe," on which he briefly commented in one of his earliest essays, the famed "Discours sur les sciences et les arts" (1750).

Unfortunately Rousseau's ideas about public opinion are much less coherent than his theory of political democracy. It is very difficult to grasp his position without a great deal of interpretation, for example, in analogy with his elaboration on the relationship between the sovereign people and government. The "law of opinion" significantly differs from all other laws in whose creation individuals are ideally directly involved: Rousseau argued in favor of public meetings in which sovereign citizens would decide what is "common good," thus expressing the general will. In contrast, he believed that public opinion is likely to arise from "people's hearts" without any public discussion; he was afraid that the latter would actually only infect individual opinions with group interests to the detriment of the general will. In Bentham's interpretation (1781/1996), "opinion publique" in the pre-Revolutionary France of the late eighteenth century referred "to that tutelary power, of which of late so much is said, and by which so much is done," but it would be better to use the term *popular opinion* to express its *constituent cause.* Yet the term "popular opinion" also has, according to Bentham, a drawback: "if *opinion* is material, it is only in virtue of the influence it exercises over action, through the medium of the affections and the will" (1781/1996, n. 12), but this conceptual dimension is lost in the term "popular opinion." There is a further complication with the notion of public opinion referring to eighteenth-century France. According to Beaud and Kaufmann, it was neither an enlightened opinion nor a tacit consensus in people's hearts that prevailed in communication among citizens, which was neither clearly public nor private. Rather, "in the seditious writings that circulate around Paris, it's not the Parliamentary debates or the state of finances that are gibed at but the personal intrigues, the private animosities, the sexual caprices that distract the king from his duties to the nation and bankrupt the public treasury" (Beaud and Kaufmann 2001, 64).[8]

It is easy to understand, now, why Rousseau vacillated between completely opposite concepts of (public) opinion. Throughout *Emile* (1762b), which Rousseau wrote at the same time as *The Social Contract*, his discussion of the ideal citizen and the means of educating the child for the state in accordance with nature is alternated with discussions of the corrupting force of public opinion based on human "love of imitating,"[9] which is "well regulated by nature; in society it becomes a *vice*" (1762b, 313; emphasis added). Terms that Rousseau uses in *Emile*—such as *the poison* of public opinion, *slave* of public opinion, *tyranny* of public opinion, *yoke* of public opinion, or *prejudices* of public opinion (1762b, 610, 703, 1195, 1235, 1615)—and his conclusion that "public opinion is the grave of a man's virtue and the throne of a woman's" (1762b, 1278) are hardly compatible with his idea of public opinion as the fourth power and a form of general will expressed in *The Social Contract.*[10]

Rousseau's ideas of public opinion as the most important type of all laws, with censors as its administrative commission in analogy with the government reduced to an administrative committee, are excessive normative idealizations. Rousseau's guiding spirit was to arrive at a legal and reliable state in which justice and legality, and liberty and equality would be in harmony. Unfortunately, he considered only political laws relevant for the social contract, and thus he was not clear about how the "fourth type of law"—public opinion—should contribute to "a good government," prevent "the abuse of government," and "check the usurpations of government." Nevertheless, Rousseau is clear in stating that no special power should belong to any arbiter, let alone the press, *in the name* of public opinion or citizens.

Controversial ideas on public opinion and his early repugnance for the press are not central to Rousseau's theories; nevertheless, these perhaps peripheral ideas reflect the specific character of Rousseau's theory of liberty, equality, property, and democracy, which influenced later conceptualizations of publicity and freedom of the press, notably with Kant and Marx, and even Mill, who did not share most of Rousseau's ideas of equality and general will.[11] Popularity of the *Contract* may also have contributed that, ever since Rousseau, the ideals of democracy and the rule of law have been linked to *public opinion.*

Consider the following conundrum: "What is the power on which everything else depends, which guarantees the execution of all laws, but at the same time confines the course of life within the limits of the most miserable uniformity?"

The most probable answer to the question construed solely of words Rousseau used to define public opinion would be, "the press!" Yet Rousseau would never choose this answer.

The censorial tribunal proposed by Rousseau resembled Bentham's idea of the Public Opinion Tribunal, whose essential part, as a sort of its executive organ, was the press. Although significant differences exist between the two "tribunals"—including the role of the press—the two concepts are not entirely exclusive. In accordance with the *greatest happiness principle,* Bentham's Public Opinion Tribunal was pragmatically intended to control all actions of the legislature in order to prevent misrule and oblige the authorities to act in the best interest of the people by forming an enlightened judgment. Rousseau's censorial tribunal was outlined more abstractly as a committee, whose main task was to apply public opinion to specific cases, thus contributing to a permanent formation and implementation of the general will (or, in contrast, the will of all). It differed from Bentham's tribunal in that is was primarily supposed to not only bring up but also breed "right" opinions, thus emphasizing the disciplinary function of public opinion that only later—but in much more critical vein—pervaded social discourse (e.g., Tocqueville, Mill, Bryce, Lippmann, Ross, and Cooley).

Rousseau did not trust newspapers or any other intermediary between citizens and the general will manifested in the decisions of the government. As a fervent herald of direct democracy, he "liberated" public opinion of any specific intermediaries and "organs" but censorial tribunal, thus also newspapers. As his rare notes on the press indicate, he was everything else but eager to include newspaper publishing and reading among citizen actions heading for general will.

Nevertheless, newspapers became the most common medium expressing or representing public opinion during the early phase of modern history. Since the first appearances of newspapers, they were not exclusively intended to supplement privately mediated news (letters), but mostly to spread news and opinions that were specifically *intended* for the public. Paradoxically, before newspapers reached a nationwide circulation, which was a condition sine qua non to public opinion as a national phenomenon (Splichal 1999), they ceased to be a genuine means of public opinion expression, since they became *organs of political parties* (what Rousseau would be afraid of) or "a large capitalist business whose direct and main goal is to create profit" (Tönnies 1922, 179–80). Freedom of the press was degraded to a category of property right and freedom of entrepreneurship, and the press to a power or estate independent of the public—thus proving that the power/estate metaphor, if taken literally, is merely a caricature of freedom, since it blurs the essence of the idea of free expression and publication pursued by great minds of the eighteenth and nineteenth centuries. Yet this happened long after Rousseau's time.

These substantial changes in the press relate to the nature of *publicness*, from which also (changes in) public opinion emanated. Of course, public deliberation as the human "body" of the abstract principle of publicity—paradoxically deemed redundant if not even detrimental by Rousseau—has never been limited to the press and mass media. Universities, associations, even coffeehouses remain the sites of the "public use of reason" until these very days. Nevertheless, the press was the most important means of the materialization of citizens' right to think and speak, and hopefully publish, freely, for it was by far the most inclusive means of expressing and influencing public opinion in terms of the size of the public and diversity of issue areas.

RIGHT TO FREEDOM: KANT'S PRINCIPLE OF PUBLICITY

Immanuel Kant (1724–1804), the last philosopher who was at the same time a natural scientist, is considered by many the most influential thinker of modern times. The essays he published on the universal value of human freedom, rights, and publicity of human acts have a significance that exceeds most of the more detailed accounts of freedom of the press in the history. Not only may (and should) Kant's general ideas on freedom, reason, judgment, and right be related to such specific social phenomena as publicity, public opinion, communication, and, specifically, the press; Kant enthusiastically tackled this task himself on several occasions, starting with the article "Beantwortung der Frage: Was ist Aufklärung?" (1784), followed by the essay "Über den Gemeinspruch: Das mag in der Theorie richtig sein, taugt aber nicht für die Praxis" (1793), and his last two publications *Zum ewigen Frieden* (1795/1983) and *Der Streit der Fakultäten* (1798/1979), not to mention his fundamental works in philosophy and ethics. Unfortunately, and despite his most elaborate discussion of publicness (or perhaps because of that), Kant remains—and Marx joined him later—the path not taken by modern defenders of freedom of the press. It is easy to understand why Kant's ideas were completely overlooked by the most eager corporate and professional defenders of independence—rather than freedom—of the press in the twentieth century: the strength of the "fourth estate" and "free marketplace" arguments is seriously worn out by Kant's coherent, deliberative model of publicity. No such "justification" could be found, however, for modern *theories* of the press.

Kant's persistent and profound concern for human *freedom* justifies classifying his work concerning publicness into the liberal current of social thought despite his strict subordination of freedom to categorical or unconditional imperatives, which express generally what constitutes obligation. Like Rousseau, who considered freedom the fundamental right of humanity, Kant defines human freedom as the only right that belongs to everyone by nature. Kant's negative conception of freedom corresponds to the common idea of "the act of volitional choice," which is not "determined by sensuous impulses or stimuli," whereas his positive conception of freedom is "given by the fact that the will is the capability of pure reason to be practical of itself," which is only possible if the maxim of action is "subjected to the condition of being practicable as a universal law" (1785/1952, 386). Kant defines freedom negatively as "independence of the compulsory will of another." Negatively defined freedom denotes freedom *from* interference by others and the absence of obstacles that may impede the satisfaction of individual interests and needs; thus individuals may define and satisfy them without any external impediment. In contrast, "positive freedom" is defined in relation to a universal law; it is "the one sole original, inborn right belonging to every man in virtue of his humanity . . . in so far as it can coexist with the freedom of all according to a universal law" (1797, 401). Freedom makes rational human beings *ends in themselves*—not because of reason but because of freedom that gives us the dignity; reason merely enables us to be conscious of our existence. The supreme principle of morality or categorical imperative, "Act according to a maxim which can be adopted at the same time as a universal law,"[12] presents an obligatory moral and legal constraint to "negative freedom." An important element of both Rousseau's and Kant's political philosophy was the importance attributed to moral sentiments. Contrary to traditional rationalism and liberalism, and despite the great value the Enlightenment gave to reason and science, both Kant and Rousseau excluded reason from the strict definition of moral virtues. According to Kant, freedom alone—under the general condition of universal agreement with the will of others—is necessary and sufficient condition for human beings to be ends in themselves.

Autonomy in Cultivated Reasoning and Construction of Shared Meanings

Human freedom is a fundamental condition for the formation of the "civil state" of society from, and in contrast to, the natural condition of mankind. Similarly to Rousseau, Kant identified in his article "Ueber den Gemeinspruch: Das mag in der Theorie richtig sein, taugt aber nicht für die Praxis"[13] (1793), and later in *To Perpetual Peace* (1795/1983, 100–102), three basic principles upon which a civil state of society should be founded: (1) the *liberty* of every member of the society as a *man*, (2) the *equality* of every member of the society with every other as a *subject* and the dependence of all on common legislation, and (3) the *self-dependency (Selbständigkeit)* of every member of the commonwealth as a *citizen*. On sovereignty, Kant again takes up a position similar to that of Rousseau, namely, that individuals made a contract with the entire social body, whose members they became *qua citizens* with the very same act and with the sole end to realize "the rights of men under public compulsory laws, by which every individual can have what is his own assigned to him and secured the encroachments or assaults of others" (1793, 30). The idea of an "external law" as universal law to which every one must obey arises exclusively from the idea of human *freedom*, which is made possible by such a contract. In Kant's view, the laws of freedom—as distinguished from the laws of nature—are both juridical (referring to external relations or actions of one person to another, and their lawfulness) and ethical (as determining principles of our actions). This duality is essential also for Kant's idea of publicness *(Öffentlichkeit)*, which he conceived simultaneously as "the principle of the legal order" and as "the method of enlightenment" (Habermas 1962/1995, 104), and discussed it on three levels: (1) as *the universal public* (commonwealth) equal to the people as the source of the rational social contract and participant (critical observer) in the formation of general will, (2) as *the universal principle of publicity* mediating between politics and morals, (3) as the *right of citizens to make their opinions public*, which is the axiomatic condition of the mediating function of publicity.

The main difference between Kant and Rousseau is in the relation between liberty and equality, and the definition of equality: liberty is defined by Kant as everybody's entitlement "to seek his own happiness in the way that seems to him best, if it does not infringe liberty of others in striving for a similar end for themselves when their liberty is capable of consisting with the right of liberty in all others according to possible universal laws" (1793/1914, 31). The principle of equality stipulates that "every member of the commonwealth has rights against every other that may be enforced by compulsory laws" (p. 32), with the exception of the sovereign. Equality under the law does not imply the enforcement of any other form of equality among individuals, specifically not equality in property; on the contrary, "it is quite compatible with the greatest inequality" in material and spiritual terms. The principle of self-dependency is, according to Kant, the basis of the unity of the will, together with freedom and equality, from which the "original contract" or the fundamental law emanates. This principle discrim inates between citizens who have a voice in legislation regardless of the size of property and "protected fellow subjects"—women, children, and all those who have no property supporting them—who have no right to vote. Kant's view of the self-dependency is quite undemocratic, relying heavily on the bourgeois middle class. Whereas everybody has the right to claim freedom and equality (as a passive subject), not all subjects are qualified to deal with the state as active citizens:

> All they have a right in their circumstances to claim may be no more than that whatever be the mode in which the positive laws are enacted, these laws must not be contrary to the natural laws that demand the freedom of all the people and the equality that is conformable thereto; and it must therefore be made *possible for them to raise themselves from this passive condition in the state to the condition of active citizenship.* (Kant 1797/1952, 437; emphasis added)

Surely enough, Kant limited active participation in the political (public) sphere to property owners. However, is (the right to) private property constitutive of human freedom, specifically freedom of speech and the press? Kant's answer is, again, similar to Rousseau's: property right is seen as the foundation of the civil state which, however, is created through public opinion but should exclude (hereditary rights to) possession. While Kant limits the right of participation to those who can compete in the marketplace, he suggests— when questioning the proprietors' right to "transmit the land for a sole exclusive use to the following generations for all time"—that the state can annul any hereditary privileges to individuals or to a class, such as nobility or clergy,

> for the foundation of their previous possession lay only in the opinion of the people, and it can be valid only so long as this opinion lasts. As soon as this public opinion in favour of such institutions dies out, or is even extinguished in the judgement of those who have the greatest claim by their acknowledged merit to lead and represent it, the putative proprietorship in question must cease, as if by a public appeal made regarding it to the state. (1797/1952, 442)

The right of resisting the law and actively participating in legislation only applies to the state or to the legislator (citizens); subjects—those to whom the right to participate in public affairs is not granted—should have no right to either of them. Kant emphasized that the right to vote belongs to the "citoyen," not the "bourgeois." In contrast to the possession of land, property is considered by Kant a *condition for a citizen to be his own master:* the quality needed for the elective franchise is, "besides of the natural (not being a child or a women), *only one:* that he must be his own master (sui juris), *thus* (mithin) he must have some property"[14] (1793, 245; emphasis added). Yet Kant admitted that "it is somewhat difficult to define the qualifications which entitle anyone to claim the status of being his own master" (1793, 246; Habermas 1962/1995, 110) and left the door open for everybody to qualify as a proprietor and citizen (except children and women). We may deduce that *the* genuine condition for the franchise is that of being one's own master (i.e., autonomous in reasoning and able to use one's own reason in public), whereas "some property" is used as an operational—not entirely reliable—criterion, as merely an indicator of his individual mastery qua citizen. The point here is certainly not to suggest that Kant was maybe more democratic than usually considered, but rather that the condition of "being one's own master" could be, in different circumstances, attained without the presumption of property and without compromising Kant's theory of publicity.

Kant differs from Rousseau by arguing that an active citizenship assumes the public use of *reason* and, consequently, citizens' *right* to make their opinions public. Kant's "public use of reason" denotes a specific type of deliberative communication, which demands at least some familiarity and understanding of the political process and citizenship. It is what Stephen Macedo calls "a certain form and quality of reasoning," emphasizing that "citizens should participate in the spirit of public justification: not simply asserting their own positions, but considering and addressing the reasonable arguments of others, including those of public officials" (quoted in Schudson 1997, 303). Specific norms of the public use of reason are not incorporated in just any form of communication.

Kant's view of publicity relying primarily on the men of letters does not seem very democratic if compared with Rousseau. However, Kant also declared the need of a universal liberation from the human impossibility of using one's own reason—the need of expanding the number of those entitled to active citizenship. The liberal Kant believed that the social basis of citizenship would expand with the privatization of civil society (Habermas 1962/1995, 111)—an idea that was definitely invalidated by Karl Marx. Nevertheless, Kant's confidence in liberal bourgeois ideals does not contradict his universal theory of publicness. His conceptualizations of "public use of reason," "principle of publicity," and "opinion" as a distinct (the lowest) level of "holding-for-true" are momentous for *any* discussion on freedom of the press.

Kant specifically elaborates the concept of opinion which, in *Critique of Pure Reason,* is defined as the lowest level of "holding-for-true" *(Für-*

wahrhalten). Kant sharply distinguishes opinion, belief, and knowledge, which are the three "modes of holding-for-true," three kinds of judgment "through which something is presented true." Similarly to Plato's definition "that the mind of the one who knows has knowledge, and that the mind of the other, who opines only, has opinion" (360 B.C./1901, 170), Kant specifies opinion as fugitive, uncertain, and contrasted negatively against the truth, or knowledge as the strongest mode of judgment of truth. Holding-for-true is, according to Kant, determined by the subjective and objective validity of judgment and has three levels (1781/1952, 241): opining *(Meinen)*, believing *(Glauben)*, and knowing *(Wissen)*. In contrast to John Locke, who did not make any distinction between "faith" and "opinion"—defining both in contrast to knowledge as "that assent which we give to any proposition as true, of whose truth yet we have no certain knowledge" (Locke 1690, 3)—Kant strictly differentiated between the two in terms of (the degree of) certainty and conviction. Certainty was the criterion Locke used to distinguish between mere guessing and true knowledge, but he did not compare the two in terms of conviction. For Kant, opinion is both subjectively and objectively insufficient,[15] and belief is subjectively sufficient but lacks objectivity; only knowledge is sufficient on both accounts. Subjective sufficiency is termed "conviction" (a judgment is sufficiently valid for myself); objective sufficiency is termed "certainty" (sufficient for everyone).[16] One can only test the degree of subjective sufficiency, that is, the difference between "conviction"—a judgment valid for every rational being and thus objectively sufficient—and "persuasion," which is merely an illusion having only private validity, if the judgment is *communicated*: persuasion cannot be distinguished from conviction so long as we do not discover its validity for others or achieve the discursive agreement of all individual judgments (1781/1952, 240).

Kant's discussion of the quality of opinion, in contrast to belief and knowledge, was later resumed by Ferdinand Tönnies, who stressed in his *Critique of Public Opinion* that opinions are *particular* and *determined by interests*, since "the recognizing subjects have their 'human flaws'" (Tönnies 1922, 187).[17] The same opinions frequently indicate the same benefits and interests, and opinion struggles largely demonstrate fights between social strata and classes. Only in the sciences can human recognition, and the opinion it forms, have a quality of necessity. Thus the idea that opinions only depend on a human aspiration for knowledge cannot represent a general practical assumption regarding public opinion. Using numerous historical examples, Tönnies demonstrated that public opinion always presupposed and included different opinions, which resulted from differences in a subjective life situation: not only were they aspects of individual differences and distinctions, but they also constituted the specificity of groups, social strata, and classes. Furthermore, there were always pressures by institutions with power to limit a public display of "inopportune" opinions. Surpassing differences and creating public opinion from individual opinions is possible only in a large public, whose members are educated and qualified for discussion.

Although Tönnies conceived of publicity on Kant's premises, his conceptualization was much more "practical" (sociological), conceiving of publicity in terms of practical activities of writing and publishing performed by journalists or, rather, "publicists." Tönnies attributed to the press, or rather to publicity, the role of "setting the public in motion"—the essence of publicity thus being (in contrast to the sciences) the pursuit not of truth but rather *influence*, although news in the press are occasionally closer to the truth than a scientific statement. However, on the normative level Tönnies discriminated between two kinds of publicity as Marx did, based on the kind of "relationship the publicist has with his own products." He considered the relationship *natural* if a publicist represents his views only out of internal needs created by his own conviction.[18] Yet publicity may also follow entirely *external* motives and impulses, which is against the natural relationship and results from external pressures, such as, for example, corporate control and corruption, which made "independent newspapers" an illusion for Tönnies—except if the "natural relationship" was protected by public law, which essentially was also Kant's idea.

Kant attributed to publicity the constitutive significance of an elementary theoretical and practical human capacity and transaction, although strangely—since Kant was quite meticulous about definitions—the concept of "publicity" remained without any definition (Habermas 1962/1995, 108; Gerhardt 1995, 190). As he made clear in *To Perpetual Peace* (1795), publicity is the *necessary condition* and *supreme principle of right*: "All actions relating to the right of other men are unjust if their maxim is not *consistent with publicity*" (emphasis added). If the condition of publicity is not fulfilled and the enacted laws are not made commonly accessible, their rightfulness is questionable if not completely lacking.

Yet Kant considered publicity not only the supreme principle of right. As it is clear from the role he attributed to communication in the process of examining the subjective sufficiency of a judgment, communication is constituent of human reasoning. This point is made clearer in Kant's *Critique of Judgment* (1790). While discussing "public sense," Kant outlined the idea of communication as the process of construction of shared meanings (an idea that reappeared in social sciences only a hundred years later!) and thus founded the modern theory of human communication, without having been ever credited for it.

In the discussion of *communicability* of human sensations, Kant suggests that the concept of "sense" would be wrongly reduced to "judgement where what attracts attention is not so much its reflective act as merely its result."[19] When we speak of a "sense of truth" or a "sense of justice," or any other "sense," we do not merely refer to sensing but also to reasoning—since no representation of this kind could ever "enter our thoughts were we not able to raise ourselves above the level of the senses to that of higher faculties of cognition." Common sense thus amounts to common (not yet cultivated) *understanding*. Then Kant brings to light two conceptual dimensions of the attribute "common," first, the "doubtful honor" of what every one would understand and, second,

> the idea of a *public* sense, i.e., a critical faculty which in its reflective act takes account (*a priori*) of the mode of representation of everyone else, in order, *as it were*, to weigh its judgement with the collective reason of mankind, and thereby avoid the illusion arising from subjective and personal conditions which could readily be taken for objective, an illusion that would exert a prejudicial influence upon its judgement. This is accomplished by weighing the judgement, not so much with actual, as rather with the merely possible, judgements of others, and by putting ourselves in the position of everyone else, as the result of a mere abstraction from the limitations which contingently affect our own estimate. (Kant 1790/1952, 519)

The latter conceptualization of "public sense" actually generalizes the procedure of examining the subjective sufficiency of a judgment, which ideally brings about "the agreement of all judgements with each other, in spite of the different characters of individuals" (1781/1952, 240) brought about by publicity—a process constitutive of public opinion.[20]

Indeed, even today one can hardly imagine a more accurate conceptualization of public opinion as a process taking place beyond the boundaries of physical settings, and "the public" as a form of imagined (intellectual) community whose members shared similar ideas and opinions without being in a direct interaction, as Tönnies—most likely influenced by Kant conceptualized it in his book named *Critique of Public Opinion* (1922) to follow the example of Kant's *Critiques*. Yet Kant was less enthusiastic about the attainments of public sense, suggesting that "the aesthetic, rather than the intellectual, judgement can bear the name of a public sense," but at the same time he suggested—as imagination and understanding unite in cognition—that "taste may be designated a *sensus communis aestheticus*, common human understanding a *sensus communis logicus*" (Kant 1790/1952, 519, 520 n.).

Even in matters of public sense, as Kant would suggest, opinion must never be presented and taken up without some knowledge; thus an opinion is never merely an "arbitrary fiction." Of course, one cannot possibly hold mere opinions in judgments of pure reason. It would be absurd, for example, to have an opinion about pure mathematics—in such a field, one must either *know* or abstain from forming a judgment altogether. According to Kant, the same rule applies to issues of morality. Consequently, the public use of reason always implies provision of reasons for one's judgment. "Public sense" and "public use of reason" differ primarily in relation to publicity. The former implies "the merely possible" publicity, the latter "actual publicity." In the process of formation of public sense, individuals mostly assume what judgments are held by others; in the public use of reason, individual judgments are publicly presented and discussed. The difference is homological to two types of judgments analytically compared by Kant, conviction and persuasion:

> Conviction may, therefore, be distinguished, from an external point of view, from persuasion, by the possibility of communicating it and by showing its validity for the reason of every man; for in this case the presumption, at least, arises that the agreement of all judgements with each other, in spite of the different characters of individuals, rests upon the common ground of the agreement of each with the object, and thus the correctness of the judgement is established. (1781/1952, 240)

In one of his earliest political essays, "An Answer to the Question: What Is Enlightenment?" (1784), Kant elaborated on the public use of reason, which he considered—similarly to rationalists and encyclopedists—primarily a matter of scholars discussing different opinions with the sole aim to find the truth. Opinion would likely become more rational or objectively certain if put to a publicity test. Without public presentation of ideas, as Kant stated in his last political tractate, *The Conflict of the Faculties* (1798), the truth would not likely come to light. Yet he did not consider the academic world self-sufficient; pursuing the truth is also in the best interest of the government and citizens at large. Scholars only act as an instrument of the universal human reason and in the service of the public; thus they have a simultaneous task of guiding and enlightening the people. Enlightenment is not primarily intended for reasoned people but is conceived of as a process of universal liberation from the human impossibility of using one's own reason without being guided by someone else. Kant argued that liberation from immaturity demands that individuals think with their own reason. Only freedom of the public use of one's reason, which a person makes use of as a scholar before the reading public, can stimulate enlightenment unhindered by the limitations of the private uses of reason.

Kant's idea of the "public use of reason" arises from his "regard to universal communicability [as] a thing which every one expects and requires from every one else, just as if it were part of an original compact dictated by humanity itself" (1790/1952, 520). Thus he defined three maxims of reflection, which are characteristic of cultivated reasoning and should be applied as principles of common sense to public use of reason: (1) the maxim of *understanding*: "to think for oneself," (2) the maxim of *judgment*: "to think from the standpoint of everyone else," (3) the maxim of *reason*: "always to think consistently" (1790/1952, 519). The first two maxims are remarkably similar to what Mead much later conceptualized as a fundamental principles of symbolic interactionism: (1) "Anything of which a human being is conscious is something which he is *indicating to himself*." (2) "Human beings *interpret each other's actions* as the means of acting toward one another" (Blumer 1969, 79; emphasis added). The first Kantian maxim claims that reason should always be active, void of prejudices and superstition, as a necessary condition of *enlightenment*, which Kant equated with "emancipation from superstition" (Kant 1790, 519). As he stated earlier (1784):

> Enlightenment is man's emergence from his self-incurred immaturity. This immaturity is self-incurred if its cause is not lack of understanding, but lack of resolution and courage to use it without the guidance of another. . . . Laziness and cowardice are the reasons why such a large proportion of men, even when nature has long emancipated them from alien guidance . . . nevertheless gladly remain immature for life.

The second maxim refers to the need that a man "detaches himself from the subjective personal conditions of his judgement, which cramp the minds of so many others, and reflects upon his own judgement from a *universal standpoint*" (1790, 519). The third maxim—consistent thought—is only attainable with a permanent pursuit of thinking autonomously and from the standpoint of others at the same time, which makes possible a continuous modification of shared opinions, or innovation, on account of new evidence discursively presented.

The Right to Public Use of Reason as a Remedy Against Human Immaturity

Kant saw the public use of reason as an alternative to the authoritatively instituted limits of discussion. He strictly differentiated between public and private uses of reason, a differentiation later used in his typology in the *Metaphysics of Morals* (1797) to justify the difference between "social" and "civil" rights. An individual is free in his public use of reason, where he acts as a transcendental being, beyond the realm of any practical restraint. Private use of reason is the use by a person in a civic post or office in the matters regulated by orders from above or by law and conducted in the interests of a community; in such cases the use of reason should be restricted, according to Kant. The reason is that "through an artificial unanimity the government may guide [civil servants] toward public ends, or at least prevent them from destroying such ends." It is a different matter with the public use of reason: here a citizen "addresses the public in the role of a scholar . . . without thereby harming the affairs for which as a passive member he is partly responsible" (1784). Or, to take another Kantian example: the citizen cannot refuse to pay the taxes imposed on him, but he would act perfectly in accordance with his

civic duty if he publicly expressed his opinion about the taxes as a scholar before the reading public. Thus the border between the public and the private
uses of reason runs inside of the individual, who has to obey orders as a civil
servant, even if he considers them wrong, but is also entitled to use his reason in public as a scholar to criticize the same orders. Passive obedience in
the civil state of society reflects "the prerogative which *nature* has given the
stronger that the weaker should obey him" (1795)—for generally Kant considers the laws of the civil state of society as regulating the same matter, the
same relations among individuals as in the natural state—but in "the *juridical* form of the coexistence of men under a common *constitution*" (emphasis
added). Consequently, the natural social state is regarded as the sphere of private, and the civil state as the sphere of public right. The difference between
public and private as conceptualized by Kant prevailed in Germany until the
end of the nineteenth century.[21]

The revolutionary significance of Kant's idea of the public use of reason is
clearly seen when compared with the modest quest for the "ministerial responsibility," by his contemporary Edmund Burke, or even with Bentham's idea of
the Public Opinion Tribunal. Burke compared in "Selections" the public's failure to ask the governors of appropriate information with someone who does
not stay the hand of suicide and could consequently be held guilty of murder.
Yet he limited his claim only to information needed for a free action—he did
not demand the right for the public to judge of its own desires and interests, but
only asked the governors not to gratify the former at the expense of the latter.
Burke acknowledged that "ministers are not only our natural rulers but our natural guides," admitting that in some cases their "silence is manly and it is wise."

Such benevolence to the sovereign power was completely at variance
with Kant's view on the public use of reason. Even Kant's empirical standards of an "enlightened prince" (he alluded to Fredrick II, king of Prussia
between 1740 and 1786) were set much higher:

A prince who does not regard it as beneath him to say that he considers it his duty,
in religious matters, not to prescribe anything to his people, but to allow them
complete freedom, a prince who thus even declines to accept the presumptuous
title of tolerant, is himself enlightened. He deserves to be praised by a grateful
present and posterity as the man who first liberated mankind from immaturity (as
far as government is concerned), and who left all men free to use their own reason in all matters of conscience. Under his rule, ecclesiastical dignitaries, notwithstanding their official duties, may in their capacity as scholars freely and publicly
submit to the judgement of the world their verdicts and opinions, even if these deviate here and there from orthodox doctrine. This applies even more to all others
who are not restricted by any official duties. This spirit of freedom is also spreading abroad, even where it has to struggle with outward obstacles imposed by governments which misunderstand their own function. For such governments can
now witness a shining example of how freedom may exist without in the least

jeopardising public concord and the unity of the commonwealth. Men will of their own accord gradually work their way out of barbarism so long as artificial measures are not deliberately adopted to keep them in it. (Kant 1784)

From the standpoint of *humanity* as a whole, which is "an end in itself" and by that also the supreme limitation of freedom of human action, liberation from immaturity means objective aspiration and progress toward the perfectly just order. Enlightened opinion endowed with publicity and scholarly prudence are, according to Kant, the most reliable sources of progress and essential prerequisites of a fully enlightened age. In spite of his inclination toward a republican and representative system (though not Rousseauean democracy and revolution), Kant did not see the driving force of development as the running of things from the bottom up but rather from the top down (1798/1979, 164). The public use of reason does not contradict the absolute power of the sovereign; yet one can expect—as Spinoza did—that an enlightened sovereign would attend to citizens' publicly expressed opinions. Similarly, education in all fields could only be successful if it were carried out in accordance with the prudently considered plans of the state. One can easily see in the ambivalence of Kant's attitudes toward the public a reflection of the ambiguous position of the public in that time—on the one hand subjected to, and protected by, the state, and on the other hand claiming the right of public expression.

Kant realized that it is difficult for many individuals to work themselves out of immaturity. They get to used to it and almost like it because they are not allowed to use their own reason. The fact that only few individuals really have succeeded in cultivating their minds and liberating themselves from immaturity suggests, as Kant believed, that the task would be better performed by or in the public; if the "freedom to use reason publicly in all matters" is granted, "enlightenment is almost inevitable." There are always people who use their own reason and are willing to spread the spirit of self-respect. Kant was aware that "a public can only attain enlightenment slowly." He also warned against the danger of manipulation with the masses and the spread of prejudices. "Perhaps a revolution can overthrow autocratic despotism and profiteering or power-grabbing oppression, but it can never truly reform a manner of thinking; instead, new prejudices, just like the old ones they replace, will serve as a leash for the great unthinking mass"(1784). Despite all obstacles, however, Kant insisted that only freedom of the *public use of one's reason*—which demands that the individual thinks with his or her own mind—could stimulate the liberation from immaturity, and requested citizens to "have the courage to use their *own* reason," which he declared the motto of Enlightenment (1784).

Should citizens become equal in the public use of reason in which they engage, the principle of publicity must be based on the abstraction from all contingencies and particularities in terms of individuals' institutional and personal interests—on "the presumption of impartiality and the expectation that the participants question and transcend whatever their initial preferences may have been" (Habermas 1992b, 449). Thus in *The Conflict of the Faculties*, Kant argues that philosophers, for example, should not become kings because "power corrupts the free judgement of reason" (1798/1979, 115). From a normative perspective, the principle of abstraction from social roles in public discourse may *justify a critique* of publicly expressed opinions on the ground that they fail to meet the requirement of impartiality and universality. From the empirical perspective, however, such claims would be confronted with the fact that, as Kant argued, opining—in contrast to knowing—is subjectively and objectively *insufficient*. The existence of *different* opinions on an issue implies an *objective* uncertainty and *subjective* insecurity, according to Kant, and reflects opinions' dependence on empirical inequalities and idiosyncrasies in terms of knowledge, values, status, and interests of those holding opinions. Tönnies (1922) partly reduced the controversy by stressing the objective grounds of opinion and thus "elevating" opinion from objectively completely insufficient judgment to judgment with a higher degree of objective sufficiency than belief. Nevertheless, like many other sociologists, Tönnies opposed the idea of publicness as an abstraction from specific interests because he did not see any possibility that individuals, while discussing practical problems to be solved, would put aside their particular personal, group, or class interests.[22] And that was not a new objection to the claim of impartiality in public discourse; the first of them appeared much earlier. Edmund Burke (1770), for example, opposed the idea that public representatives should have no friendly or commercial relations and connections with the people's interests, arguing that it is not only empirically indefensible, but also theoretically groundless—since what are they supposed to represent if they have "no connection with the sentiments and opinions of the people?" As Burke suggested, private reputation was the basis for public confidence.

Kant did not attribute much theoretical significance to *public opinion*, although he considered it a powerful moral force in similar ways as Rousseau. It may, as a kind of substitute for legal judgment, "inflict the loss of honor" upon those who committed a moral offense, according to the lex talionis, or it may impel the state to act in accordance to it (1797, 429).[23] In the same way as Rousseau, Kant regarded public opinion as a force inflicting itself on legislation and as the foundation of private property.[24] He even used Rousseau's example of dueling to demonstrate the power of public opinion and to explain the opposition between the subjective motive principles of honor among the people (expressed in public opinion compelling the insulted person to obtain satisfaction) and the categorical imperative of penal justice (that the killing of any person contrary to the law must be punished with death) with the fact that "the legislation itself and the civil constitution generally . . . are still barbarous and incomplete."

As Bentham and Rousseau, Kant argued that public opinion has no sense independently of legislation. The process of public opinion in

Kant's science of right may be seen and understood in homology with his construction of the "original contract" as the basis on which a civil state has been established. Such a "contract" as an *empirical fact* is neither possible nor necessary to presuppose. The idea of a "coalition of all the private and particular wills of a people into one common and public will" is, according to Kant, "merely an idea of reason; but it has undoubtedly a practical reality. For it ought to bind every legislator by the condition that he shall enact such laws as might have arisen from the united will of whole people; and it will likewise be binding upon every subject, in so far as he will be a citizen, so that he shall regard the law as if he had consented to it of his own will" (1793/1914, 40). Correspondingly, public opinion operates in both ways—influencing every legislator as well as every citizen.

Kant is absolutely clear about the superior status of the sovereign that cannot be challenged. Kant "defended" himself against reproaches pointing to his excessive flattering of the monarch by suggesting that he also might be reproached by the opposite side because he asserted "too much in favor of the people." The main "retribution" that Kant granted to citizens was the *right of public expression*. He suggested a sort of contract of rational despotism with free reason: free public use of autonomous reason ought to be the best guarantee of obedience—on condition that the political principle that must be obeyed itself be in conformity with universal reason, which can be achieved through the principle of publicity and public use of reason.

As the right to communicate existed as a *natural right* of human beings that they could not alienate—or they would cease to exist as human beings—the right to express opinion should be a *civil right* of citizens. Since infallibility cannot be considered a necessary quality of the sovereign and pursuing truth is an act congruent with the categorical principle, the right to publish opinions has to be granted to the citizens. Indeed, the most important part of Kant's defense of the rights of subjects acting under the surveillance of government is their right of publication and freedom of the press:

> Consequently, the *right [Befugnis]* must be conceded to the citizen, and with the direct consent of the sovereign, that he shall be able to *make his opinion publicly known [seine Meinung öffentlich bekannt zu machen]* regarding what appears to him to be a wrong committed against the commonwealth by the enactments and administration of the sovereign. For to assume that the sovereign power can never err, or never be ignorant of anything, would amount to regarding that power as favored with heavenly inspiration and as exalted above the reach of mankind, which is absurd. Hence *the liberty of the press [die Freiheit der Feder[25]] is the sole palladium of the rights of the people.* (1793/1914, 40; emphasis added)

The true sense of freedom of the press is not, according to Kant, surveil-lance of the sovereign, but the *right of citizens to publish their critical opin-ions*. As Kant's concept of right "comprehends the whole of the conditions under which the voluntary actions of any one person can be harmonized in reality with the voluntary actions of every other person, according to a uni-versal law of freedom" (1797/1952, 397–98), the right to make opinion pub-lic calls for public regulation. If this liberty were refused to citizens—Kant took on Hobbes's argument—they would be alienated from the claim to right in relation to the supreme power altogether. He argued earlier that freedom to express ideas in public is even constitutive of freedom of thought, for "how much, and how correctly, would we think if we did not think, at the same time, in community with others" (1786, 325). Thus com-munication of ideas is not something purely external to the production of ideas in human mind; rather, the former is a necessary condition of the lat-ter. As Tarde (1969, 180) put it simply: "Any fine combination of ideas must first shine out in the mind of individual before it can illuminate the mind of a nation; and *its chance of being produced in the individual mind depends upon the frequency of the intellectual exchanges between minds*" (emphasis added). Consequently, if no freedom existed to express ideas in public, free-dom of thought (i.e., thinking in private) would be severely restricted too.

Yet the right to express opinion in public is not absolute, a "lawless use of reason," since "no game can long go without any law." There are only two possibilities: either the reason has "to subject to the laws that it has en-acted," or it has "to pass under the yoke of the laws enacted by others" (1786, 326). Thus the right has to be exercised "within the limits of rever-ence and love for the constitution," and citizens have to set limits to free-dom of their own accord in order not to lose it. Kant adds to Hobbes's ar-gument an additional one: since the sovereign power is legitimized by representation of the general will, the sovereign would lose the basis of his legitimacy if alienated from the only source of knowledge, which he needs to make right decisions. Eventually this may also cause distrust and hatred of the sovereign power. To avoid these detrimental consequences, Kant de-fined a general principle: "What a people could not ordain over itself ought not to be ordained by the legislator over the people" (1793/1914, 51), which suggests that all laws that are not congruent with the "original contract" le-gitimizing the sovereign cannot be regarded as "the proper will of the monarch," and thus they have to be opposed "by the influence of general and public judgments." As a consequence, laws will become more just if discussed in public. Yet opposition should not imply *resistance* either in words or in deeds. On the one hand, there must be "obedience to coercive laws relating to the whole people." On the other hand, "there must be a spirit of liberty among the people; for in things relating to universal human duty every one needs to be *convinced by reason* that such coercion is *in accordance with right"* (p. 52; emphasis added). Again, Kant relates this to the generic ability of human beings to communicate:

> Obedience without the spirit of liberty is the cause and occasion of all secret societies. For there is *a natural tendency implanted in mankind to communicate to one another* what is in them, especially in what bears upon men generally.[26] . . . And how can governments obtain the knowledge which is necessary for furthering their own essential object otherwise than by giving scope in its origin and it effects to this estimable spirit of human liberty?" (1793/1914, 52; emphasis added)

The right to express opinion can only be regulated as a personal right. "Freedom of the press," as reads the 1917 translation of Kant's essay into English, was "freedom of the pen" *(Feder)* for Kant—not freedom of the publisher or newspaper but freedom of the author or citizen to publish with the aid of the press. Similarly, the right to publish can only exist as an extension of "personal right," but not as a "real right."[27] Kant not only clearly distinguished between the right of property and right of expression—based on the nature of relationship established between the producer, the product, and the consumer in material and mental human actions—but also subordinated the right of publisher (the "real right") to the right of the author (the "personal right"). His perspective, which emphasizes the specificity of communicative actions also in legal proprietary terms, is extremely important in view of later theoretical developments, particularly in the twentieth century, in which freedom of the press ceased to exist as a personal right while it was transformed into a real right, in Kant's terms, or at least subordinated to it.

Kant starts his argument with a commonsense *wrong* impression that the possession of a copy of a book may be considered a *real right* as a right in a thing "as against every possessor of it" (1797/1952, 411, 426). In fact, a book is truly mine only in the sense of *personal right*, which—as a positive right against another—can never be derived from the ownership of a thing (e.g., a copy of the book). My personal writing (my book) is made available to others by the publisher and the printer as "external things," but the possessors of those "things" merely possess the products of mechanical art. For Kant, external things are those which are different or other than myself; "anything external may be originally *acquired* when it is an object that no other person has yet made his," but "there is nothing external that is as such originally mine" (p. 409). It would be obviously mistaken to consider "my book" just an external object because a specific intellectual relationship exists between the author and his writing materialized in the form of book, which goes beyond the relation of ownership. Printing and publishing is not a common right—which some believe because of the fact that a book is materially an external product that can be duplicated—because "a book is not merely an external thing, but is a *discourse* of the publisher to the public, and he is only entitled to do this publicly under the mandate of the author" (p. 426). What is delivered to a reader is not "a thing," but *opera*—a speech. Even if printing and publishing are considered business, Kant suggests that it is not "the trading with goods in one's own name, but as *the transacting of business in the name of another, namely, the author*" (1785; emphasis added).[28] Half a century later, Marx ironically inverted this assertion (without reference to Kant) in his critique of the attempts to reduce freedom of the press to a species of commercial freedom suggesting that, when it comes to freedom of printers' and booksellers' business, that is not any more a matter of authors, but of printers and booksellers (Marx 1842a/1974, 71).

Publicity as Moral Principle and Legal Norm

Fundamental to any normative discussion of freedom of the press is Kant's universal "principle of publicity" mediating between politics and morals in public law. He defined publicity in his essay on *Perpetual Peace* (1795) in terms of a "transcendental concept of public right" based on citizens' fundamental dignity and moral sovereignty. Kant conceived of publicity as a moral principle and legal norm, as an "instrument" to achieve both individual independent reasoning and legal order in the social realm. Much later, John Dewey defined "the public" on similar grounds. His definition of the public as a social entity consisting of "all those who are affected by the indirect consequences of transactions to such an extent that it is deemed necessary to have those consequences systematically cared for" (Dewey 1927/1991, 15–16) arose from the assumption that the public could be democratically organized only on the basis of full publicity in respect to all "transactions with indirect consequences" concerning the public and freedom of expression.

Kant argued that principle of publicity is a "mechanism of nature," which should be used as a means to create *a legal maxim* that all the people would accept and obey. He postulated the *"transcendental formula* of public justice as both ethical and juridical principle that warned: 'All actions that affect the rights of other men are wrong if their maxim is not consistent with publicity'" (1795/1983, 135). Anything that does not fulfill the condition of publicness can be neither ethically nor legally right. Publicity is therefore also a necessary condition of right. And more than that, publicity is a criterion of rationality because, on the one hand, what is right should not contradict reason; on the other hand, what is rational is always publicly communicable. The transcendental formula proceeds from the fundamental law of pure practical reason, which Kant formulated in his *Critique of Practical Reason*—"Act so that the maxim of thy will can always at the same time hold good as a principle of universal legislation" (1788/1952, 302)—and the universal principle of right defined in the *Metaphysics of Morals*: "Every action is *right* which in itself, or in the maxim on which it proceeds, is such that it can coexist along with the freedom of the will of each and all in action, according to a universal law" (1797/1952, 398).

The principle of *publicity* has the same supreme status in Kant's ethics as the principle of *utility* in Bentham's ethics. Publicity in Bentham's ethics is derived from the general principle of *utility*; as Bentham argued, whatever principle differed from the principle of utility would necessarily be a wrong one. Bentham's principle of utility was aimed at the maximization of the people's happiness, and, only because publicity is instrumental to utility, it could be used as a "standard of right and wrong." In contrast to Bentham, the standard of right and wrong is for Kant publicity in their own right: all actions are wrong if their maxim is not conformable to the principle of publicity.

Happiness cannot be a basis of a universal principle and the guidance of legislation because opinions on what constitutes happiness widely differ among individuals and constantly change in time. Furthermore, "the principle of happiness, which is properly incapable of any definite determination as a principle, may be the occasion of much evil in the sphere of political right, just as it is in the sphere of morals" (Kant 1793, 47). The supreme principle, from which all other maxims relating to the commonwealth must proceed and has to be secured to every individual, could only be the *principle of right* because "it is only not contradictory in itself that a whole people should agree to such a law, however unpleasant may be its results in fact, [thus] it would as such be conformable to right" (Kant 1793, 43). That also prohibits active resistance against law and gives the state the necessary and exclusive legitimate power of coercion.

Whereas the principle of publicity had an instrumental function for the utilitarians and even a disciplinarian role for Bentham, Kant lifted it to a transcendent principle of public justice mediating between politics and morals in public law. Unlike Rousseau, Kant did not believe that man was by nature good (yet he was grateful to Rousseau for helping him overcome his own blind dismissal of the illiterate masses and set him on the path toward respect for the human being and his rights). Thus Kant did not defend the principle of publicity for the sake of the moral improvement of the people but argued that it is necessary to use this "mechanism of nature" as a means to create a legal maxim that people would obey. Without the possibility of publicity, without the principle of public agency, there would be no justice.[29] The reverse is also true: if a goal can only be achieved in the public realm, with the help of publicity, it means that there is no distrust in the underlying political maxims that are congruent with the goals and rights of all. Publicity alone therefore can guarantee harmony between politics and morals: on the one hand it guarantees legal order while on the other hand it fulfills an enlightened role.

The idea of publicness in Kant's principle of publicity is fundamental to *citizen rights* and represents the fundamental principle of a *democratic order*. Any regulation of relationships in a (political) community would contradict the public interest and citizens' freedom if citizens cannot be convinced by reason in the public realm, or if they are kept alienated and isolated from public communications that would enable them to discuss matters of common concern in public. The legitimacy of the state can only be grounded on the principle of publicity because the government can only hold authority over people if it represents the general will of the community. The reverse is also the case: only governments that are not acting in the public interest may fear "independent and public thought." Thus Kant's principle of publicity reconciles politics with democratic legitimacy: whereas politics is coercion, democracy is the moral basis of association. The two spheres can only be reconciled by fundamental human rights embodied in the principle of publicity—freedom of thought and freedom of public expression; neither can exist without the other.

Kant's differentiation between politics (power) and morals (justice) is particularly important from the perspective of the twentieth-century reconceptualizations of public opinion into a form of social control and surveillance that ensure the functioning of power, that is, its transformation from an associative into a coercive concept. Such a conceptual transformation strongly contradicts Kant's and the Enlightenment belief, also held by American pragmatists, that citizens must be *convinced by reason* in the exercise of public debate that public policies are just, or the state loses its moral legitimacy.

WHY FREEDOM OF ENTERPRISE IS NOT A SPECIES OF FREEDOM OF THE PRESS: MARX

In contrast to most of his fellow strugglers for freedom of expression and publication in the eighteenth and nineteenth centuries, Karl Marx (1818–1883) had a considerable and painful personal experience with press censorship and political persecution.[30] During his twenties, while he was contributing to and editing the *Rheinische Zeitung* and other newspapers and journals, he extensively discussed the issues of the press as a mode of individuals' humane existence and a tool of revolutionary social change, censorship, and other forms of suppression of the press, and the modes of its emancipation embedded in the process of human emancipation in general. In Marx's time, preventive state and church censorship was still a powerful instrument everywhere, even in the most advanced European countries. By examining the political and moral appropriateness of books and newspapers, censorship effectively impeded the formation of the bourgeois public as a "weapon" of the middle class directed against the absolute princely authority. Nevertheless, the press openly demonstrated its political character before the revocation of censorship—not merely as a *new* power to control the already existing powers, but also as an *oppositional* power, particularly in France. The struggle for the abolition of censorship brought to the light the true bourgeois nature of freedom of the press as an individual right linked to freedom of ownership, although in that time the profitability of newspapers was still subordinate to the political effects expected to be brought about by publicity. Even if personal division of labor between the newspaper's owner and the author (editor or journalist) had been accomplished, it did not imply the domination of the former over the latter. Indeed, for the liberal bourgeois press of the late eighteenth and early nineteenth centuries, profitability was a "side effect" (which often even did not appear) of a revolutionary political orientation. *Rheinische Zeitung*, a liberal democratic bourgeois paper published in the Rhine Province and edited by Karl Marx for a short period between 1842 and 1843, was a brilliant example: a clear oppositional political orientation helped increase its popularity and circulation up to the point when it was banned.[31]

Of all great minds usually considered the founders of the idea of press freedom in the period before the mass press, Marx was actually the only one who wrote about *the press* (newspapers) and not merely about publishing. He defended freedom of the press on its own merit, as a specific form of human existence, and as a freedom *sui generis*—in contrast to all those prevailing in his time, who only implicitly defended freedom of the press while reducing it to a mere extension of personal freedom to publish opinions. Paradoxically, Marx was never considered a theorist of press freedom in the liberal bourgeois tradition—because he criticized the reduction of press freedom to freedom of enterprise.

Marx's ideas on freedom of the press were eclectic and radical at the same time. He did not write a comprehensive tractate on freedom of expression and publication; rather, his ideas on press freedom are scattered in tens, perhaps even hundreds of articles and commentaries published in newspapers and journals, while none of his principal works contains a discussion of that subject. He conceptualized freedom of the press as essentially a *personal right* to make one's opinions and judgments public, free of any external intervention or restraint. At the same time, he emphasized the social nature of the newspaper as a means used by individuals to communicate with each other, since only in community with others—in communication—the alienated private (bourgeois) "man" can achieve the emancipation of the "citizen." Apart from this basic proposition, four distinct approaches to freedom of the press can be identified in Marx's essays:

- On the one hand, we can find clear vestiges of *rationalism* and *enlightenment* in his somewhat elitist claim for freedom of the press.
- On the other hand, his severe criticism of censorship also reflected—although not so clearly as Engels's essays—the Benthamian idea of *public control* over government.
- In addition, Marx also pleaded for a *revolutionary* role of the press, which ought to contribute to democratization of the political system and human emancipation.

- Perhaps most importantly, Marx argued against the *subordination of the press to freedom of ownership* as a peril no less frightful than censorship.

After the defense of his dissertation in philosophy in 1842 in Jena, Marx entered the profession of journalism. His radical political views expressed in the papers compelled him to live in almost perpetual exile, and he never succeeded in achieving an academic career. With a series of essays in *Rheinische Zeitung* he brought into focus the debates in the Rhine Province Assembly on freedom of the press. His first article on the issue of press freedom was published on May 5, 1842, a few months before he was appointed the editor of the newspaper. It was the beginning of a series of feuilletons devoted to "Die Verhandlungen des 6. rheinischen Landtags—Debatten über Pressfreiheit und Publikation der Landständischen Verhandlungen" and published during the next two weeks, which represented a systematic critique of dogmatic and narrow-minded understandings of freedom of the press. All these feuilletons were published anonymously, signed "By a Rhinelander," and they received a very positive response in the progressive German community.[32]

Marx worked as a journalist and an editor for a number of newspapers during the 1840s, notably the *Rheinische Zeitung* (1842–1843) and—after he was temporarily back to Germany from exile—the *Neue Rheinische Zeitung* (1848–1849). As he later wrote, "In the year 1842–43, as editor of the *Rheinische Zeitung*, I first found myself in the embarrassing position of having to discuss what is known as *material interests*," which later led him to study political economy. During that period he also published extensively on freedom of the press in the newspapers. In contrast, his major philosophical and social theoretical manuscripts written during that period were published only partially. For example, Marx's first substantive work (with Engels), *Die deutsche Ideologie* (*The German Ideology*), developing the principles of historical materialism and criticizing philosophers Ludwig Feuerbach, Bruno Bauer, and Max Stirner, as well as the theory of the "true socialists," was completed in 1845. But the book's publication in Germany was prevented by severe censorship. The complete book first appeared posthumously in the Soviet Union in 1932. In the 1840s Marx also finished his manuscript on *Poverty of Philosophy* (1847) as a critical response to Pierre Proudhon's book *The Philosophy of Poverty*, and—with Engels—*The Communist Manifesto* (1848). Soon after the failed revolution of 1848 and his renewed exile from Germany and later from France to England (1849), Marx ended his professional journalistic career, occasionally contributing to the newspapers in Europe and the United States. As a consequence, his interest in freedom of the press also disappeared from his later political analyses and theoretical writing. His last major treatise was a vindication of the charges of insulting the authorities in the *Neue Rheinische Zeitung* at the trial in February 1849 in Cologne, where Marx defended, together with his coeditor Engels, not only their *Zeitung* but freedom of the press in Germany. The jury gave a verdict of not guilty, but nevertheless a few months later Marx was again expelled from Germany.

The termination of his newspaper career was important but probably was not the only reason for Marx's loss of interest in press freedom. The press in England, where he spent most of his time, enjoyed more freedom than in any other European country at that time; thus the question of press freedom was not so pressing there as, for example, in Germany. Marx devoted his critical attention to fundamental issues of capitalism as a system of exploitation, particularly those of (material) production, exploitation, and the relationship between capital and wage labor. During the first half of 1840s, Marx collaborated with the liberal German bourgeoisie and supported their "thankless and painful task of conquering liberty, step by step, within the limits imposed by the constitution" (Waldron 1987, 121). By 1844, however, Marx accepted much more radical ideas of materialism and communism. While he agreed with Hegel's critique of considering isolated individuals and their rights as the basis of the state and society, he did not see the inaccuracy of such a conceptualization in the absence of a unifying ethical will (as Hegel did), but in a failure to recognize the fundamental importance of *production*, whose character determines the character of the relationship between human beings and nature, and between human beings themselves.[33] Thus the question of "the *positive* possibility of German emancipation" was not an ethical issue, but primarily a question of the property of production means, which could only be "resolved," according to Marx, with a revolutionary overthrow of the existing political and economic order (1844a/1974, 391). In the trial of the *Neue Rheinische Zeitung* on February 7, 1849, Marx had to defend himself against the charges of calumniation, and his main argument against the charges was that "the duty of the press is to come forward on behalf of the oppressed."[34] He joined passionately the struggle for revolutionary changes, particularly economic changes; he concluded his defense with the idea of revolution, arguing that "the first duty of the press now is to undermine *all the foundations of the existing political state of affairs*" (1849/1974, 234). The defense was published in the *Neue Rheinische Zeitung* of February 14, 1849, and was Marx's last essay on freedom of the press.

While recognizing that economic forces and material conditions determine the reality of human life, including (in particular) political freedom, Marx fervently attacked the essentially bourgeois idea that the press might attain its freedom more easily by adopting the laws of free economic operations that rested on the right to private property. Yet the more he became intrigued by the laws of capitalist economic order, including exploitation of the labor force and alienation in the work process, the less he was involved in "liberal" philosophical and humanistic themes dominant in his early writings, including freedom of the press. This is not to say that Marx in his later writings renounced the ideas of freedom and emancipation, since those ideas could still be found occasionally though less explicitly in his works. After all, his problems with censorship continued until his death. Nevertheless, in his critique of capitalism after the 1840s, which he believed would lead to a radical transformation of society in economic and political terms, the issues of free expression and publication did not reappear. A substantial part of that transformation ought to be, according to Marx, the historical "withering away" of the State, which had the central role in Hegel's philosophy of right. In contrast to Hegel, Marx saw in the state an "illusion of communal life" resulting from the contradictions between the interest of the individual and that of the community, but at the same time divorced from the real interests of both individual and community. His former trust in legal regulation of press freedom by press law as "the positive existence of freedom" would not be easily incorporated in his critique of capitalism and capitalist state, in particular, as his demand for the undermining of "all the foundations of the existing political state of affairs" by the agency of the press indicates. On the other hand, the critique of the reduction of freedom of the press to freedom of ownership propagated by the new bourgeois class is a constituent element of Marx's general critique of "the so-called *rights of man*," which he considered "nothing but the rights of a *member of bourgeois society*[35]—i.e., the rights of egoistic man, of man separated from other men and from the community" (1844a/1974, 364).

Free Press: A Privilege or a Realization of Human Freedom?

Marx never clearly formulated his views on rights—and liberties as the consequences of rights—in a generalized way. He was much clearer about the nature of freedom of the press, which may also shed some light on his differentiating the *rights of man* from the *rights of the citizen*. Instead of the earlier customary differentiation between natural and civil rights, Marx conclusively distinguished between rights of men that are based on the *separation* of man from man, their private interests, and egoistic selves, and rights of the citizen (political rights) that can only be exercised in *community* with others. The most typical "right of man" is the right to private property as the basis of bourgeois society—the right "to enjoy one's property and to dispose of it at one's discretion" independently of society; it is the "right of self-interest" that "makes every man see in other men not the *realization*, but the restraint of his own freedom" (p. 365). Marx's opposition against founding freedom of the press on the ground of the right to private property essentially did not deviate from Kant's distinction" between author's (today we would say "intellectual property") right and publisher's right (related to corporeal thing "the book") based on the nature of the relationship established between the producer, the product, and the consumer in material and mental human actions. However, Marx's critique of the right to private property was much more radical: whereas Kant rejected it merely as the foundation of intellectual freedom because "it is impossible to think of a being endowed with personal freedom as produced merely by a physical process"[36] (1790/ 1952, 420), Marx rejected it entirely.

The contradiction between the collective nature of the rights of the citizen and the "monadic" character of the rights of man is clearly expressed when freedom of the press is at stake. Marx criticized "the political emancipators" who reduced citizenship and the political community to a mere means for maintaining the "rights of man" and thus considered the private *bourgeois* rather than the citizen the "true man." But even in reducing the citizen to "the servant of egoistic man," they were not consistent, as the case of freedom of the press made clear:

> While "liberté *indéfinie* de la presse"[37] is guaranteed as a consequence of the right of man, individual liberty, freedom of the press is totally destroyed, because "la liberté de la presse ne doit pas être permise lorsqu'elle compromet la liberté publique."[38] That is to say: The right of man to liberty ceases to be a right as soon as it comes into conflict with *political* life; whereas in theory political life is only the guarantee of human rights, the rights of the individual man, it must be abandoned as soon as it comes into contradiction with its *aims*, with these rights of man. (p. 367)

If freedom of the press is considered a right of private man instead of a right of the citizen, the aim (free press) is reduced to a means of private interests. In contrast, in his defense of freedom of the press Marx emphasized the *social* nature of the newspaper and thus emancipatory role of free communication. Freedom of the press is not a form of liberty as "the right to do everything that harms no one else," which is "the liberty of man as an isolated monad, withdrawn into himself." It is not a "privilege of particular individuals," but rather a "universal right" and a "privilege of the human mind" (1842a/1974, 51). Marx's strong support for freedom of the press disallows the idea that the lack of the examination of human and citizen liberties in general may indicate his repugnance for issues of human rights.

Marx saw in the press "a realization of human freedom"; consequently, censorship or any other restriction of press freedom represents "the real mortal danger for mankind" (p. 60). Marx insisted on the centrality of the press in the pursuit of freedom and that press freedom, like every kind of freedom, has always existed—but either as a *common right* or as a *privilege*, which is the fundamental difference between different understandings of freedom of the press and the ways it had been materialized. The great significance Marx and Engels attributed not only to the press but to communication in general is reflected in their statement that *writing* marks the first all-inclusive transformation of human relations in history—the transition from a primeval, classless human community to civilization and class society (Marx and Engels 1848/1998, 34 n.). As communication in general, the press is a tissue interlacing all cells of society. Any attempt at limiting potential "inconveniences" produced by a free press would inevitably lead to an almost inconceivable loss in the social well-being of individuals and society. Thus the true sense of legal regulation of freedom of the press is not in limiting or subordinating it—as in censorship—but in recognizing the innate laws in which the essential nature of writing and communicating is expressed. It is these innate laws that determine the importance of newspapers for individual and society, which was invaluable in Marx's eyes:

> The free press is the ever-present vigilant eye of the people's spirit, the embodiment of a people's trust in itself, the communication link that binds the individual with the state and the world, the embodied culture that transforms material struggles into intellectual struggles and idealizes their crude material form. It is the people's frank self-confession, and the redeeming power of confession is well known. It is the mental mirror, in which a people can see itself, and self-examination is the first condition of wisdom. It is the spirit of the state, which can be delivered into every cottage cheaper than coal gas. It is all-sided, ubiquitous, omniscient. It is the ideal world which incessantly wells out of the real world and flows back into it as an ever richer, inspiring spirit. (1842a/1974, 60–61)

Marx's earliest writing on freedom of the press was focused on its defense against *censorship*. He wrote his first essay on censorship as "*official* criticism" already in the beginning of 1842. However, the essay "Comments on the Latest Prussian Censorship Instruction," which represents the beginning of his revolutionary political engagement on the eve of the bourgeois revolution of 1848, was not published before 1843. In the essay Marx denoted the *Instruction*, which made the main criterion of censor's judgment not writers' *actions as such*, but rather his *conscience (Gesinnung)*, a "law against tendency" that gave no objective norms according to which censor's decision could be made, and thus it did not differ from martial law or terrorism. If the law punishes the writer not for what he *did*, but for what he *may think*, the writer "has fallen victim to the most *frightful terrorism*, and is subjected to the *jurisdiction of suspicion*" (1842b/1974, 14). In addition, Marx argued that the "law against a conviction *is not a law of the state promulgated for its citizens*, but the *law of one party against another party*" (p. 14). With such a law, a person is not punished for what he *does*, but rather for what he *may think*. Yet the law that punishes the implied intention instead of wrongdoing denies the principle of citizens' equality before the law. Such a law divides rather than unites, and every law that divides is reactionary. In fact, it is not a law but a *privilege*.

As reported by Marx in his essays devoted to the debates over freedom of the press in the Sixth Assembly of Rhine Province (1842a), the speaker from the knightly estate defended censorship in exactly the same way—stressing that "the siren song of evil" (the "bad press") has a powerful effect on the masses because "human imperfection"—as those against whom Milton directed *Areopagitica* two hundred years earlier (Milton 1644/1999, 20). Marx replied that censorship could not eliminate any "peril" that would be greater than censorship itself: censorship is the real *mortal danger for human mankind*.[39] But even the abolition of censorship that prevented the press from developing according to its own principles does not bring yet necessarily a full-fledged freedom of the press. One form of nonfreedom might be replaced by another. Marx criticized the idea of freedom of the press degrading freedom to a "special privilege," which is an individual's right only inasmuch as it is not the right of another individual at the same time. In other words, freedom of one person would be based on nonfreedom of the other, which would be no different from state censorship as the principal danger.

Marx's response to the defender of censorship has a strong resemblance to what Milton wrote in *Areopagitica* or Spinoza in the *Theologico-Political Treatise*. In his 1842 polemics against the members of the Rhine Province Assembly Marx paraphrased Ludwig Wieland's[40] rationalist thought resembling Kant's ideas in the essay on Enlightenment connecting publicity with maturity of the people at large, and censorship with its immaturity: "If the immaturity of the human race is the mystical ground for opposing freedom of the press, then certainly the censorship is a highly reasonable means against the maturity of the human race" (1842a/1974, 49). This would be the same as arguing that to kill a man is the best, if not the only, way to free him from his state of imperfection.

Criticism that the press is not allowed to publish would become, if the censorship instruction remained in force, a daily obligation of censors as "official critics." In this way, government clerks are given a *limitless trust*, but all others a *limitless distrust*. The former receive an official attestation of "scientific qualification" and infallibility; the latter are permanently considered imperfect, immature, and fallible. As Milton wrote, one could hardly believe that even if such highly learned and judicious men existed, they would be willing to waste their time on such a boring work as censoring other people's writings. Similarly, Marx ridiculed the instruction's requirement that "the post of censor shall be entrusted only to men of tested conviction and *ability*, who fully correspond to the honorable trust which that office presupposes; to men who are both right-thinking and keen-sighted, who are able to discern the form from the essence of the matter" (1842b/1974, 22). Marx particularly pointed to different kinds and levels of "qualification" required by the instruction of editors and censors, and to differences between the old and new censorship instruction. Whereas *scientific qualification* is demanded by the new instruction of the writer, the censor only has to acquire "ability without further definition." That was a significant change from the former decree, which called for "scientifically trained" and even "enlightened" censors—qualifications which, according to the new instruction, only remained to be acquired by the writer. The reason why this change had to happen was explained already by Milton.

Whereas in "Comments" Marx analyzed the general relationship between freedom of the press and censorship, his "Debates on Freedom of the Press" published in the *Rheinische Zeitung* had partly a different focus. The Sixth Rhine Province Assembly held debates on publication of the proceedings of the assemblies, which was a right granted by the royal edict of April 30, 1841, and on petitions of a number of towns on freedom of the press. Marx's critique of aberrations expressed in the debates was essentially an analysis carried out by "a historical spectator" of the course of the debates. Marx justified such a method with the nature of the debates in the Assembly. Whereas all the representatives in other debates were "on about the same level," in the debates about freedom of the press the opponents of a free press had a considerable advantage. The opponents of press freedom expressed "a pathological emotion, a passionate partisanship, which gives them a real, not an imaginary, attitude to the press," whereas the defenders of the press had no experience with what they were defending, and consequently their defense was only "a matter of the head, in which the heart plays no part," based on very general and vague arguments.[41] And there was another reason to bring into focus not only the matter at issue but also the social provenance of the speakers: in the debates on the press freedom, *specific estate spirit* was fully expressed. Marx was particularly attracted by specific interests of particular estates and their "natural one-sidedness," which clearly sprang up in the arguments opposing freedom of the press and freedom in general. Thus he followed the proceedings and revealed polemics of different (i.e., the princely, knightly, and urban) estates, arguing that "it is not the *individual*, but the social *estate* that conducts the polemic. What mirror, therefore, could reflect the inner nature of the Assembly better than the debates on the press?" (1842a/1974, 34).[42]

In analyzing the attitudes of the speakers from the princely and knightly estates who defended censorship, arguing that censorship is a lesser evil than potential excesses on the part of the press, Marx discloses their estate spirit and interest in protecting their own privileges (pp. 34–65). Freedom of the press ought to be, they claimed, a privilege of particular human beings and not a privilege of humankind—it ought to be a *special*, not a *general*, right. Even if freedom of speech and writing was limited in history, the speakers believed, this did not limit the "true and noble spiritual development" of Germany. In other words, they regarded censorship as a basis for improving the German press. Marx made fun of the speakers' logic with an analogy: since Mirabeau developed his rhetorical talent in prison, are therefore prisons schools of eloquence?

The speaker from the knightly estate even opposed an unabridged and daily publication of the Assembly debates in the *Staats-Zeitung* (State Gazette) provided by the royal edict of 1841, arguing instead for an internal censorship of the Provincial Assembly to "make a wise use of the permission granted." He argued that words uttered in the Assembly had to be judged only by those for whom they were intended (i.e., he defended censorship) in order to enable freedom of discussion in the Assembly and to avoid the overanxious weighing of words it would necessitate. The knightly speaker argued against a free publication of the Assembly debates citing friendly interpersonal relationship among members of the assembly: "from many years' acquaintance, a good personal understanding has developed" among the members and they would communicate with one another more frankly the less subject they were to external influences. The speaker added that only those "external influences" on the Assembly would be useful that were not expressed "in the form of a dogmatic judgment, of praise or blame, seeking to influence our personality through public opinion." What ought to be allowed is only "well-meaning counsel, not in the abstract sense that it means well for the country, but in the fuller-sounding sense that it expresses a passionate tenderness for the members of the estates, a specially high opinion of their excellence." Most importantly, "no praise or blame, no influence of the public on our *persona sacrosancta*" should be permitted (Marx 1842a/1974, 45). In addition, the speaker maintained, the assembly should be *protected* against publicity because parliamentary freedom is only in its first period of development, and thus publicity could be particularly detrimental until a full independence and internal strength is achieved.

Marx's rejoinder was passionate and full of sarcasm:

> A publication of the Assembly proceedings that depends on the arbitrary ruling of the Assembly of the Estates, however, is worse than none at all, for if the Assembly tells me not what it is in reality, but what it wants to seem to be in my eyes, I shall take it for what it gives itself out to be, for mere semblance, and it is bad when semblance has a legal existence. . . . The unabridged publication of the Assembly proceedings can thus only be, in its true consistent meaning, the *full publicness of the Assembly*. (1844a/1974, 44)

Marx followed Bentham's belief that authentic publication of transactions of the assembly is needed, and access to debates must be secured not only to the official press. "Nothing is more contradictory than that the *highest public* activity of the province is secret, that in private lawsuits the doors of the court are open to the province, but that in its own lawsuit the province has to remain outside" (p. 44). If the members of the Assembly decided themselves on what to make public and what not, Marx suggested, publication of the debates would become "a privilege of the Assembly of the Estates, which has the right, if it thinks fit, to have its wisdom echoed by the many voices of the press." Consequently, "the privileges of the Assembly of the Estates decrease in proportion as the rights of the province increase."

The publication of the debates should be intended for the province—for the real reading public, not just for a fictitious public—and not for the estates themselves; it should not be a *privilege* of the assembly of the estates but a *right* of the public. If the Assembly does not represent the will of the public, and the decision on whether or not to make the debates public remains with the estates, there would be no reason to esteem a monarchy *with* a provincial assembly higher than a monarchy *without* a provincial assembly.

Whereas Marx's attitude in favor of authentic publication of the assembly debates in newspapers was vigorous and unambiguous, his view of the role of public opinion was ambivalent, yet predominantly favorable. He perceived the democratic nature of public opinion as a normatively defined concept, but he also recognized that this democratic project was not materialized in practice, which gave opportunities to those who attempted at manipulating public opinion.

> Of course, the development of parliamentary freedom in the old French sense, independence from public opinion, and the stagnation of the caste spirit, advance most thoroughly through isolation, but to warn against precisely this development cannot be premature. A truly political assembly flourishes only under the great protection of the public spirit, just as living things flourish only under the protection of the open air. Only "exotic" plants, which have been transferred to a climate that is foreign to them, require the protection and care of a greenhouse. (Marx 1842a/1974, 46–47)

Unfortunately, Marx never formulated his views on public opinion in a systematic way. His *Contribution to the Critique of Hegel's Philosophy of Right* (1844) written in the form of commentaries to Hegel's *Philosophy of Right* ends just before the passage in which Hegel presented his view of publicity and public opinion (§ 315). Habermas thinks that "Marx denounced public opinion as false consciousness" and considered it merely "a mask of bourgeois interests" under which its "true character" was hidden (Habermas 1962/1995, 124). Yet that is by no means clear; in fact, Habermas's judgment is not only an excessive oversimplification but an erroneous inference drawn primarily from Marx's later works. Marx's position in his essays defending freedom of the press was rather the opposite. Like Bentham, he saw in publicity, public opinion, and the press means to force the government to serve the public interest and not misuse its power. Marx considered the press "the *only effective control*" of officials and bureaucracy (1849/1974, 241). The "storm of public opinion," always representing a combination of rationality and passion, may even have the power to achieve the abolition of censorship (1849a, 351). Marx was never so explicit about the need to expose government to public surveillance as Engels, who considered—like Bentham—the "primary duty" of the press "the protection of citizens against excesses committed by officials." As long as censorship existed, the press did not have the power to survey authorities and make their actions public, but "since the winning of freedom of the press the actions of officials also can be placed before the forum of public opinion" (Engels 1849).

Marx agreed with the knightly speaker in the Rhine Province Assembly that the assembly should become "an immediate object of the public spirit" and its "personification"; it should be put "in the light of the general consciousness" and forsake its particular nature in favor of the general one. However, he criticized him for regarding the Assembly as a kind of *private club* and demanded that it be deprived of the *aristocratic privilege* of secret proceedings, so that the privilege of the Assembly would be transformed into a right of the province or the public (Marx 1842a/1974, 43). Decisive for Marx's respect for the role of public opinion was the free press as both the product and the source of public opinion. To make the press a medium of free exchange of opinions, it has to be entirely independent not only in the sense of the absence of censorship, which of course is a necessary (but not sufficient) condition. Another condition constitutive for freedom of the press is derived from Kant's public use of reason and Hegel's account of public opinion as a channel in which "everyone is free to express and make good his subjective opinion concerning the universal" (1821/2001, 248). As Marx argued, the press can only be truly free if it is emancipated from the private interests of those participating in public discourse, including the print medium, so that they all would appear equal as "exponents of reason."

> The rulers and the ruled alike . . . are in need of a *third* element, which is *political* without being official, hence not based on bureaucratic premises, an element which is of a *civil* nature without being bound up with private interests and their pressing need. This supplementary element to the head of a citizen of the state and to civic heart is the *free press*. In the realm of the press, rulers and ruled alike can criticize their principles and demands, yet no longer in a relation of subordination, but on terms of equality as *citizens of the state;* no longer as *individuals*, but as *intellectual forces,* as exponents of reason. The "free press" is the product of public opinion and, at the same time, also produces public opinion; it can transform a particular interest to a common interest. (Marx 1843/1974, 189–90)

Marx insisted on the recognition of personal *rights to write and publish* because he considered the press the common means of individuals to communicate their spiritual existence and to participate in collective (spiritual) life, which is the determining factor of everyone's identity. Marx considered the press the "most general way for individuals to communicate their intellectual being. It knows no reputation of a person, but only the reputation of intelligence. . . . What I cannot be for others, I am not for myself and cannot be for myself. . . . Just as everyone learns to read and write, so everyone *must have the right* to write and read" (1842a/1974, 73). Sharing this right makes citizens equal—provided that it is a *universal* right, since this right always existed, but only as a special right and thus a privilege of elites. Marx's concept of press freedom suggests that participation in public communication is determinative for the relationship among individuals in a group, community, and society. This is not limited to political participation in the sense of raising citizen initiatives and individual participation in the processes of political decision making, for example, public expressions of opinion and participation in voting and elections. Although the political dimensions of participation are most widely seen and most often discussed, participation extends deeper into the existence of human beings and beyond politics: through participation the individual enters from privacy into publicness.

According to Marx, a genuine press freedom could only exist if it overcame partial interests of the *estates* in a particular kind of freedom. He argued against the representatives of the three estates in the Rhine Province Assembly because of their narrow-mindedness, which "opposes the press in one case, and defends it in another." But in fact, *"whenever a particular freedom is put in question, freedom in general is put in question"* (1842a/1974, 76; emphasis added). Since the press is "only" a realization of the *general* freedom, it cannot be anyone's privilege. Only the speeches of the commission's spokesman and of some members of the "fourth estate"—the *peasant estate*—contradicted the general negative spirit of the Assembly. A representative of the peasant estate proclaimed that "the human spirit must develop freely in accordance with its inherent laws and be allowed to communicate its achievements, otherwise a clear, vitalizing stream will become a pestiferous swamp" (Marx 1842a/1974, 76).

The Primary Freedom of the Press Is Not to Be a Business

After analyzing the positions advocated by the defenders of censorship in the Rhine Province Assembly, Marx developed a spirited critique of the attitudes expressed by the speaker presenting the interests of the bourgeois class, who seemed to defend freedom of the press but in fact only advanced freedom of ownership. From the perspective of press development, Marx's critique, focused on the relation between freedom of ownership and freedom of the press, is even more penetrative than his polemics against censorship. Marx argued that the true interest of the bourgeoisie was not to abolish the nonfreedom of the press as a whole, but rather to *substitute* one form of nonfreedom for another one—the external nonfreedom (censorship) that limits the right of property in the sphere of the press for the internal nonfreedom. Thus the bourgeois affirmation of freedom of the press is primarily the affirmation of freedom of *enterprise*, and indeed nothing but freedom of enterprise. In such a position against freedom of the press Marx identified "the opposition of the *bourgeois*, not of the *citoyen*" (p. 86)—a distinction he elaborated in more detail a couple of years later in the *Jewish Question*

(1844b). Degrading press freedom by subsuming it under freedom of enterprise consistently completed the process of the transformation of the early bourgeois publicity into universal availability and "decency" of the press—a negation rather than an affirmation of freedom. Both in the case of censorship and subjection to freedom of property the press is not free: instead of being subject to its own laws, it is dominated by external laws.

Marx raised the issue of freedom of ownership in relation to freedom of the press as well as to freedom and human rights in general. His critique of the bourgeois "so-called rights of man" focused on equality, liberty, security, and property. Central to his concern was the right to private property as the "practical application of man's right to liberty." Both of them constitute the basis of bourgeois society; they *appear* to bring into force human freedom, but both of them actually *obstruct* true emancipation. The contradiction between freedom of the press and freedom of ownership reflects the general contradiction between the *communal* character of the rights of the *citizen* and the *egoistic* character of the rights of *man*. As Marx emphasized, the *political* annulment of private property in suffrage actually provided its full recognition. With the declaration that every member of society is an equal participant in national sovereignty regardless of his or her property, education, or occupation, which are all pictured as merely "nonpolitical distinctions," the state actually allows them to act in their way. In fact, Marx argued, "the state only exists on the presupposition of their existence; it feels itself to be a political state and asserts its universality only in opposition to these elements of its being" (1844b/1974, 354).

The speaker representing the urban estate in the Assembly requested "that *the business of freedom of the press* (das *Gewerbe des Pressfreiheit*) should not be excluded from the *general freedom of business* (*Freiheit der Gewerbe*)" in order to abolish the situation in which "the work of arms and legs is free, but that of the brain is under tutelage" (1842a/1974, 67). Marx admitted the originality and even some validity to the bourgeois conceptualization of press freedom, first, because "why should our speaker not depict freedom in a form which is dear and familiar to him [if] Rembrandt painted the Madonna as a Dutch peasant woman?" The more so, since Germans had no experience with freedom of the press, but they were well apprised of "freedom of business" or "freedom of ownership." Second, if the press is regarded only as business, then indeed intellectual business (*Kopfgewerbe*) ought to deserve "greater freedom than business run by arm and leg," since "the emancipation of arm and leg only becomes humanly significant through the emancipation of the head" (pp. 67–68). There was even a *tactical* reason to present the issue of freedom of the press merely as a kind of freedom of ownership, which Marx did not consider. One of the key arguments against freedom of expression as an "extension" of freedom of thought, or an "intermediate matter" between thought and action, was that the principle of freedom of thought should not be applied to expression because that would imply the enforcement of one's right to impose his views on others, and thus inevitably lead to conflicts and wars. The presentation of the issue of freedom of the press as purely a matter of (at that time widely accepted) the right of private property and free entrepreneurship would shift the emphasis from the controversial matter of whether or not the expression of opinions implies an attempt to impose them on others, and would thus make freedom of the press more acceptable. Yet if freedom of the press is not only familiarized in the form of freedom of ownership but believed to reside in entrepreneurial freedom, than it can only be a *privilege*, a special right—not a right of every human being, but only the right of the owner, of bourgeois. Marx was certainly right in insisting that the subsumption of freedom of the press under the "general freedom" of ownership was a tyranny against the free press, which was only in the interest of the bourgeois class and not in the interest of citizens.

Marx draws a strict distinction between freedom of ownership and freedom of expression and the press that is similar to Kant's differentiation between the right of publisher and the right of author; but in addition to Kant's *ethical* principle of publicity, he also demanded *legal* regulation of press freedom. The liberal jurist Marx particularly praised the historical view of the spokesman in the Rhine Assembly who asserted that "whenever the inevitable progress of time causes a new, important interest to develop and gives rise to a new need, for which no adequate provision is contained in the existing legislation, *new laws are necessary to regulate this new state of society*" (p. 75; emphasis added). In contrast to censorship edicts, Marx considered the press law the legal recognition of freedom of the press. In particular, it has to make sure that *no class of citizens is granted more rights than another*. The true sense of the press law is not restricting the freedom of the press (as in censorship) to prevent criminal acts through fear of punishment. Marx adopted Kant's insistence that any actual legislation be consistent with a "universal law" by emphasizing that "laws are the positive, clear, universal norms in which freedom has acquired an impersonal, theoretical existence independent of the arbitrariness of the individual." An absence of the press law from the actual legislation indicates "the exclusion of freedom of the press from the sphere of legal freedom, for legally recognized freedom exists in the state as law" (p. 58).

The idea that freedom of business and ownership ought to become the common denominator and the keystone against which all other "freedoms" should be "measured" was in Marx's eyes at least as dangerous to freedom of the press as censorship. As he argued, the ideas expressed in the Assembly were much more than just individual discussions: they represented specific social estates. Inversely, Marx's critique of a *bourgeois* conceptualization of press freedom may be seen as not only *a critique* of such an understanding (or rather misunderstanding) of the nature of the press and its freedom, but *the critique* of the bourgeois class. While this idea was not clearly present in his analysis of debates on press freedom and censorship, it emerged unequivocally a couple of years later:

> The bourgeoisie, wherever it has got the upper hand . . . has resolved personal worth into exchange value, and in place of the numberless indefeasible chartered freedoms, has set up that single, unconscionable freedom—free trade. In one word, for exploitation, veiled by religious and political illusions, it has substituted naked, shameless, direct, brutal exploitation.
>
> The bourgeoisie has stripped of its halo every occupation hitherto honored and looked up to with reverent awe. It has converted the physician, the lawyer, the priest, the poet, the man of science, into its paid wage laborers. (Marx and Engels 1848/1998, 38)

Freedom of the press can only be defended if the true nature of the sphere of the press is comprehended. It means that we must proceed from the generic or "essential character" of the press rather than its "external relations." Marx insisted on separating discussions of freedom of specific spheres of human activity and therefore rejected the idea that press freedom was a kind of commercial freedom. He admitted that the latter also existed since "the press also exists as business," but then (Marx argued in accordance with Kant's distinction between publisher's and writer's rights) "it is not a matter of writers, but of printers and booksellers. However, the concern here is not with the freedom of printers' and booksellers' business, but with freedom of the press" (1842a/1974, 71). The writer has to earn in order to live and write, but he must by no means reduce his life and work to business; even more—Marx obviously refers to his own life—he has to sacrifice his own existence to the existence of his works. "Every particular sphere of freedom is freedom of a particular sphere," claimed Marx. Otherwise "one could also put the matter the other way round and call freedom of business *a kind of freedom of the press*." Or, for example, why the carpenter, who demands freedom for his craftsmanship, would not be rather given the freedom of the philosopher? Consequently, freedom of doing business has nothing to do with the true nature of the press and its freedom; on the contrary, "*the primary freedom of the press is not to be a business*" (p. 71).

Marx's critique of "commercialization" of press freedom and his appeal against the dependence of writers on "material interests" may sound romantic and slackly argued today. We should not forget, though, that at the time he wrote the essay no one could imagine complex "news factories" competing on the press market for consumers described by Bücher half a century later. Thus it would not make sense to expect from Marx a systematic analysis of what did not exist yet. Marx was primarily attentive to the existing political and legal situation in the Prussian state rather than to specific economic conditions needed for a free press to develop. On the other hand, just the opposite could be also argued; namely, that Marx was already aware of the danger whose age was only to come—the negative social consequences of capitalist production guided by the principle of maximization of profit. Indeed, it is possible to see a connection between his early critique of the reduction of press freedom to freedom of entrepreneurship and his later critique of political economy of capitalism. This connection suggesting a continuity in Marx's critical thought seems more plausible than the idea that the subsequent aversion for criticism and thus suppression of intellectual freedom in the socialist movement probably derive from Marx's belittlement of the importance of human or citizen rights. It would be difficult to derive Lenin's fear of conspiracy of criticism— arguing that the request "for a durable unity, there must be freedom of criticism" is nothing but "opportunism" (Lenin 1902, 3–4)—from Marx's belief that *criticism* is the "true censorship," which is based on the essence of press freedom and resulting from it as "the tribunal," in contrast to "censorship," which is criticism monopolized by the government (Marx 1842a/1974, 55). This is not to say that Marx in his "mature" age "inherited" all the liberal ideas of journalist and editor Marx of the 1840s. Yet he certainly remained convinced of the extreme importance of a free and critical press not only within the framework of capitalism, but also in the period to follow capitalism; but this issue was of secondary concern in the period when Marx passionately concentrated on the struggle of the working class against the capitalist class and its state, and its world historic importance. In *that* context, he did not show much tolerance to "muddleheads from the alleged 'learned' caste," as he called[43] "professional literary men" who gave up practical work for, and with, the proletariat.

Marx was not the only social theorist whose work stimulated discussions about a radical break between ideas developed in different periods of a writer's lifetime. The idea of "two Marxes"—the young liberal versus the old orthodox Marx—is comparable to the belief (see Himmelfarb in Rinderle 2000, 138) that a fundamental ethical difference exists between Mill's *Liberty* (1859) and his *Utilitarianism* (1863), a difference between the rational-liberal asserting freedom of conscience and expression as a fundamental human right, and the elitist-conservative Mill's believing that human instincts have to be "controlled and enlightened by a higher reason" to sustain progress in civilization.

LIBERTY AND TOLERANCE AIMED AT TRUTH: MILL

The history of human ideas is full of paradoxes. For instance, Edmund Burke, who resolutely defended the unity of power, was unjustly declared the founding father of the "fourth estate," an idea of the press rooted in the separation of powers. It is believed that the founder of the principle of publicity,

Immanuel Kant, never used the term "public opinion" in his theory of publicity, but he did it. Karl Marx, who passionately struggled for press freedom, is unjustly held responsible for Marxism's lack of interest in human rights and generally progressive social theory, while the concept of the "free marketplace of ideas" was unjustly attributed to John Stuart Mill, although it neither derives directly from any of his texts nor it does reflect appropriately his views on freedom of thought and expression. Equating Mill's justification of freedom of expression with the "free marketplace of ideas" rather than diversity and plurality in general is the same as suggesting that the well-known Chinese saying "Let a thousand flowers flourish" pertains to the free marketplace. Similarly to the "fourth estate," which became current only after its putative father, Burke, the "free marketplace of ideas" metaphor became popular not before Justice Oliver Wendell Holmes, who in 1919 substantiated his dissenting voice in *Abrams vs. United States* by arguing that "the best test of truth is the power of the thought to get itself accepted in the competition on the market" (in Trager and Dickerson 1999, 102). In contrast, Mill not only persuasively defended freedom of expression as everybody's right but, at the same time, also determined "the grounds and limits of the *laisser-faire* or noninterference principle." In his *Principles of Political Economy* (1847), he discussed the necessity of the governmental intervention and emphasized the need for proper regulation to adjust individual independence to societal interests and control. Although his essay *On Liberty* often appears as a major philosophical justification of freedom of expression *and* freedom of the press,[44] Mill's innate interest was, in fact, limited to free expression (including free *individual* publication of opinion) and consumption of ideas *irrespective of the press*.

His famous essay *On Liberty* is not a plea for the press to be free, but a vigorous defense of individuals' right to make their personal opinions available to others. At the center of Mill's writings are "civil liberty" and its relation to the authorities of *power* (government and society) and *reason*, which only refers to two aspects of "negative freedom" in Kant's complex principle of publicity (without Mill's reference to it)—the pursuit of truth and unconditional dependence of freedom of thought on freedom of speech. Mill's "categorical" (to use Kant's term) *principle of noninterference* clearly indicates his deviations from Kant. Compared with earlier dissertations on freedom of speech and press, the most remarkable characteristic of Mill's defense of individual freedom is that he did not defend it against the Church, the state, or, as Marx did, against freedom of entrepreneurship. Early seventeenth-century treatises on freedom of expression focused on the issue of religious liberty and tolerance, and the struggle for freedom of speech and publication was marked by the demand of tolerance addressed to the Church. Since the beginning of the eighteenth century, the debates concentrated on political liberty, and the struggle for freedom of the press became part of the political struggle leveled primarily against secular authorities. Following Tocqueville, however, Mill saw the most harmful danger to the individual coming from an intolerant society and particularly from public opinion. Thus he directed the struggle for liberty against the people's majority, "tyranny of majority," and against the excessive power of public opinion or the public itself. In contrast to Bentham's *criticism* directed against government or Marx's call for mutual *criticism* between the rulers and the ruled in the realm of the press on terms of equality, Mill demanded *tolerance* for those expressing dissenting or minority opinions. This major shift in the perception of possible threats to freedom was not so much a matter of setting a different paradigm per se, but quite obviously a consequence of empirical changes and specificities of British society in the first half of the nineteenth century.

Mill's intellectual life was characterized by ambivalence. Until his father's death, he was loyal to the philosophies of Jeremy Bentham and James Mill, of which he was "predestined" to be the heir (Sabine 1961, 706). Later he attempted to modify, somehow eclectically, empiricism and utilitarianism, primarily with Kantian and post-Kantian German philosophy. Mill was a rather regular contributor to newspapers participating in political discussions of the time, as he reported in his *Autobiography* (1873). His first writings appeared toward the end of 1822, when he was only sixteen, in the *Traveller*, edited by Bentham's former amanuensis Walter Coulson. At that time Mill also offered a series of five letters (under the signature of Wickliffe) discussing the issue of free publication of religious opinions to the *Morning Chronicle* (at that time the Whig organ, but after 1823 "a vehicle of the opinions of the Utilitarian radicals"); three of them were published in January and February 1823, but the remaining two never appeared because the editors considered them "too outspoken for that journal." When in 1823 Bentham established the *Westminster Review*, the radical political organ to become the counterweight against the Whig *Edinburgh Review*, Mill became, following his father James, one of the main contributors. After the French Revolution of July 1830 he wrote articles for several weeks on French affairs for the *Examiner*, whose proprietor, editor, and main author became Albany Fonblanque, the former writer of the *Chronicle*, but shortly ceased the writing because of "the uninteresting nature of all the passing events in that country."[45] Mill self-critically remarked in his *Autobiography* that "mere newspaper articles on the occurrences or questions of the moment, gave no opportunity for the development of any general mode of thought."

At first glance, Mill seems to fully accept the principle of utility or, as Bentham later called it, the greatest happiness principle. While stressing that much more should be said on the ideas of pain and pleasure, which are central to utility as a moral standard, he immediately emphasized that "these supplementary explanations do not affect the theory of life on which this theory of morality is grounded—namely, that pleasure, and freedom from pain, are the only things desirable as ends" (Mill 1863, 10). Mill criticized Bentham's abstract utilitarianism striving, as it did, for an increase in human happiness but at the same time overlooking real human beings. As Anderson

(1983, 343) stresses, central to Mill's critical understanding of real human beings was "the notion that man was a creator of purposes and a maker of ends; a *self*-improving and *self*-perfecting being" (emphasis added). Consequently, Mill was primarily interested in freedom as stimulating personal faculties and capabilities rather than an institutionalized form of disciplinary technology. The principle of utility was transformed from a *moral* principle into an *axiological* principle—"utility as the ultimate appeal on all ethical questions; but it must be utility in the largest sense, grounded on the permanent interests of a man as a progressive being" (Mill 1859/2001, 14). Only on the grounds of such interests, individual spontaneity may be restrained by external control, yet only "in respect to those actions of each, which concern the interest of other people."

Mill also did not endorse the utilitarian position favoring effectiveness of government—as a means to "augment the happiness of the community"— over intellectual and political freedom. His defense of personal freedom was clearly *non*utilitarian. He defended the liberty of opinion in the name of the search for *truth* on moral and epistemological grounds. The primary utility of one's opinion is its truth, which is, due to its complexity, fully comprehensible only to a limited number of "minds sufficiently capacious and impartial to make the adjustment with an approach to correctness" (1859/2001, 45); this is why Mill was so concerned with the education of lower classes. In defending personal freedom of speech, he said that even if "all mankind minus one were of one opinion, and only one person were of the contrary opinion, mankind would be no more justified in silencing that one person, than he, if he had the power, would be justified in silencing mankind" (1859, 18)—a claim that is obviously not aimed at bringing "a maximum of happiness" to the people, since the majority would be dissatisfied in such cases. Whereas Bentham claimed in his *Principles of Morals and Legislation* (1781) that "the interest of the community then is . . . the sum of the interests of the several members who compose it," thus making the individual less important in comparison to "the sum," Mill was closer to Spinoza's belief that "every man should think what he likes and say what he thinks" regardless of the interest or opinion of the majority or government, emphasizing that "originality of mind and individuality of character . . . are the only source of any real progress, and of most of the qualities which make the human race much superior to any herd of animals" (Mill 1847, 5, 11:3).

Mill was particularly critical (not quite justly) of Bentham's efforts to subject the government and the minority of elected public functionaries to the Public Opinion Tribunal. As already noted, Bentham did not exclude "every possibility of the exercise of the slightest or most temporary influence either by a minority, or by the functionary's own notions of right," as Mill claims in his essay on Bentham (1838/1859). Bentham certainly treated the government as constantly exploiting opportunities to promote sinister interests, but he did not consider publicity only as a means of control, nor did he reduce the role of public opinion exclusively to the function of surveillance. His ideas of the "melioration-suggestive" function of public opinion and the press, and the press as an "instrument of public instruction," indicate that innovative ideas are also considered part of the public opinion process, and *innovation* can only emanate from the *minority*.

Mill's critique of Bentham's "failure" to point out the means by which democratic institutions could strengthen "respect for the personality of the individual" and "deference to superiority of cultivated intelligence" is not entirely justified. It is true that Bentham did not devote his main concern to these two "sentiments" in which Mill had been most interested (intellectual liberty of the best-educated individuals in the first place), but this is not to say that he entirely neglected them. After all, Bentham's idea of society was not only that of *the sum* of individuals, but also that of *individuals pursuing their separate interests*, of which Mill was critical just because Bentham's neglect of interests other than individual. It could be a matter of permanent dispute if such a shift of focus from the majority to cultivated individuals (the elite) would make Bentham "the Montesquieu of our own times," as Mill believed, while giving that epithet to Tocqueville instead. Nevertheless, Mill credited Bentham and his followers with the increasing awareness of the public "that their laws and institutions are in great part not the product of intellect and virtue, but of modern corruption grafted upon ancient barbarism," emphasizing that "to Bentham more than to any other source might be traced the questioning spirit, the disposition to demand the why of everything, which had gained so much ground and was producing such important consequences in these times" (Mill 1838/1859). Mill did not consider him a "destructive philosopher" who merely perceived anomalies; he praised Bentham for having been able to perceive the truths that would rectify anomalies.

The idea(l)s Mill followed differed from those of Bentham, but they were more radically different from those pursued by Marx, although the two great minds have certainly more in common than one may judge by appearances. Both were interested in economy and human freedom, but in a different order. Marx's early writings were devoted to freedom of citizens and freedom of the press; only later did he switch to political economy, largely under the influence of his practical work for newspapers. Mill's first comprehensive treatise, *Principles of Political Economy*, was first published in 1847, which reached a number of revised editions (see Ellis 1906) and reflected Mill's increasing inclination toward socialism and interest in human liberty, culminating in *On Liberty* (1859). Marx's writings on freedom of the press were as eclectic as Mill's writings on political economy. Nevertheless, there are more discrepancies than congruities between the two contemporaries who—though they both lived in London for quite a while—never met each other. The degree of their disagreement is perhaps best demonstrated by the fact that Marx bitingly, although rarely, referred to Mill as a "philanthropic economist" and "the best representative of shallow syncretism" attempting to "reconcile irreconcilables,"[46] whereas Mill in his entire writings did not make a single reference to Marx.

In contrast to Marx, who criticized the reductionist ideas according to which citizenship and political community were mere means of maintaining the rights of the "bourgeois society" based on the *right to private property*, Mill saw private property as "the guarantee to individuals of the fruits of their own labour and abstinence" (1847, 2, 1:2).[47] Mill was inclined toward "systems of community of property" as substitutes for the organization of the economy based on private ownership due to the development "of the various natural superiorities residing in each individual." He even proposed a ban on collateral inheritance, strict limitation of the amount of inheritance, and severe taxation on inheritance. He believed that "the political economist, for a considerable time to come, will be chiefly concerned with the conditions of existence and progress belonging to a society founded on private property and individual competition; and that the object to be principally aimed at in the present stage of human improvement, is *not the subversion* of the system of individual property, but the *improvement* of it, and the full participation of every member of the community in its benefits" (1847, 2, 1:4; emphasis added). Mill did not consider freedom of private ownership an intrinsic value of human beings, but he favored it on account of stimulating productivity of labor. For pragmatic reasons he did not see any possibility for practical abolition of private property without the existence of a higher standard of justice, a higher moral condition of human nature, and the renovation of the system of education. Up to that time in a very distant future, Mill did not see any sense in contemplating the abolition of private property but, on the contrary, suggested—like the French socialists whose ideas he embraced rather favorably—to consider it a substantial element of the systems of production and distribution of goods. Marx, who lived and worked in London at the same time, counted Mill among "bourgeois economists" and objected to his theory of *psychologizing* economic categories. Mill had argued that while the laws of the production of wealth are a matter of natural necessity, the laws pertaining to the sphere of the distribution of wealth are a matter of human freedom and political responsibility; he did not see them determined by the laws and conditions of production, as Marx did.

Notwithstanding significant disagreements on fundamental ideas, we may identify a threefold, at least rudimentary agreement between Marx and Mill regarding their perception of the role of communication (and more specifically, the press) in society. Both Marx and Mill

- believed in the general importance of human ideas and their consequences, particularly when diffused broadly, for the well-being of society (although on different grounds)

- related the notion of press freedom to personal freedom of expression (in different ways)
- considered freedom of the press, together with freedom of association and assembly, a necessary condition for a democratic society (but they disagreed on what exactly constituted it)

Bentham defended publicity as a means of maximizing the *happiness and felicity* of the people as the foundation of any physical or mental operation and the ultimate standard of right and wrong. Mill, however, considered freedom of thought, expression, and publication positive values in their own right—a conception of freedom mainly influenced by rationalism and Immanuel Kant. Mill believed that no society in which intellectual and political freedom are not respected enjoys freedom, but in contrast to Marx, he emphasized the liberal-individualistic nature of freedom: "The only freedom which deserves the name, is that of pursuing our own good in our own way, so long as we do not attempt to deprive others of theirs, or impede their efforts to obtain it" (Mill 1859/2001, 16). No member of society can be rightfully "compelled to do or forbear because it will be better for him to do so, because it will make him happier, because, in the opinions of others, to do so would be wise, or even right. These are good reasons for remonstrating with him, or reasoning with him, or persuading him, or entreating him, but not for compelling him, or visiting him with any evil in case he do otherwise" (Mill 1859/2001, 13). Hardly any prohibitory regulation could be congruent with the principle of utility. Thus the fundamental principle regulating governmental interference with the liberty of action of any member of society could only be based on preventing harm to others, since only in that case it is reasonable to expect ordinary people to believe that "the thing prohibited is a thing which they ought not to wish to do" (1847, 5, 11:2).

Mill firmly believed that in a democratic society, *"laisser-faire . . .* should be the general practice: every departure from it, unless required by some great good, is a certain evil." However, he also admitted that market competition is not the best solution in *all cases*: for example, in the case of a commodity "in the quality of which society has much at stake, the balance of advantages may be in favour of some mode and degree of intervention, by the authorized representatives of the collective interest of the state" (1847, 5, 11:7). The single exception in human existence that must be completely protected from authoritative intrusion is that part of the life of every person which concerns only his "inward or outward life . . . and does not affect the interests of others, or affects them only through the moral influence of example" (1847, 5, 11:2; also 1859, 15). Typical examples of inward life are *thoughts* and *feelings*, and of outward life, involving no painful consequences for others, are personal *opinions* expressed in public. "I hold that it is allowable in all, and in the more thoughtful and cultivated often a duty, to assert and promulgate, with all the force they are capable of, their opinion of what is good or bad, admirable or contemptible, but not to compel others to conform to that opinion; whether the force used is that of extra-legal coercion, or exerts itself by means of the law" (1847, 5, 11:2). In *On Liberty*, Mill once more emphasized the inseparable connectedness between forming and expressing (or publishing) opinion, yet without any specific reference to the *publication* of opinions and reasons why it should not follow the rules pertaining to actions affecting the interests of others. By omitting any distinctive characteristic of opinion *publication in the press,* in contrast to its mere (often private) *expression,* Mill seems to agree with Hobbes on the historical triviality of the printing press, namely, that the "invention of printing is no great matter compared with the invention of letters" (Hobbes 1651/1992, 24).

Freedom to Express and Publish Opinions as an Extension of Freedom of Thought

Similar to Spinoza's differentiation between "the mental state" and "the outward act" in his *Theologico-Political Treatise* of 1670, and Locke's distinction between the "inward persuasion of the mind" and "outward" actions in his *Letter Concerning Toleration* (1689), Mill distinguished "internal" convictions from "external" actions. Like his predecessors, Mill thought it absurd to assume that inward opinions could be directly controlled by external means, such as laws (although legislation could be a powerful tool of individual motivation). He, too, was primarily concerned to confine the interference of government and society with "external actions," which he divided into two specific regions. On the whole, there are three regions in Mill: (1) the "inward domain of consciousness" of individuals, which also includes the communication of ideas, and the outward domain consisting of (2) the sphere of free actions based on freedom of "tastes and pursuits" and "framing the plan of our life to suit our own character" (so long as what we do does not harm others, even though they may think our conduct to be foolish, perverse, or wrong), and (3) the domain of the "combination among individuals" who have to be free to unite for any purpose provided that it does not have harmful consequences for others. All three regions of human liberty should be free of any direct intervention by society or the state because they either do not affect other people or they affect them only with their free consent and participation. More specifically, the first domain of human liberty comprises

> liberty of conscience in the most comprehensive sense; liberty of thought and feeling; absolute freedom of opinion and sentiment on all subjects, practical or speculative, scientific, moral, or theological. *The liberty of expressing and publishing opinions* may seem to fall under a different principle, since it belongs to

that part of the conduct of an individual which concerns other people; but, being almost of as much importance as the liberty of thought itself, and resting in
great part on the same reasons, is practically inseparable from it. (Mill
1859/2001, 15–16; emphasis added)

In reference to free expression of opinions, Mill obviously had the same
sort of hesitation that his critics had afterward with his distinction between
actions concerning others and actions concerning only the actor himself,
which is impossible to exclusively separate. Mill had the same difficulty
when stating that the entire sphere of internal and external actions did not
contain any action in which individuals' participation would not be fully free
and unrestrained but somehow forced or controlled. This would potentially
justify or even call for societal interference because if one looked at the final
consequences, no such action would really exist. In the long run, whatever
affects an individual may also "affect others through himself" (1859/2001,
15). Thus he emphasized that he meant only "direct effects" of an action on
others, or effects "in the first instance," which the expression of opinions
does not seem to have. Other types of human conduct do, but those actions
were beyond Mill's concern. We can certainly agree with the latter restriction
to "direct actions," yet this does not help define either theoretically or practically the boundary between the two sorts of actions Mill wants to discrimi-
nate.

External intervention must not take place in the mental domain or in the
entire region of human liberty to impede actions of individual members of
society, except for the sake of protecting other members. In analogy with
Locke's and Spinoza's quest for religious tolerance, Mill emphasized the
need for toleration rather than the need for a critique of government, or rational critical debate, as emphasized by Bentham and Marx. Similarly to Spinoza (1670/1883, 263), Mill argued that if the power of free *judgment* is withheld from the individual, the government becomes more tyrannical, but in
contrast to Spinoza he extended the argument to human *action* as well. To
some extent, even *trade* could be seen as a part of the region of human liberty, according to Mill, although it is not the *true* domain of individual liberty, and thus "the principle of individual liberty is not involved in the doctrine of Free Trade." Since trade is a social act and thus affects the interest of
other persons not (directly) involved in a transaction, and even of society as
a whole, it could be regarded as a domain that calls for governmental interference. Yet Mill was decisively negative: "But it is now recognised, though
not till after a long struggle, that both the cheapness and the good quality of
commodities are most effectually provided for by leaving the producers and
sellers perfectly free, under the sole check of equal freedom to the buyers for
supplying themselves elsewhere. This is the so-called *doctrine of Free Trade*,
which rests on grounds different from, though equally solid with, the prin-

ciple of individual liberty" (1859/2001, 87; emphasis added). Restrictions on trade and economy, in general, are "an evil," although they are legitimate, simply because all restraints are "an evil" that should be avoided whenever possible; leaving people to act on their own is always better than controlling and directing them. But for Mill this is essentially not an issue of individual liberty, since there is no doubt that this kind of interaction may be legitimately controlled for certain ends.

For Mill, the question of liberty was in essence the question of *negative individual freedom* in the sphere of intellectual life. The Liberty Principle, as defined in Mill's *On Liberty*, comprises two components: *(un)accountability* and *(non)interfererence*. On the subject of accountability, the principle implies (1) individual unaccountability to society for actions not concerning the interests of other persons and (2) accountability for actions (potentially) damaging to the interests of others. In the matter of interference, Mill concedes the exercise of power—either by government or other institutions—over any member of society against his or her will only to prevent a (potential) harm resulting from his or her actions for society or even him- or herself. Of the two opposing principles implied—society tolerating everyone to decide what is good for him- or herself and to live accordingly (noninterference) or compelling everyone to live according to what is good in the view of majority (interference)—Mill strongly preferred the former.[48] His main concern was to strengthen and protect the citizen against the power of government or fellow citizens tending to impose their own opinions and preferences as a rule of conduct on others.

Mill's crucial argument for intellectual and political freedom and tolerance was not addressed to the government or the state but rather to *society*—to "the nature and limits of the power which can be legitimately *exercised by society over the individual*" (1859, 6; emphasis added). Not only in his essay *On Liberty* (1859), but even in *Representative Government* (1861) and already in *Principles of Political Economy* (1847) he identified the numerical *majority* of the population, or public opinion—as result of his reading of Tocqueville's *Democracy in America* (1835, 1840)—as a powerful source of political oppression and a major threat to liberty. Thus Mill did not disapprove of all kinds of governmental interference with actions performed by individuals; on the contrary, he specified a number of cases that directly call for such an intervention to increase their beneficial consequences and make society more tolerant.

Mill differentiated between two kinds of government interventions: the authoritative control of free actions of individuals and nonauthoritative intervention. The best example of the former is *legal* regulation, issuing a command and enforcing it by penalties, whereas the latter comprises various activities, from giving advice and promulgating information to establishing governmental agencies competing with individuals' "free actions."

Mill defended the noninterference principle with three main arguments. First, if something has to be done, it is likely to be done better by individuals rather than the government. Those who do the work are likely to know how to do it better than the government. Even if the government possessed the best available knowledge and skills, it is likely that individual producers would be more successful, since they would soon increase their knowledge due to their strong and direct interest in the effectiveness and quality of production. Second, even if individuals did worse than government, their involvement would serve to educate them, and thus they should do it themselves. And third (the most important reason for Mill), government interference has to be restricted a priori wherever possible in order to minimize "the great evil of adding unnecessarily to its power" (1859/2001, 100–101; 1847, 5, 11:7).

On the other hand, Mill listed a number of cases in which the noninterference principle should not necessarily or universally apply, and different reasons substantiating the need for authoritative or nonauthoritative intervention, without an attempt to systemize them. Mill's basic proposition that "the workman is generally the best selector of means" does not imply that the consumer is the most competent judge of goods or services. Since it is quite obvious, as Mill argued, that the consumer is not always appropriately educated to form a valid judgment, "the presumption in favour of the competition of the market does not apply" or is acceptable only with numerous exceptions. If the whole society has a special interest in specific goods or services, the best achievements may result from the balance between some degree of governmental intervention or control and individual action. Mill's list of harmful consequences of free actions is much longer than a contemporary "free marketplace" characterization of his ideas would imply. As Gordon convincingly states, "What Mill rejected as an unnecessary and undesirable consequence of the free market now seems to pass as unexceptional, even natural" (Gordon 1997, 246). For example, late-twentieth-century market ideology rules out *cooperation* in contrast to Mill, who emphasized that the government should financially stimulate private enterprises to learn how to accomplish great tasks not only through individual energy but also by different forms of voluntary cooperation (Mill 1847, 5, 11:16).

In addition to the economy, "there are other things, of the worth of which the demand of the market is by no means a test; things of which the utility does not consist in ministering to inclinations, nor in serving the daily uses of life, and the want of which is least felt where the need is greatest. This is peculiarly true of those things which are chiefly useful as tending to raise the character of human beings" (Mill 1847, 5, 11:8). *Education* would be a typical case for the kind of products or services for which the market cannot be seen as a test of their value, since the uneducated cannot judge matters of education. As Mill noted, those who need educational services most usually desire them least, due precisely to the lack of education; therefore, education is "one of those things which it is admissible in principle that a government should provide for the people."

The principle of noninterference may also be questionable when individuals are unable to judge about their own interests and the means needed to realize them, such as children, mentally impaired, and occasionally women. Another exception occurs when an individual attempts to decide what is best for him or her into the future and enters into an irrevocable contract without having any real knowledge about what may happen in the future—such as marriage. Or similarly, when individuals can only participate indirectly in decision making (e.g., as shareholders in a joint-stock company). As Mill believed, the drawbacks of government management are not greater, if greater at all, than those of management by joint stock.

There are some matters in which state interference must be required—not to protect the interest of those who are unable to manage it themselves but to give effect to their decision or judgment. Workers, for example, cannot negotiate working hours with employers individually but only in an organized way, under protection of the law. The principle that individuals are the best judge of their own interests cannot apply to acts of public charity and similar acts by individuals not in their own interest but in the interest of other people.

Finally, Mill specifies two classes of acts in which government *should* interfere: actions performed by individuals in their own interest, which involve consequences that exceed their own interests, such as the colonization of other countries, or important public services lacking in interest for those potentially rendering those services and those who would pay for them, such as scientific explorations or traffic regulation.

Two classes of characteristics may be recognized in Mill's "typology" of human actions that justify, or even call for, the governmental intervention. On the one hand, Mill identified transactions, such as educational process, in which potential customers are not well informed about the supply of goods or services and thus they cannot make qualified decisions. On the other hand, in some cases service suppliers could have malefic or sinister interests that users may be unable to discover. Neither of them "qualifies" the press, according to Mill, for a legitimate intervention by the state, although the reasons for intervention acknowledged by Mill as legitimate for (public) education and traffic were later implied particularly in the conceptualization of public service broadcasting, which dominated the development of radio and television in Europe until the late 1900s.

In contrast to either Bentham or Marx, who attributed to the press (albeit from different perspectives) a quintessential task of political or generally spiritual *mediation in society*, recognizing the need for its regulation, the press for Mill represented a blind spot in the relationship between citizens and government, as did it for Rousseau. Mill considered newspapers of little avail to the "origination of new ideas" (1847, 5, 5:2). Mill suggested that the nonintervention principle should *not* be applied in a number of specific cases but did not

include the agency of the press, although he realized how important but difficult it was to enable and persuade people to hear arguments for and against
an opinion. Moreover, he demanded that special attention to be paid to minority opinions and neglected interests. "Truth . . . is so much a question of the
reconciling and combining of opposites, that very few have minds sufficiently
capacious and impartial to make the adjustment with an approach to correctness, and it has to be made by the rough process of a struggle between com-
batants fighting under hostile banners" (1859/2001, 45). Remarkably, writing
On Liberty, Mill concluded that "the time, it is to be hoped, is gone by, when
any defence would be necessary of the 'liberty of the press' as one of the securities against corrupt or tyrannical government" (1859/2001, 18). Why did
(liberty of) the press *have no more* need of securities against governments or
other threats? Mill had identified the danger of the tyranny of the majority—but
was it in no relation to the liberty of the press? Were there no other "corrupt
and tyrannical" interests that could impede a free press than those of a tyrannical government? Did the liberty of the press become secure by de facto exclusion of the "tyrannical majority"—not really able to judge its own interests,
let alone important political issues—from active participation in the press? If
the sphere of the press is not listed among those specific cases that allow for,
or even require, *specific* intervention by society or government—does it imply
that the press should be regarded as just another form of *trade*, so that it is not
a matter of liberty in the strict sense any more? Mill's reticence about freedom
of the press indicates a position later adopted by U.S. Supreme Court Justices
Hugo Black and William O. Douglas, arguing that literally *no* restriction should
be imposed on the media, so that even the offence of defamation should be
abolished to protect the press from the chilling effect of liability (Powe 1991,
124). Unfortunately, any attempt at reconstructing what would have been
Mill's answers to these questions can hardly exceed pure speculation inferred
from his rare incidental attitudes toward newspapers and much more elaborate discussion of the governmental (non)intervention.

Mill advocated the liberty of expressing and publishing *all* opinions, but
primarily *minority* opinions. He claimed that the opinion to be "encouraged
and countenanced" should always be "the one which happens at the particular time and place to be in a minority. That is the opinion which, for the
time being, represents the neglected interests, the side of human well-being
which is in danger of obtaining less than its share" (1859/2001, 45). Clearly,
any "interference" by government or society in stimulating people to listen
to "both sides" and ensuring individual liberty of opinion expression to those
representing the minority would not be an infringement of individual liberty
for Mill. Yet he never consequently resolved the tension between the principle of governmental noninterference and its responsibility to encourage expression of dissenting opinions, what he attempted for a number of other
"cases" specified above, such as education or colonization.

Mill attributed no importance to the press as a means of paving the way for expressing minority opinions to the public. On the contrary, he was only concerned with the problem of how to make newspapers available to *readers*—in fact, to the *majority* of readers. In a way, newspapers had already solved the problem of how to encourage minority opinions, since the opinions presented in newspapers had been formed and expressed by an *elite minority*—writers like Mill. The only remaining problem was how to disseminate those opinions to less educated classes. That was Mill's main argument against newspaper taxes:

A tax on newspapers is objectionable, not so much where it does fall as where is does not, that is, where it prevents newspapers from being used. To the generality of those who buy them, newspapers are a luxury which they can as well afford to pay for as any other indulgence, and which is as unexceptionable a source of revenue. But to that large part of the community who have been taught to read, but have received little other intellectual education, newspapers are the source of nearly all the general information which they possess, and of nearly all their acquaintance with the ideas and topics current among mankind; and an interest is more easily excited in newspapers, than in books or other more recondite sources of instruction. Newspapers contribute so little, in a direct way, to the origination of useful ideas, that many persons undervalue the importance of their office in disseminating them. They correct many prejudices and superstitions, and keep up a habit of discussion, and interest in public concerns, the absence of which is a great cause of stagnation of mind usually found in the lower and middle, if not in all, ranks, of those countries where newspapers of an important or interesting character do not exist. There ought to be no taxes (as in this country there now are not) which render this great diffuser of information, of mental excitement, and mental exercise, less accessible to that portion of the public which most needs to be carried into a region of ideas and interests beyond its own limited horizon. (1847, 5, 5:2)

For Mill, it is not freedom of the press that constitutes a substantial part of the "region of human liberty," but only the *personal liberty of expressing and publishing opinions*.[49] Although the latter is not directly part of the "inward domain of consciousness" (comprising liberty of conscience, liberty of thought and feeling, and freedom of opinion and sentiment), because it always concerns *other* people, Mill emphasizes that it is no less important than liberty of thought and is inseparable from it. This *may* also imply publication of opinions in newspapers, yet the fact remains that Mill's conceptualization of human liberty concerns the press neither directly nor substantially. The reason for excluding freedom of the press from the realm of individual liberty had been identified already by Marx (1842a/1974, 51): freedom of the press is not a form of liberty as "the right to do everything that harms no one else"—which is "the liberty of man as an isolated monad, withdrawn into himself"—nor "a privilege of particular individuals," but a "*universal* right" and "a privilege of the *human mind*" (emphasis added).

It seems, then, a matter of consistency that in Mill's *On Liberty* the idea of freedom of the press is only mentioned twice in passing: first, in the chapter "Of the Liberty of Thought and Discussion," in which Mill expresses his belief that the "liberty of the press" does not need to be defended against tyrannical government any more, and, second, in the concluding chapter "Applications," in which Mill states that "not all freedom of the press . . . would make this or any other country free otherwise than in name," if governmental interference with the economy, education, and charities is not restricted. As Mill makes clear in the very beginning of the essay, his subject is "civil or social liberty," by which he conceives of "the nature and limits of the power which can be legitimately *exercised by society over the individual*" (1859/2001, 6; emphasis added). His primary concern is for "the only freedom which deserves the name," meaning, "that of *pursuing our own good in our own way*, so long as we do not attempt to deprive others of theirs, or impede their efforts to obtain it" (p. 16). Thus he was primarily concerned with the "inward domain of consciousness" from among the three domains in the region of human liberty. Under that designation he discussed in different works specific "freedoms" or "liberties," for example, of thinking, opinion and sentiment, religion and worship, expressing and publishing opinions, speaking and writing, and liberty of public discussion. Other individual liberties in Mill's work include the freedom to unite, freedom of action, liberty of tastes and pursuits, liberty of private life, and the liberty of the seller and buyer.

"Newspapers Contribute So Little to the Origination of Useful Ideas . . ."

One could assess Mill's ideas on liberty as not directly relevant to press freedom, since he did not see freedom of the press as an ally of personal liberty. But since the issue of freedom in general (if not confined to personal liberty) is obviously pertinent to the press, one could rather investigate the consequences of Mill's conceptualization of freedom for the press or ask—which may eventually be the same—which concept of freedom of the press is implied by Mill's liberty principle. It seems rather obvious that it cannot be freedom in the sense of the "free marketplace of ideas," since the latter does not guarantee what Mill had in mind, primarily, the right of a minority to voice its opinion in public. The ideological nature of the "free marketplace of ideas" metaphor was brought to light by the same process that disclosed the corruptness of the fourth estate model—the process of press *monopolization*. In all "democratic countries," leading newspapers sooner or later acquired a monopoly in the marketplace and effectively erased one of the essential elements of fourth estate and "free marketplace of ideas" concepts: a *diversity* of ideas presented through a *variety* of newspapers. Mill considered this process as essentially (only) a spiritual and moral one, rather than an economic one. He criticized developments in the press market because they stimulated a process of lowering the general level of education and increasing intolerance, but he did not realize that this process was determined by the costs and capitalization involved in technological developments (Williams 1978, 47) and—because of the concentration of ownership—limiting the feasibility of producing newspapers for the majority of the population. Mill was not even concerned about close relationships between political parties, government, and newspapers, which shifted the press "from its natural position of complete independency to become part of 'the political machine.'"[50] Thus Mill called for a specific intervention to protect personal freedom only because "the present civilization tends so strongly to make the power of persons acting in masses the only substantial power in society, that there never was more *necessity for surrounding individual independence of thought, speech, and conduct*, with the most powerful defences, in order to maintain that originality of mind and individuality of character" (1847, 5, 11:3; emphasis added). Yet, even in aspiring to protect individual intellectual independence, he was never specific about the installation of "the most powerful defences" to effectively protect personal liberty. He left the issue with merely a conviction that "genuine private affections" and a "sincere interest in the public good" are possibly congruent on the condition that individuals would be properly brought up (1863/2001, 17).

Putting aside Mill's theoretical idiosyncrasy and his struggle with public opinion, whose powerful tool became precisely the (penny)[51] press, there is also no particular *practical* reason why one should expect him to defend freedom of the press as vigorously as Marx did or as strenuously as he defended personal freedom of expression. His personal existence (unlike Marx's) never depended on the press, nor was freedom of the press in England in his time restricted as sharply as it was in Germany. As we have seen, Mill even believed that the press was free to such an extent that there was no longer a need to discuss the issue of freedom of the press. Mill had contributed to English newspapers and journals since his youth, yet his attitudes toward the press remained ambivalent. On the one hand, he praised newspapers as a modern equivalent of the ancient Greek agora, but on the other hand, he saw in the press a vehicle of subordination of individuals to the masses, a part of

the general tendency of things throughout the world to render mediocrity the ascendant power among mankind. In ancient history, in the Middle Ages, and in a diminishing degree through the long transition from feudality to the present time, the individual was a power in himself; and if he had either great talents or a high social position, he was a considerable power. At present individuals are lost in the crowd. In politics it is almost a triviality to say that public opinion now rules the world. The only power deserving the name is that of masses, and of governments while they make themselves the organ of the tendencies and instincts of masses. Those whose opinions go by the name of public opinion . . . are always a mass, that is to say, collective mediocrity. And what is a still greater novelty, the mass do not now take their opinions from dignitaries in Church or State, from ostensible leaders, or from books. Their thinking is done for them by men much like themselves, addressing them or speaking in their name, on the spur of the moment, *through the newspapers.* (1859/2001, 61; emphasis added)

Mill credited newspapers on different occasions and, more or less incidentally, with different functions. His parenthetical discussions of the press are not marked by the controversy in his writings about the ideals of negative individual liberty and active and disinterested participation in public affairs. Although the libertarian and participatory dimensions are reflected in his attitudes toward the press, they are minimized and thus the ambivalence is reduced: Mill endorses the participatory potential of the press with the proviso that it is limited to certain functions, and the liberty of opinion expression in the press with the proviso that it may have some harmful consequences. Instead of advancing individuals' right to pursue their own interests, the utility of the press is reduced to a potentially injurious tool for the promotion and dissemination of ideas: "Newspapers *contribute so little,* in a direct way, *to the origination of useful ideas,* that many persons undervalue the importance of their office in *disseminating them*" (1847, 5, 5:2; emphasis added). The press is considered a tool to help educate the masses rather than enable their active participation in the political process. Mill's ambivalent attitude toward the utility of the press is also clearly reflected in his distinction between the good (respectable) and more problematic (pauper) press, which is obviously not based on Mill's principle of everyone's right to pursue his or her own good.

In his *Representative Government* Mill considered reading newspapers and "perhaps writing to them," alongside public gatherings and solicitations to authorities, as mediating the political process—"the extent of the participation of private citizens in general politics during the interval between one parliamentary election and another" (1861/2001, 170–71). He believed newspapers could help bridge the gap between ancient Athenian democracy, where neither the need nor conditions existed "for the formation and propagation of a public opinion, except among those who could be brought together to discuss public matters in the same agora," and a modern representative democracy in which "the press, and even the newspaper press [became] the real equivalent, though not in all respects an adequate one, of the Pnyx and the Forum"[52] (1861/2001, 10). Newspapers, for Mill, are not really the site to *organize public debates,* not even during the period between parliamentary elections.

Similarly to Rousseau and Kant, Mill claimed that the enforcement of *universal education* of citizens be admitted by the state as a fundamental condition for freedom of opinion formation and expression, and the only way to achieve "the mental well-being of mankind (on which all their other well-being depends)" (1859/2001, 49). Yet Mill also attributed an educational role to the press as its primary function; as he stated, "the instruction obtained from newspapers and political tracts may not be the most solid kind of instruction, but it is an immense improvement upon none at all" (1847, 4, 7:2). The press is not considered an instrument of realizing personal freedom of expression, but a tool to "awaken public spirit, to diffuse a variety of ideas among the mass, and to excite thought and reflection in the more intelligent."[53] Mill feared that the rise of the *penny press* would be destructive of the newspapers' worthwhile pedagogic services to their readers, although he also praised "the salutary measure of fiscal emancipation which gave existence to the penny press" (1847, 4, 7: 2), namely, the abolition of the Newspaper Stamp Duties Act of 1819 which was, according to Lord Ellenborough's explanation, not directed against the "respectable press" but against the popular "pauper press" that after 1815 reached a large new audience of primarily lower classes (Williams 1978, 46). Mill was also afraid that political franchises to a less educated class of people would reduce interests in education and newspaper reading, while admitting that

> the working classes are now part of the public; in all discussions on matters of general interest they, or a portion of them, are now partakers; all who use the press as an instrument may, if it so happens, have them for an audience; the avenues of instruction through which the middle classes acquire such ideas as they have, are accessible to, at least, the operatives in the towns. With these resources, it cannot be doubted that they will increase in intelligence, even by their own unaided efforts. (1847, 4, 7: 2)

Mill thought that education provided by the "respectable" press would stimulate citizen participation and provide the only security against "political slavery." Although he criticized Bentham's idea of public surveillance that would force authorities to follow the public interest, he adopted it in principle, adding that it should be based on "the diffusion of intelligence, activity, and public spirit among the governed" (1847, 5, 11:6). In other words, surveillance should not be in the hands of the population at large, but rather a privilege of the knowledgeable minority because "political checks will no more act of themselves than a bridle will direct a horse without a rider," if checking functionaries are not properly qualified (1861/2001, 24). In contrast to Bentham, who defined publicity as the "central characteristic" and "indispensable instrument" of the Public Opinion Tribunal to prevent the government from pursuing its own interests (which every government will try to do if not put under surveillance), Mill looked for perfect harmony between the interest of the functionaries and their duties; the utility of publicity is not in being an impediment to evil or stimulus to good in itself, but in helping the electorate find appropriate functionaries.

Mill detected two basic difficulties with Bentham's broad category of the Public Opinion Tribunal as the guardian of public functionaries: its members lack competency and there is no guarantee that their moral standing is high enough. "If the checking functionaries are as corrupt or as negligent as those whom they ought to check, and if the public, the mainspring of the whole checking machinery, are too ignorant, too passive, or too careless and inattentive, to do their part, little benefit will be derived from the best administrative apparatus" (1861/2001, 24). He suggested, however, that the Parliament should watch and control the government; he vested the representative assembly with the functions Bentham had attributed to the Public Opinion Tribunal.[54] According to Mill, publicity in the Benthamian sense of being answerable to *the public* is only conducive to "enforcing a servile conformity" to the public. Thus it should be replaced with publicity in the sense of "being under the eyes of *others*," that is, responsibility to the public (the majority) should be replaced with responsibility to those in opposition. This argument—earlier developed in *On Liberty*—is persuasive: those acting in opposition to the opinion of others are always required to have sound arguments and a sure ground of their own (1861/2001, 129).[55]

As society experienced general progress, education and knowledge increased in importance; hence Mill also emphasized the importance of diffusing knowledge in society "down to the lowest classes," through not only through the press but also institutions established by the government. He held the government responsible for encouraging people to educate themselves and "to manage as many as possible of their joint concerns by voluntary co-operation; since this discussion and management of collective interests is the great school of that public spirit, and the great source of that intelligence of public affairs, which are always regarded as the distinctive character of the public of free countries" (1847, 5, 11:6). In *Representative Government* Mill defined the most important criterion of the goodness of a government: "the degree in which it tends to increase the sum of good qualities in the governed, collectively and individually" (1861/2001, 23). As he later proclaimed in *Utilitarianism*, "there is absolutely no reason in the nature of things why an amount of mental culture sufficient to give an intelligent interest in these objects of contemplation, should not be the inheritance of every one born in a civilised country" (1863/2001, 17). Mill's writings generally suggest that any form of governmental intervention that stimulates the development of citizens' knowledge cannot be detrimental to their freedoms.

Apparently the ambivalence of Mill's conceptualization of the press and its tasks in society reflects the British press in the mid-nineteenth century. Mill's time witnessed an extremely fast rise in the number of publications in general and newspapers in particular: annual titles of publications increased from 370 in 1790 to over 500 in 1820 and to more than 2,600 by the 1850s! After 1815 the more radical "pauper press" began to rise, evading the Stamp Duty then in force primarily as a political tax by excluding news and publishing only opinion (Williams 1978, 46). The established newspapers aimed at the educated middle class, such as *The Times*, pretended to perform the role of the fourth estate but, in fact, "the natural position of the nineteenth-century [British] press was that of being part of the political machine" (Boyce

1978, 26). At the same time, the popular (particularly Sunday) press developed for a different kind of *mass* readership, followed by the new cheap evening press in the 1860s. In parliamentary debates on press taxes both traditionalists and reformers in Parliament wanted to destroy radical working-class journalism and trade unionism (Curran 1978, 55). Yet not only press taxation—which contrary to the goal of excluding the working class from reading newspapers merely ensured that the popular newspapers were effectively controlled by the working class—but also and perhaps primarily the industrialization of the press, and the expansion of the "free market" after the termination of newspaper taxation led to decline of the radical press in Britain. Mill's ambivalence is more than merely a reflection of that empirical situation; it is also an elitist[56] defense of the status quo, legitimizing the process in which "the *principle* of the public sphere, that is, critical publicity, seemed to lose its strength in the measure that it expanded as a *sphere* and even undermined the private realm" (Habermas 1962/1995, 140, 136). As Habermas further argues, liberal (and specifically Mill's) theorizations of that process may be considered reactionary because they "reacted to the power of the idea of a critically debating public's self-determination . . . as soon as this public was subverted by the propertyless uneducated masses."

Regardless of Mill's failure to grasp the social substance of the press and his rather unfavorable assessment of newspapers as unsuitable for the development of any general mode of thought, his arguments for freedom of expression may be applied to the press—not conceived of as the "fourth estate" or as the "marketplace of ideas," but as an implement, a genuine *medium* of a free public discussion. It is as if we deleted the interpolation in Mill's sentence that in modern representative democracy "the press, and even the newspaper press [became] the real equivalent, *though not in all respects an adequate one,* of the Pnyx and the Forum." In fact, Mill never explained in *which respects* newspapers are "adequately" and "inadequately" equivalent of the antique Greek forms of democratic deliberation; nor whether this was a deficiency inherent in the press or only specific to the British press of his time. Thus we may read Mill's *On Liberty*, which concerns justifiable constraints of power exercised by society over the *individual* in his or her pursuit of the truth through public discussion—to test his arguments pertaining to the category of personal intellectual rights (holding and freely propagating opinions) with regard to freedom of the press.

How to Make Invisible Hands behind the "Marketplace of Ideas" Visible

Mill distinguished three dimensions in the liberty of opinion and speech—the mental process of thinking, its external manifestation through speech, and nonverbal actions provoked by the expressed opinions—which are *all* constitutive of intellectual liberty. In fact, the proper domain of freedom of opinion is the *expression* of opinion, since the mental process of thinking cannot be subject to "compulsion and control, whether the means used be physical force in the form of legal penalties, or the moral coercion of public opinion." Thus the fundamental "very simple principle" to govern all dealings of society with the individual as defined by Mill states

> that the sole end for which mankind are warranted, individually or collectively, in interfering with the liberty of action of any of their number, is self-protection. That the only purpose for which power can be rightfully exercised over any member of a civilised community, against his will, is to prevent harm to others. (1859/2001, 13)

Could (or should) this "very simple principle" regulating the relationship between individual and society also be applied, qua fundamental principle, to the press—as it has been in the First Amendment to the U.S. Constitution? It is not difficult to see important differences between the *expression* of opinion and *publication* of opinion (expression in the press or, today, other media) in terms of (1) the feasibility of two kinds of "external manifestation" of opinion to be exercised universally and equally by all members of society, and in terms of (2) the degree of potentially pernicious consequences of such an exercise.

For instance, Mill considered the press "pernicious" due to its unfavorable cultural consequences. The penny press, Mill believed, induces mediocrity that should be prevented. His scruples against the press do not refer to individual actions in which the press is used as a means of opinion expression, but to its *corporate* or *institutional* existence: the press as institution may cause harm to those exposed to it. Mill's cure for similar cases—for example, in the sphere of education—was as simple as his fundamental principle: direct or indirect state intervention.

On the other hand, Mill did not believe that even the most extensive exercise of personal freedom (of expressing opinion) would cause the kind of injuries that would warrant civil restraints. Thus Mill defended freedom of expression on ethical grounds (leaving individuals ignorant is a moral evil) and pragmatic utilitarian grounds (the public good is better served by unrestricted expression of opinion). But when compared with the press, he saw more potentially pernicious consequences of opinions expressed in public than published in newspapers—an idea completely at variance with later legal regulations of defamatory and libelous speech considering an offense more harmful and thus requiring greater punishment if committed through the media.[57] Referring to the distinction between opinion and action, Mill followed his habitual rhetoric of exemplification:

> No one pretends that actions should be as free as opinions. On the contrary, even opinions lose their immunity when the circumstances in which they are expressed are such as to constitute their expression a positive instigation to

some mischievous act. An opinion that corn-dealers are starvers of the poor, or that private property is robbery, ought to be unmolested when simply circulated through the press, but may justly incur punishment when delivered orally to an excited mob assembled before the house of a corndealer, or when handed about among the same mob in the form of a placard. (1859/2001, 52)

As he put it more generally, "the manner of asserting an opinion, even though it be a true one, may be very objectionable, and may justly incur severe censure" (p. 50). Mill identified two possible reasons why the expression of opinions could be restricted, but he emphasized that it is practically impossible to establish a firm line between what is acceptable or objectionable because it would always depend on those whose opinions are attacked, and they would always—if they had strong feelings on the subject—consider attacks on their opinion intemperate. One reason is the stigmatization of opponents as bad and immoral persons because they hold different opinions; the other is the suppression of facts or arguments, misstatement of elements of a case, or misrepresentation of opposite opinions. As Mill argues, the latter case is also important and should be restrained—but that is practically impossible because it could be only revealed by those who suppressed or mispresented facts. In the interest of truth and justice, the employment of vituperative language should be restrained, particularly if used by those holding the prevailing opinion, so as to not discourage people from advancing opposing opinions and from listening to those who express them.

Indeed, Mill always insisted on the need for *social support* for *nonconformity*, arguing that the entire human race has no right to silence one dissenter. Similarly to Marx's argument against the ideas of "imperfection and immaturity of the mankind" as a fictitious reason for press censorship, Mill argued for a *legal guarantee* of personal freedom of expression and publication of opinions because it is essential for the *search for truth*. Thus "every opinion which embodies somewhat of the portion of truth which the common opinion omits, ought to be considered precious, with whatever amount of error and confusion that truth may be blended" (1859/2001, 44).

Mill's arguments for the freedom of expressing and publishing opinions are based on the belief that it is necessary for the advancement of human knowledge. This, of course, was a grand Enlightenment idea(l) that has always been obstructed by particularistic and/or class interests (the Church, for example) and has never been fully recognized institutionally. On the contrary, throughout history attempts of powerful actors, or "powers," to limit the diversity of opinions prevailed. Diverse institutions obligated to disseminate human knowledge were primarily interested in the promotion of what Kant conceived of as "beliefs" and "opinions" (i.e., unreliable forms of human wisdom), in contrast to what he termed objectively and subjectively reliable knowledge. What such institutions, including newspapers, pursued was not the "whole truth" but only those "truths" congruent with central *beliefs*. Even the most sacrosanct institutions of knowledge, academies of science, were not immune from such censorship, as in the famous case of the French Academy of Science against Frantz-Anton Mesmer, an Austrian physician propagating therapeutic use of magnetism in medicine, in 1784 (see Bensaude-Vincent 2000, 24–25).

In his convincing argument for liberty of thought and discussion, Mill identified four reasons against attempts to silence the expression of an opinion: (1) If any opinion is compelled to silence, that opinion may happen to be true. Anyone who denies this possibility is to assume his or her own infallibility. (2) If the opinion not allowed to be made public is right, we are deprived of the opportunity of exchanging error for truth. However true the opinion protected by silencing its opponents may be—it will soon become a dead dogma if it is not thoroughly, recurrently, and fearlessly discussed. (3) Even if the opinion in question is wrong, its suppression renders impossible a clearer perception and livelier impression of truth, which would become more telling when confronted with an erroneous opinion. (4) When the conflicting opinions share the truth, the nonconforming opinion is needed to supply the remainder of the truth, of which the prevailing opinion embodies only a part.

Since Mill was interested only in *negative* freedom, he believed—with a specific reference to freedom of the press—that "no argument . . . can now be needed, against permitting a legislature or an executive, not identified in interest with the people, to prescribe opinions to them, and determine what doctrines or what arguments they shall be allowed to hear" (1859/2001, 18). One can hardly disagree with this assertion derived from his fundamental principle of noninterference. However, freedom *from* "prescribed opinions" does not equal freedom *to* express opinions. Mill's strict principle of noninterference in the process of opinion expression does not help much in pursuing his subordinated principle, namely, that freedom of expression is essential not only because it stimulates nonconformity, but because it stimulates the search for truth. He argued that "the only way in which a human being can make some approach to knowing the whole of a subject, is by *hearing what can be said about it by persons of every variety of opinion*" (1859/2001, 22; emphasis added). He also made clear—in his critique of the uneducated masses—that freedom of expression should not only be considered in the sense of the availability of truth to those in search of it; it should also be accepted as a universal *moral obligation*. Yet Mill was only concerned with the need to abolish any possible prevention of opinions from being heard, with "the mischief of denying a hearing to opinions because we, in our own judgment, have condemned them" (p. 24)—as if the whole variety of opinions were simply *there*. But it is not. In order to enable human beings to be(come) informed, it is not enough not to suppress opinions. According to Dewey, "The belief that thought and its communication are now free simply because legal restrictions which once obtained have been done away with is absurd. . . . No man and no mind was ever emancipated merely by being left alone. Removal of formal limitations is but a negative condition; positive freedom is not a state but an act which involves *methods* and *instrumentalities* for control of conditions" (1927/1991, 168; emphasis added). As Mill frequently discovered—as in the cases of education and science—for various reasons "supply" (of opinions, too) may not meet existing demands, or there may not be appropriate demands for existing supplies. In such cases, except for the press, Mill argued for the "interference" by society or authorities. Consequently, he should suggest that it is the responsibility of society or the authorities not only to refrain from suppressing opinions but also to engage in making different opinions *available* to "many foolish individuals, called the public."

If freedom of the press is justified on ethical and pragmatic grounds with the need to make different opinions available, as Mill suggests, than we are allowed to compare the publication of opinions (in the press) with two other historically institutionalized processes of public expression of opinions. According to Mill, "the publicity and discussion . . . are a natural accompaniment of any, even nominal, representation" (1861/2001, 49); political assembly is a "Congress of Opinions," and Mill devoted a large part of *Representative Government* to a detailed account of Parliament as an arena where "every interest and shade of opinion in the country" can be presented "in the face of the government and of all other interests and opinions" (p. 69)—a perfectly *organized* expression of opinions. Thus parliaments are an institutionalized form of the (public) opinion process, where expression and exchange of opinions are not merely *unrestrained* but *enabled* to come about in the first place.

Public opinion polls offer an even more persuasive argument for the *historical need* to organize the process of opinion expression beyond merely allowing it. As Ginsberg argues, new formal channels for the expression of opinions, such as political representative bodies and elections, which were constructed by the state, together with the education of the masses in their use, made "the expression of mass opinion . . . less disruptive" and enabled the state "to reduce the threat that informed expressions of mass opinion often posed to the political order" (1986, 57, 48). These transformations were perpetuated and strengthened by *polling*, which became largely institutionalized in all democratic societies after the 1930s. One of the first prominent U.S. pollsters, George Gallup, believed that polling was a political (rather than merely a research) construct that ought to compensate for the growing limitations of a parliamentary democracy and suggested that polling might help reestablish antique Greek town meetings on a national scale. Controversies over value and function of opinion polls for democratic political processes are as old as polling itself, and they follow much older efforts at theorizing public opinion and democratic government.[58] Albig (1956) and Key (1967) argued that public opinion polls were an indication of democratic developments based on "the ethical imperative that government heed the opinion of the public (which) has its origins in democratic ideology as well as in the practical necessity that governments obtain support of influential elements in society" (Key 1967, 4). In contrast, Rogers (1949)—who defended the libertarian criticism of the tyranny of public opinion proclaimed earlier by Burke, Tocqueville, Bryce, and Lippmann that political representatives should not follow the dictates of the public—considered "completely false" Gallup's ideas that polling was a remedy against fallacies of democratic system because polling in fact prevents *discussion* and *agreement,* which are essential to a democratic government. "*Vox populi* cannot help democratic governments to decide what they ought to do. Political and intellectual leaders must propose alternative policies. They must educate the electorate, and if the leadership and education are effective, then the people will demonstrate their 'essential wisdom'" (Rogers 1949, 235). Notwithstanding the completely opposite interpretations of the (non)democratic merits of polling, both streams of thought agree that polling is an *organized form of opinion expression,* for better or worse, of a democratic system.

There still is substantial disagreement over the democratic value of the press. It is mainly to Mill's credit that newspapers were regarded as a site of public discussion—not because Mill would argue for it, but because the rapid development of the press "enforced" the application of Mill's libertarian theory to the press—unfortunately primarily through the metaphor of the "free marketplace of ideas," which in the long run helped justify restrictions of freedom of expression of opinions. But even Mill's intellectual heirs did not fully support the idea of the press as the pursuer of truth. Lippmann, who was one of the most ardent followers of Mill's liberal doubt about the virtues of public opinion, warned against a naive "ancient belief that truth is not earned, but inspired, revealed, supplied gratis," which he called an "economic prejudice" spread particularly among newspaper readers, and the failure to see that "news and truth are not the same thing" (1922/1991, 320, 358). In contrast, Lippmann argued that the press might try best to reveal the *truth,* in addition to publishing *news,* but the two endeavors are not necessarily in consonance and may even contradict each other. The fundamental question remained, Where and how could individuals or newspapers get information they needed, and who was supposed to provide and pay for it? Citizen freedom and freedom of the press do not suffice; an expert and independent "intelligence bureau"—comparable to the stock exchange and elections—would be needed to ensure a continuous flow of reliable information for political decision making.

I am not referring to Lippmann because I agree with his idea of a perfectly impartial, scientific "intelligence bureau," which is close to Mill's trust in expert knowledge and no less naive than the idea that truth is "supplied gratis." What is important in Lippmann's argument is that it reflected a widely accepted idea at the beginning of the twentieth century—both among American pragmatists and Lippmann in the United States, and representatives of German *Zeitungswissenschaft* and sociologists, like Gabriel Tarde and Ferdinand Tönnies, who realized what Mill had failed to see half a century earlier—that searching for truth and expressing and disseminating opinions must be socially organized.

What kind of organization of the press—and the media in general—is needed to maximize its democratic potential? What kind of interventions should be prohibited because they would endanger personal freedoms of expression and publication, and what kind of interventions are suitable to stimulate citizens' equality in freedom to use their reason in public, and should be thus enacted? I will focus on these questions in the next chapter.

NOTES

1. I am not referring here specifically to rationalistic philosophy of the seventeenth century, but to diverse approaches to publicity inferring freedom of expression of individuals from their status as rational beings. Yet "rationalists" disagree on the question of whether this fact implies that freedom of expression discriminates individuals according to their capacity for reasoning.

2. Rousseau was one of the first modern writers who attacked private property and therefore may be considered a forefather of modern socialism and communism. Yet his views on private property were ambivalent. In *A Discourse on Political Economy* (1755), for example, he still claimed that "it is certain that the right of property is the most sacred of all the rights of citizenship, and even more important in some respects than liberty itself." In *Emile* (1762b), however, he was convinced that "man is the cheapest commodity on the market, and among all our important rights of property, the rights of the individual are always considered last of all," and that "the demon of property spoils everything he lays hands upon" (1762b, 884, 1242). Yet in *The Social Contract* (published at the same time as *Emile*), Rousseau set "the proprietorship of all [a person] possesses" next to civil liberty, emphasizing the substantial difference between *possession* ("which is merely the effect of force or the right of the first occupier") and property ("which can be founded only on a positive title").

3. *Social Contract* (1762a) also includes a fearful reintroduction of the "state of nature" into the community of citizens in the case of breach of loyalty to the sovereign. Rousseau claimed that "every malefactor, by attacking social rights, becomes on forfeit a rebel and a traitor to his country; by violating its laws he ceases to be a member of it; he even makes war upon it. In such a case the preservation of the State is inconsistent with his own, and one or the other must perish; in putting the guilty to death, we slay not so much the citizen as an enemy. The trial and the judgment are the proofs that he has broken the social treaty, and is in consequence no longer a member of the State. Since, then, he has recognised himself to be such by living

there, he must be removed by exile as a violator of the compact, or by death as a public enemy; for such an enemy is not a moral person, but merely a man; and in such a case the right of war is to kill the vanquished."

4. In January 1766, when Rousseau has been exiled from Bern, he accepted the asylum offered to him by David Hume in England, where he spent four years.

5. The question of whether Rousseau "permits" private property or not is one of the most controversial issues in interpretations of Rousseau's theory. I agree with those suggesting that Rousseau assumed the inevitability of private property while he warned against excessive differences between individuals in terms of property as an important source of inequality and thus of liberty, which was the reason he required legal restrictions of wealth. However, the question of private property does not directly pertain to his concept of public opinion.

6. I am only familiar with one Rousseau comment on the consequences of the press, which he published in the essay "Discours sur les sciences et les arts" (1750). He argued that the arts and sciences injured human morals and manners, the progress of knowledge made governments more powerful and restricted individual liberty, material progress undermined equality and friendship, and he proclaimed his famous declaration of "back to nature." In accordance with this "naturalistic" idea, Rousseau wrote: "To consider the horrid disorders which the press has already caused in Europe, to judge of what may happen, by the progress this evil makes every day, one may easily foresee that princes must take as much pains to root up this destructive weed as ever they did to plant it." In later works, Rousseau renounced the idea of the "natural man" in favor of a "moral man."

7. As Rousseau argues, "When in the popular assembly a law is proposed, what the people is asked is not exactly whether it approves or rejects the proposal, but whether it is in conformity with the general will, which is their will. Each man, in giving his vote, states his opinion on that point; and *the general will is found by counting votes*" (1762a; emphasis added).

8. In *Emile* (1762b, 1338) Rousseau recognized a close connection between public opinion and prejudices, as well as the dependence of the former on the latter: "There exists for the whole human race a rule anterior to that of public opinion. The inflexible direction of this rule is what all the others should relate to. It is the judge even of prejudice, and only in so far as the esteem of men is in accordance with this rule has it any authority for us."

9. The negative connotation of imitation unduly pervaded social theory ever since. In contrast to such a negative view, Gabriel Tarde defined imitation, along with opposition and innovation, as *universal sociological principles* and laws of social development, and specifically of public opinion. He suggested that innovations are more likely to be imitated if they are more similar to those already imitated, the closer they are to the most advanced technological aspects of society, and the more they meet the predominant cultural emphasis on novelty as opposed to tradition. As Tarde further maintained, imitation is always based on a desire to achieve a certain goal or to solve a problem, and always arises from innovation. See Tarde 1969.

10. Rousseau's book *Emile, or, On Education*, published in Amsterdam the same year as *The Social Contract* (1762), was ordered to be burned by the French parliament. To escape arrestment, Rousseau fled to Neuchatel and later to England, and he did not return to France before 1770.

11. Despite criticism of "erroneous ideas," Mill praised Rousseau in *On Liberty*: "The superior worth of simplicity of life, the enervating and demoralizing effect of the trammels and hypocrisies of artificial society, are ideas which have never been entirely absent from cultivated minds since Rousseau wrote; and they will in time produce their due effect, though at present needing to be asserted as much as ever, and to be asserted by deeds, for words, on this subject, have nearly exhausted their power" (Mill 1859/2001, 2:35).

12. See Guyer 2000, 172–206, for a comprehensive analysis of Kant's three different conceptions of the categorical imperative.

13. "On the common saying: this may be true in theory, but it does not apply to practice."

14. The English translation of Habermas (1962/1995, 110) wrongly suggests that Kant speaks of two separate qualities, "that he must be his own master" *and* "property."

15. A century and a half later, Kant's concept was adopted by one of the founding fathers of the German science of journalism, Emil Dovifat: "Opinion is still an insufficient 'holding-for-true' *(Fürwahrhalten)*, which tends to establish through witnesses and confirmation" (1931/1967, 117).

16. A counterreason to the holding-for-true is *doubt*. Inversely to certainty, Kant distinguishes between subjective and objective doubt; the former is the state of an undecided mind and the latter the insufficiency of the grounds of holding something to be true.

17. Tönnies "rationalized" Kant's opinion and defined it as "a matter of reason" in contrast to belief which is, according to Tönnies, "a matter of heart," so that opinion is closer to knowledge than belief on Tönnies's scale. In fact, it could be said that belief is more characteristic of *Gemeinschaft*, whereas opinion belongs to *Gesellschaft* in Tönnies's famed typology of social structures.

18. As we shall see, Marx similarly argued in his discussion of freedom of the press that the press can only be free if it is regulated by the laws of its own sphere rather than other spheres of human activities, so that an author would not consider his texts as a *means*; his texts are a *means in themselves*: "and they are so far from being a means for himself or the others that he sacrifices *his own* existence for *their* existence if necessary" (Marx 1842a/1974, 70).

19. In the *Critique of Judgment*, Kant differentiates between the "taste of sense" and the "taste of reflection," suggesting that "in respect of the agreeable, every one is allowed to have his own opinion, and no one insists upon others agreeing with his judgement of taste, which is what is invariably done in the judgement of taste about beauty. The first of these I may call the taste of sense, the second, the taste of reflection: the first laying down judgements merely private, the second, on the other hand, judgements ostensibly of general validity (public), but both alike being aesthetic (not practical) judgements about an object merely in respect of the bearings of its representation on the feeling of pleasure or displeasure" (1790/1952, 481).

20. Habermas (1962/1995, 108) erroneously suggests that Kant's theorization of the process of agreement formation "only lacked the name of 'public opinion.'" Kant obviously did not use the term "public opinion" until his very last writings, but he did use it in several passages of one of his last works, *Metaphysics of Morals* (1797/1952, 442). For example, when discussing the hereditary privileges in the first part of the book, "The Science of Right," he stated that the foundation of such possession "lay

only in the *opinion of the people [Volksmeinung]*, and it can be valid only so long as this opinion lasts. As soon as this *public opinion [öffentliche Meinung]* in favour of such institutions dies out . . . the putative proprietorship in question must cease." Cf. Imannuel Kant, *Die Metaphysik der Sitten* (Stuttgart: Reclam, 1990), 183–84.

21. In his voluminous book *Bau und Leben des sozialen Körpers*, Albert Schäffle (1875, 445) defined publicity in its narrower sense as "the dissemination of socially effective ideas beyond the boundaries of the circle that professionally execute professional work; communication between the members of the parliament in a closed session, or generally, communication between members of closed circles of any kind is not regarded as a public, but a secret procedure. Publicity in its narrow sense is dissemination of social currents of thoughts beyond the boundaries of the closed circles of professional intellectual work, opening up these circles to the increasingly wide circles of the social body and their response to this professional work. 'Public' messages do not imply that *everybody* knows and is aware of them, yet everybody who is interested in them must have a possibility to be acquainted with them. A prerequisite for publicness is openness, that is, the possibility for the dissemination of ideas beyond the closed circles of professional mental work."

22. Empirically oriented communication research rather postulates the need for *coorientation* and *empathy*, which can ensure an effective communication and *consensus*. See Splichal 1999, 41–45. This postulate becomes almost self-evident in the period of globalization, when new forms of cooperation are needed to solve *problems beyond national* economies, politics, and cultures.

23. Latin phrase meaning "law of retaliation," a retributive concept of punishment, according to which anyone who causes harm to another should suffer the same harm in return.

24. Thus Kant argued in "The Science of Right" that "there cannot be any corporation in the state, nor any class or order, that as proprietors can transmit the land for a sole exclusive use to the following generations for all time (ad infinitum), according to certain fixed statutes. . . . Those [e.g., nobility or the church] who in this connection fall under the movement of reform are not entitled to complain that their property is taken from them; for their previous possession lay only in the opinion of the people, and it can be valid only so long as this opinion lasts. As soon as this public opinion in favour of such institutions dies out, or is even extinguished in the judgement of those who have the greatest claim by their acknowledged merit to lead and represent it, the putative proprietorship in question must cease, as if by a public appeal made regarding it to the state" (1797, 442). Similarly in the *Perpetual Peace* (1795, sec. 1).

25. *Die Freiheit der Feder* (freedom of pen) is in boldface type in the German original (Kant 1793, 265).

26. In an analysis of the difference between the institution of property and freedom of thought and opinion in Kant's theory, Paul Guyer came to a fascinating conclusion that, according to Kant, "the institution of property . . . is always a collective exercise of freedom of action and thus always indeed requires public regulation rather then merely permitting it," whereas "freedom of thought and opinion is not an intrinsically collective exercise of freedom and thus does not legitimately invite public regulation" (2000, 12). In fact, however, Kant suggests exactly the opposite with his rhetorical question, "How much, and how correctly, would we think if we did not

think, *at the same time, in community with others?*" (1786, 325; emphasis added). As Habermas (1962/1995, 104) commented on that, "in regard to enlightenment, therefore, thinking for oneself seemed to coincide with *thinking aloud* and the use of reason with its *public use*" (emphasis added). How can the *public* use of reason be an *individual* and *not* a *collective* exercise? Notwithstanding, as I made clear earlier, it is not freedom of *holding* thought and opinion that Kant declared "the *right [Befugnis]* of the citizen," but freedom to "*make his opinion publicly known [seine Meinung öffentlich bekannt zu machen].*" Quite obviously—following Guyer's argument—this collective, *public* exercise of freedom requires *public* regulation.

27. Kant first discussed the difference between the rights of the publisher and the author in terms of personal versus real rights in his article "Of the Injustice of Counterfeiting Books" (1785) and later included that discussion in "The Science of Right" (1797/1952).

28. Kant argues that the publisher has no right to profit, to which only the author is entitled: "As the agent who intrudes himself acts in the name of another in a manner not permitted, he has no claim to the profit which arises from this business; but he in whose name he carries on the business . . . possesses the right to appropriate this profit to himself as the fruit of his property. . . . This lies beyond a doubt in the elementary conceptions of natural right" (Kant 1785b).

29. Much earlier, Edmund Burke (n.d.) expressed the importance of publicity in a similar though much more restricted way in his discussion of "government favouritism," arguing against "the *discretionary* power of the Crown . . . abused by bad or weak men, [which] has given rise to a system which, *without directly violating the letter of any law*, operates against the spirit of the whole constitution. . . . It is therefore next in order . . . that the discretionary powers which are necessarily vested in the monarch, whether for the execution of the laws, or for the nomination of the magistracy and office, or for conducting the affairs of peace and war, or for ordering the revenue, should all be exercised upon *public principles* and rational grounds, and not on the likings or prejudices, the intrigues or policies, of a court" (emphasis added).

30. I devoted a short chapter in my book on *Mass Communication between Freedom and Alienation* to Marx's conceptualization of freedom of the press (published in Slovene only; Splichal 1981, 100–105). The present chapter is based on that analysis.

31. The newspaper *Rheinische Zeitung für Politik, Handel und Gewerbe* [The Rhine Newspaper for Politics, Commerce and Business] was founded in January 1842. Marx became its editor in October 1842 and kept the position until the newspaper was banned in March 1843.

32. Marx devoted three series of feuilletons to the debates of the Sixth Rhine Province Assembly, but only the first and the third were published. In the first series of essays Marx continued his critique of the Prussian censorship which he had begun in "Comments on the Latest Prussian Censorship Instruction." Marx wrote the comments between January 15 and February 10, 1842, but they were published only later as an article in *Anekdota zur neuesten deutschen Philosophie und Publizistik*, vol. 1 (1843). The second series of articles, devoted to the conflict between the Prussian government and the Catholic Church, was banned by the censors. The manuscript of this article has not survived, but the general outline of it is given by Marx in his letter

to Ruge of July 9, 1842. The third series of articles was devoted to the debates of the Rhine Province Assembly on the law on wood thefts and published in the *Rheinische Zeitung* between October 25 and November 3, 1842. See *Marx-Engels Werke* 1974, 1:109, 601 n., 627–28.

33. In the preface to *A Contribution to the Critique of Political Economy* we can find the famous sentence by Marx explaining his reconceptualization of Hegel's concept of "civil society" and the relationship between the "economic structure" and "political superstructure" of a society: "My inquiry led me to the conclusion that neither legal relations nor political forms could be comprehended whether by themselves or on the basis of a so-called general development of the human mind, but that on the contrary they originate in the material conditions of life, the totality of which Hegel, following the example of English and French thinkers of the eighteenth century, embraces within the term 'civil society' *(bürgerliche Gesellschaft)*; that the anatomy of this civil society, however, has to be sought in political economy. . . . The general conclusion at which I arrived and which, once reached, became the guiding principle of my studies can be summarized as follows. In the social production of their existence, men inevitably enter into definite relations, which are independent of their will, namely relations of production appropriate to a given stage in the development of their material forces of production. The totality of these relations of production constitutes the economic structure of society, the real foundation, on which a legal and political superstructure arises and to which definite forms of social consciousness correspond. The mode of production of material life conditions the general process of social, political and intellectual life. It is not the consciousness of men that determines their existence, but their social existence that determines their consciousness" (1859/1974, 8).

34. In the trial, Karl Marx, editor in chief, Frederick Engels, coeditor, and Hermann Korff, responsible publisher, were tried by the Cologne jury court. They were accused of insulting chief public prosecutor Zweiffel and calumniating the police officers who arrested Gottschalk and Anneke in the article "Arrests" published in the *Neue Rheinische Zeitung*, July 5, 1848. The jury acquitted the defendants. At: www.marxists.org/archive/marx/works/cw/volume08/footnote.htm#284.

35. In German: *bürgerliche Gesellschaft*, which stands for both "civil society" and "bourgeois society." Bourgeois society refers to society of *Stadtbürger* (*Stadt* = city), whereas civil society refers to *Staatsbürger* (*Staat* = the state; see Kant 1793, 245). The concept of "*bürgerliche Gesellschaft*" has different meanings in Marx's writings: it changed from a basically Hegelian understanding of civil society stressing its contrast with the "state" to a much more descriptive term, particularly in his later works, referring to the anatomy of capitalist society; in the introduction to *Grundrisse* Marx wrote that "the bourgeois society is the most developed and diversified historic organization of production. . . . In this society of free competition, the individual appears detached from the natural bonds etc., which in earlier historical periods make him the accessory of a definite and limited human conglomerate. . . . Only in the eighteenth century, in 'bourgeois society,' the individual is faced with the various forms of social interdependence as a mere means towards his private purposes, as external necessity" (Marx 1857–1858/1974, 25, 1, 3). Although there may be objections against applying Marx's "self-interpretation" to his ten-year earlier text, I still find the term "bourgeois society" more appropriate when discussing Marx's critique of the concept

of right reduced to the rights of "egoistic man" centered around the right of private property. The term "civil society," out of its specific historical context and because of its contemporary connotation of constituting the foundations of democracy, would cast a shadow of misunderstanding on Marx's critique of freedom of ownership.

36. This was Kant's argument in his discussion of the nature of relationship between parents and children, but the problem is essentially the same. As "parents cannot regard their child as . . . a thing of their own making; for a being endowed with freedom cannot be so regarded," a newspaper owner or a publisher cannot regard the discourse produced by the author—who is "endowed with freedom" and addressed his ideas to a particular public—his own property. As Marx later pointed out, free press had to be legally regulated according to the nature of *communication* and not as a form of property.

On the general question of Kant's influence on Marx's defense of press freedom: Marx never refers to Kant's arguments in his articles, but similarity with Kant's ideas is quite evident in many cases.

37. "Unlimited freedom of the press." Quotation from the French Constitution of 1793, Article 122.

38. "Freedom of the press should not be permitted when it endangers public liberty." Marx's quotation from "Robespierre jeune," in Buchez and Roux, *Historie parlementaire de la revolution française*, 28:159.

39. As Marx has stated later, there was one danger more frightful than censorship—*precensorship*: "When . . . there is no censorship because there is no press, although the need for a free and therefore *censurable* press exists, one must expect to find a *precensorship* in circumstances which have suppressed by fear the expression of thought even in its more unpretentious forms" (1843, 195).

40. See S. Müller-Doohm 1972, 134.

41. Marx compared those "disinterested" defenders of freedom of the press with an artist who never experienced beauty: "Goethe once said that the painter succeeds only with a type of feminine beauty which he has loved in at least one living being. Freedom of the press, too, is a beauty—if not exactly a feminine one—which one must have loved to be able to defend it. If I truly love something, I feel that its existence is indispensable, that it is something which I need, without which my nature can have no full, satisfied, complete existence. The above-mentioned defenders of freedom of the press seem to enjoy a complete existence even in the absence of any freedom of the press" (1842a/1974, 33).

42. Prussia formed eight provincial assemblies in 1823, which embraced the heads of princely families, representatives of the knightly estate (the nobility), towns, and rural communities. The election system provided for a majority of the nobility in the assemblies whose competencies were restricted to local affairs and expressing desires on government.

43. Letter from Marx to Sorge on October 19, 1877.

44. For example, Rivers and Schramm 1969, 38; Gleason 1990, 37; Ingelhart 1987.

45. In the late 1820s and early 1830s Mill planned to write a history of the French Revolution of 1789; he had been literally obsessed by the subject for quite some time. After the July Revolution of 1830 he dropped the plan, probably because of his disillusionment, but he still wrote on France regularly. See Coleman 1983 for details.

46. Marx's postscript to the second German edition of *Capital* (1873), in *Marx-Engels Werke*, 23:21; also p. 777 (Berlin: Dietz Verlag 1973).

47. All quotations from Mill's *Principles of Political Economy* refer to the Web version of the book available at: www.ecn.bris.ac.uk/het/mill. The first number stands for the book, the second for the chapter, and the third for the section from which quotation is taken.

48. Confronted with the elitism advocated by Walter Lippmann in a way similar to Mill, almost a century after Mill, John Dewey argued that it is not the point to *tolerate* the diversity of opinions, but to comprehend the social welfare as evolving from conflicting opinions. It is not only that "toleration in matters of judgment and belief" (which was largely perceived a disturbing "negative matter") should become a "positive matter." More importantly, opinion diversity should become fundamental to democratic life: "We agree to leave one another alone (within limits) more from recognition of evil consequences which have resulted from the opposite course rather than from any profound belief in its positive social beneficence. As long as the latter consequence is not widely perceived, the so-called natural right to private judgment will remain a somewhat precarious rationalization of the moderate amount of toleration which has come into being" (Dewey, 1927/1991, 51).

49. Since Mill specifically mentioned that no special defense of freedom of the press was needed any more (1859/2001, 18), it would be inconsistent to assume that Mill used the words *speech* and *press* without making any clear distinction between the two, which would imply that his justification of personal freedom of speech is directly transferable to the case of press freedom.

50. This has been asserted by Frederick Greenwood (1830–1909), one of the most respected journalists of his day and editor of the *Pall Mall Gazette* (1865–1880), as quoted in Boyce 1978, 26.

51. By the end of 1830, control of the press in Britain was very much relaxed; the newspaper stamp was reduced to one penny, so that the price of newspapers decreased, which made an increase in circulation possible. See Boyce 1978.

52. Pnyx was a large, theater-like area on the hill west of the Acropolis in ancient Athens, where the Assembly of the Athenians held its meetings. Forum Romanum was a large open space between the Capitoline and Palatine, the two hills of Romulus and Remus in ancient Rome, that was predominantly used for government and political meetings. The Roman forum consisted of a large number of remarkable buildings, including Curia, where the Senate of Rome used to meet.

53. Mill's ideas clearly reflected the parliamentary debates on the Stamp Duties Act and how to deal with the working-class press. In the 1830s debates against the taxation of the press, "the cause of a free market press was synonymous with the suppression of trade unionism: the dream for which they fought was an unfettered capitalist press that would police the capitalist system" (Curran 1978, 56).

54. Mill wrote in *Representative Government*: "Instead of the function of governing, for which it is radically unfit, the proper office of a representative assembly is to watch and control the government: to throw the light of publicity on its acts: to compel a full exposition and justification of all of them which any one considers questionable; to censure them if found condemnable, and, if the men who compose the government abuse their trust, or fulfil it in a manner which conflicts with the deliberate sense of the nation, to expel them from office, and either expressly or virtually

appoint their successors. This is surely ample power, and security enough for the liberty of the nation. In addition to this, the Parliament has an office, not inferior even to this in importance; to be at once the nation's Committee of Grievances, and its Congress of Opinions; an arena in which not only the general opinion of the nation, but that of every section of it, and as far as possible of every eminent individual whom it contains, can produce itself in full light and challenge discussion; where every person in the country may count upon finding somebody who speaks his mind, as well or better than he could speak it himself—not to friends and partisans exclusively, but in the face of opponents, to be tested by adverse controversy; where those whose opinion is overruled, feel satisfied that it is heard, and set aside not by a mere act of will, but for what are thought superior reasons, and commend themselves as such to the representatives of the majority of the nation; where every party or opinion in the country can muster its strength, and be cured of any illusion concerning the number or power of its adherents; where the opinion which prevails in the nation makes itself manifest as prevailing, and marshals its hosts in the presence of the government, which is thus enabled and compelled to give way to it on the mere manifestation, without the actual employment, of its strength; where statesmen can assure themselves, far more certainly than by any other signs, what elements of opinion and power are growing, and what declining, and are enabled to shape their measures with some regard not solely to present exigencies, but to tendencies in progress"(Mill 1861/2001, 68).

55. The analysis of intellectual influences on Mill indicates that his emphasis on the importance of diversity and opposition appears to have been significantly influenced by the French historian François Guizot, who stressed the importance of "systematic antagonism" for human progress. See Varouxakis 1999.

56. Mill's elitism is most explicit in his argument for an electoral system weighted in favor of the most educated voters in his *Representative Government*. He did not see anything undemocratic in the proposal; on the contrary: "Entire exclusion from a voice in the common concerns is one thing; the concession to others of a more potential voice, on the ground of greater capacity for the management of the joint interests, is another" (1861/2001, 109–110).

57. It is not difficult to see a fundamental difference between the impact newspapers had in the mid-nineteenth century England and the role media acquired with the development of a mass press, film, and radio in the period when democratic media legislation originated. The impact of a newspaper with several *thousand* copies sold was not comparable to a massive rally that might comprise several *hundred thousand* present, whereas today the relationship is inverted. According to Williams's calculations, the newspaper-reading public in Britain was no more than one percent of adult population in 1820; the daily public increased to 3 percent and the Sunday public to 12 percent by 1860. In 1820, the circulation of *The Times* was no more than seven thousand copies (Williams 1978, 42, 47).

58. I have elaborated on the issue of the political significance of polling in the chapter on "Political Institutionalization of Public Opinion: Controversies on Polling" in my book *Public Opinion: Developments and Controversies in the Twentieth Century* (1999).

4

From the Republic of Letters to the Public of Letters to the Editor

What is to be done? This question may appear an awkward beginning for the closing chapter, but not to those who are familiar with Lenin's essay criticizing the idea of "freedom of criticism" bearing the above famed title. In the name of "scientific truth," which he believed could not exist in the plural, Lenin did not tolerate any critique from within the proletarian movement and equated it with revisionism. He insinuated that "'freedom' is a grand word, but under the banner of freedom for industry the most predatory wars were waged, under the banner of freedom of labour, the working people were robbed. The modern use of the term 'freedom of criticism' contains the same inherent falsehood. Those who are really convinced that they have made progress in science would not demand freedom for the new views to continue side by side with the old, but the substitution of the new views for the old" (Lenin 1902, 3). Lenin's idea presents exactly *what is not to be done.* Since the subjective persuasion is not a proof of its objective sufficiency or certainty, as Kant made clear, nobody should ever dare to follow Lenin's suggestion to act toward others on the basis of a subjectively sufficient judgment. The universal principle of *publicity*, if materialized in social communication, is the most effective remedy against such an aberration.

Publicity has an important, though always limited influence on all politically relevant actions, and the same is true for the absence of publicity. The *principle* of publicity became a "universal good" of the Western Hemisphere with the Enlightenment idea of the people as the ultimate source of sovereignty, and of publicity serving the people's needs—an idea that was also in the germ of any conception of press freedom. The universality of the principle of publicity was most clearly stated in Immanuel Kant's and Jeremy Bentham's theories. They both attempted a universal definition of the principle

163

of publicity, although on substantially different grounds—Bentham on the basis of its utility for the maximization of the people's happiness, Kant on the principle of right and the need of using one's reason in public. The two great architects of the publicity principle also differed in terms of practical solutions to implement the principle; only Bentham grappled with a detailed plan to make the principle of publicity efficient in practice. The development of modern mass media immensely widened the *implied* practical consequences of the principle, both for the media and the society at large. Yet besides new opportunities, changes in the political, economic, and social environments also create new problems in terms of consequences of the practical application of the principle, the most important concerning the relation between the right to property and the personal right to communicate.

As a matter of principle, it would be mistaken to promulgate any specific historical form of publicity as a universal functional requirement for the maintenance of publicness in general. The notion of the universality of the principle does not imply uniformity of its empirical appearances. On the other hand, it would be also a failure to renounce all pretensions to the universal normative concepts of "publicness" and "publicity" altogether due to historical variations. In his defense of the concept of the constitution, Kant concluded that "although a perfect state may never exist, the idea is not on that account the less just, which holds up this maximum as the archetype or standard of a constitution, in order to bring legislative government always nearer and nearer to the greatest possible perfection" (1781/1952, 114). We can find a similar idea later in Habermas's "counterfactual" defense of the concept of the procedurally grounded quality of public opinion that should enable the measurement of the actual influence of public opinion on the political system, or in his idea of the unity of public opinion as a counterfactual entity in democratic theory that ought to enable distinguishing between "genuine processes of public communication and those that have been subverted by power" (1992b, 440). It does not mean that we should look for such an *archetype* of publicity as a ready-made ideal model constructed in the past that could be applied as a universal solution to the present problems. In the end, what social theorists and philosophers thought and said in the past is perhaps not important per se. Rather, it is the future we have to face. But we would be barking up the same wrong tree if we conceived of the future independently from the past, since the ideas of freedom of the press that were popular and contested in the eighteenth and nineteenth centuries are reflected and (mis)interpreted by contemporary concerns for human rights and the right to communicate in particular. Due to numerous conceptual changes and controversies that arose during the past centuries, a clearly defined concept of publicity would be needed primarily for *normative* purposes. All democratic societies are facing the problem of how can the media, old and new, be made accessible to citizens and how they can be used for the benefit of citizens and not only as a vehicle to reach and persuade potential consumers and voters, and to generate profit and power. The question then arises if an *archetype* of (the principle of) publicity may be outlined. What follows is such an attempt based on the ideas generated in the eighteenth and nineteenth centuries, which I scrutinized in the previous chapters.

THE IDEA OF THE RIGHT TO COMMUNICATE

The concept of the fourth estate lost its moral vigor long ago. The surveillance objectives of the early 1800s "deteriorated" into the Progressive utopia of egalitarian social control of the early 1900s, and both were challenged by the critique of the tyranny of majority. Trust in the visions of surveillance subsided due to accumulated power in the hands of the state and incorporated economic power of private capital, with the owners of media corporations becoming part of the power elite composed of top political, economic, and military people. Inordinate *individualism* brought about by deregulated capitalism of the late 1900s made no case for personal liberties beyond freedom of enterprise. Freedom of expression and publication as a personal right has been largely neglected on account of freedom of the fourth estate as the real right, but the latter has been rendered increasingly ineffective in its mission of surveillance because of the profit maximizing operations of private media capital and consecutive alliances with power elites muted the bark of the "watchdog." As C. Wright Mills suggested, the rise of the *power elite* led to a complete absence of a civil service that would not be politically biased and to "the increased official secrecy behind which great decisions are made without benefit of public or even Congressional debate" (Mills 1956/2000, 296). In other words, the once dignified great power of the Public Opinion Tribunal and its main vehicle, the press, in securing public confidence vanished.

Similarly, the free marketplace model of the press "remains an essentially idealist transposition of the model of face-to-face communication to that of mediated communication" (Garnham 1992, 361). This practical model failed to conform to radical changes introduced into the public sphere with the development of the mass press and broadcast media, corporate capitalism, and the modern state. Insisting that market competition of the media is the most important precondition of their freedom assumes, without warrant, that the right to *private property*—because *everyone* has this right—guarantees both freedom of the media (their independence from the state) and freedom of citizens (free choice between different media and contents). Apparently this is an "ideal type of free market" of the media, which in practice does not exist due to the processes of capital concentration and centralization. As a consequence,

the "free" media market is largely oligopolized, and the "free" choice is severely limited by constrained supply. "Commercial media conventionally por-
tray themselves as virtual slaves to the 'market,' and thus—as providing people with exactly what they want. They quietly gloss over the power of major
advertisers and corporations to define *poor* people's media wants as irrelevant,
compared to those of the more affluent sectors of the market. . . . Only the ex-
traordinarily gullible believe in the democratic passions of commercial media
executives" (Downing 1984, 5–6). Even for producers, the free market does
not ensure free access to the "deregulated" marketplace because of the levels
of investment required to enter the market, rising program production costs,
and already existing oligopolies. In Blumler's words, organizational concentration and conglomeration in mass communication tend to limit the opportunities of independent producers to profitably offer something different from
mainstream supply, foster standardization of program supply across the entire
media (particularly television) industry, and create a risk that the main channels of access to the public may eventually be controlled by a small number of
strategically placed and minimally accountable gatekeepers (Blumler 1991, 9).

In contrast to the rather abstract Kantian ethical principle of publicity—as
an "instrument" to achieve individuals' independent reasoning and legal order in the social realm and to regulate relations between politics and morals
through public law—the concrete material form of publicity that has been institutionalized when the powerful mass media entirely suppressed its ethical
foundation. This new form of communication, which became a momentous
element of the political and economic system, transformed the very nature
of the publicity "mechanism" itself: instead of enabling citizens to use their
own reason in public, the media *represented* them in public following the
example of boundless political representation; instead of securing for citizens the personal right to publish opinions, they effectively deprived them
of that right. The press lost its "natural freedom" tied to the personal liberty
of the author: a complex network of relations between the media and political and economic actors transformed the former relatively simple process of
mediation between authors and small circles of readers, and between politics and morals, into complex, widespread processes of (public) mediation
between economy and politics, which utterly enervated the idea of immediate and universal citizens' participation.

In contrast, Enlightenment conceptualizations of freedom of the press—
centered around the concept of "publicity" and derived from *personal* right
of reasoning, writing, and publishing opinions—brought forth by grand
social theories of the eighteenth and nineteenth centuries did not pass an
empirical test of history. In addition or, better, in contrast to the narrow conceptualization of the press as only a means of democratic surveillance, freedom of the press may be conceptualized—as derived from these theories—
as a specific historical form and an extension of personal freedom of thought

and expression—an extension not merely in the quantitative sense of more of the sameness, but in the sense of diversified opportunities for communication. It is not considered the final stage of the development of human positive freedom of expression, and it is only one among different possible— and different historical—operationalizations of the principle of publicity as the supreme normative concept. An operationalization of the principle of publicity supplementary to *freedom of the press* is Kant's *right to communicate*, which later appears in a Deweyan conceptualization of the public as increasing the level of social knowledge and inclusion of actors and areas of popular participation.

A personal right to communicate is derivable from Kant's idea of publicness centered on the universal principle of publicity. Publicity is the necessary condition and principle of all actions relating to the right of other men: if the enacted decisions and laws are not made commonly accessible, their rightfulness is at least questionable if not completely lacking. Yet the principle of publicity can only become the supreme principle of right and legal order, if citizens are able to make their own judgments on the validity of publicly presented claims—which can only be based on a reflective, reasoned act.

Communication as the process of construction of shared meanings is constitutive of human reasoning, which is particularly important in the process of examining the subjective sufficiency of judgments and the pursuit of truth or objective sufficiency of judgments. Human reasoning must be communicable to others, who must be able to be attracted to it through communication. Certain subjective (personal) and objective (societal) conditions should be met for such communication to take place. Every person must be able to attain active citizenship, that is, to become a member, in Bentham's words, of the "tribunal of the public . . . forming an enlightened judgment."

Besides language competence of actors, communicability of human understanding requires "the courage" to use one's own reason in public and accept the attention attracted by such uses. Only if the three conditions are met can publicity serve as the principle of right (in contrast to obedience that is characteristic of the "private use" of reason, in Kant's sense). In addition, those taking part in transactions having significant consequences for those not participating have an ethical obligation to make those judgments or actions public.

The public formed of self-dependent citizens who participate in the process of will formation is the condition for the principle of publicity to become universal; and it is congruent with the categorical imperative—"Act only on that maxim through which you can at the same time will that it should become a universal law"—only if it is universal. In Kant's system of publicness, there are two principal components of the principle of publicity: the systemic principle of justice and the personal right to public use of reason or, in its contemporary version, the right to communicate. I see five clusters of rights and corresponding conditions pertinent to the modern complex world of mass media that may be listed as constituent elements of the citizen right to communicate:

1. *Right to be given information* and related rights and duties:
   - *Accessibility/Surveillance:* All actions (in the political assembly or elsewhere) with implications for those not participating must be subject to the surveillance by the public. If the enacted laws and actions are not made commonly accessible, their rightfulness is questionable. Surveillance is an interactive process: all those who are exposed to surveillance may take an active part in publicity, having the right of transmitting information and opinion in public.
   - *Hospitality:* Foreigners and noncitizens must have access to national publics.
2. *Right of transmitting information and expressing opinion* and related rights and duties:
   - *Tolerance* for judgments of approbation and disapprobation.
   - *Tolerance* of nonauthentic publications.
   - *Tolerance and receptiveness* for judgments expressing dissenting or minority opinions and different cultural identities.
   - *Freedom of social inquiry* and of dissemination of its findings.
3. *Right of free access to the media* and related rights and duties:
   - *Accessibility:* If communication means are not made commonly accessible communicability of opinions cannot be materialized. Right of access can only be restricted if not violating the principle of equality of citizens.
4. Rights and duties enabling citizens to *participate in public communication, decision making,* and *in the management of the media*:
   - *Regulatory rules:* Publicness not only implies the involvement in the regulation of long-term consequences of transactions in which individuals are directly not involved yet seriously affected in a general sense, but particularly participation in systematic regulation of communicative actions. Publicity is a means to regulate human actions that exist independently of publicity, but regulatory rules are also constitutive for the publicity itself, and citizens must have the right to discuss them.
   - *Regulatory bodies:* Censorial or controlling function of public opinion has to be performed not only outwardly (thus legitimizing rightfulness of public actions), but also inwardly (protection against abuses of publicness). Citizens must have the right to be informed about, and to participate in, decision making or other actions of press and broadcasting councils, courts of honor, and management organs of public service media.

5. Corollary related to constitutive *conditions* of public expression of judgments:
   - *Rationality/Reflexivity* (in the sense of Kant's "method of enlightenment") is not only allowed but requested of all participants in the public discourse. Publicity serves as an asymptotic criterion of rationality because it fosters critical faculty of weighing every judgment with the collective reason—"not so much with actual, as rather with the merely possible, judgments of others, and by putting ourselves in the position of everyone else" (Kant 1790/1952, 519).
   - *Communicability:* Universal communicability is what everyone expects and requires from everyone else in public discourse, which makes public communication possible. Kant believed that what is rational is always publicly communicable. Dewey would strongly disagree; he realized that "presentation is fundamentally important, and presentation is a question of art" (Dewey 1927/1991, 188); a "scientific" presentation could not attract the attention and stimulate (re)actions of members of the public, with the exception of a few intellectuals. Forming opinions on public matters calls for "a subtle, delicate, vivid and responsive art of communication" (p. 184). Otherwise, social sciences would be assimilated to physical sciences, which is but another form of *absolutism*.
   - *Educativeness:* The involvement in public discussion of social problems at least creates a public "spirit" inclined to rational discussion. Public debates have to be regulated in a way to make the media and the public sphere accessible to the groups remote from parliamentary institutions, and to stimulate an increase in individuals' knowledge. Intelligence and reflexivity are not "personal endowments" that one inherits but are social in their very nature; thus an appropriate system of education is essential for the development of human ability and need to communicate.

The realization of the civil right to communicate in modern democratic societies requires a level of resources proportional to the increase in its complexity since it had existed as a *natural right* to communicate. The right to communicate existed as a natural right of human beings, which they could not alienate (or else they would cease to exist as human beings), as long as the individual's relation to his or her language was only determined by his or her membership in community, that is, as a component of the relation of a "natural" member to his or her human community.

With the development of writing, human generic ability and need to communicate ceased to exist as a natural right, which is why Marx and Engels considered the development of writing the birthmark of both civilization *and* class society. The idea of communication as a natural human ability possessed and practiced equally by every member of a collectivity merely because of his or her membership of the collectivity became definitely untenable. Writing transformed communication from an entirely natural relationship (as it had been in a primitive collectivity) into a social (or as Kant would argue, "civil") relationship because it moved communication from the sphere of no-property (the mere ability to speak is not possible to alienate, thus it cannot be appropriated externally) to the sphere of property. Writing enabled the separation and thus alienation of the message from the sender, just as any other good can be separated from the producer. This helped create the illusion that the messages in their material form of "things" (e.g., in the form of books or newspapers) could be subject to *real right*, and consequently that freedom of the press could be a species of freedom of ownership. As a matter of principle, however, "a personal positive right against another can never be derived from the ownership of a thing only" (Kant 1785). The negative ownership of a book or newspaper (a copy of it) justifies the negative right to resist anyone who would hinder me from the use of this thing at pleasure, whereas a corresponding positive real right could only proceed from a particular (additional) contract, but not from the mere ownership of the thing. In the case of communication, such an additional contract can only be based on the communication contents thus could not obviate the author.

Even more delusive than the idea of equating messages and communication with movable things is the idea of likening the communication *organs* of the human body to the things one can freely dispose of:

> Does it mean that the rights of private property are superior to our right of freedom of speech? The short answer is YES. . . . But a subtler answer is that on the liberty view, they are really both cases of the same thing. Ownership is the right to dispose at will of the owned *thing*. In the one case, what we own is our horses, businesses or whatever; in the present case [of speech], it is our *organs and powers* to speech and expression. (Narveson 1994, 67; emphasis added)

Narveson intermingled two concepts strictly differentiated by Kant: "a man may be his own *master* . . . but *not the proprietor* of himself" (Kant 1797/1952, 415; emphasis added). Yet even if we accepted the narrow-minded idea that one owns his or her bodily organs as property—like any external things, which implies their potential alienation—that could only apply to the organs one indeed can separate from, which is not the case with "our organs . . . to speech and expression"—in contrast, for example, to kidneys. Thus, even if we take seriously the above gallows humor, the conclusion must be the same:

Since communication belongs to the sphere of *inalienable personal* rights, all forms of communication, including the press or media generally, should be *primarily* regulated according to the principles of *personal right*. On that account, expressing opinions should become a *civil right* of citizens in the civil state of society, as it had been a natural right in the natural state of society. And that is exactly what Kant proposed in his transcendental formula of public law, which requires that all actions relating to the right of others be congruent with the *principle of publicity*. Indeed, publicity should be considered the central part of public right, which is aimed at the establishment of the harmony between morality and politics.

With the emergence of new media, lines between different forms of media are blurring, making it increasingly difficult to construe medium-specific definitions of rights. This process actually reveals the *unity* and *totality* of different—from interpersonal to mass mediated—forms of communication, which makes highly problematic any preferential treatment of professionalized and institutionalized forms of "the press" or "the media" against citizens' public yet much less formal practices of communication on the Internet. In other words, after two centuries, technology is now forcing us to reconsider the division between personal rights of thought and expression, and the real rights of the media, which have been established in consequence of an earlier technological innovation—the development of the mass-produced and profit-oriented newspapers.

IS THE PROPERTY RIGHT SUPERIOR TO THE RIGHT TO COMMUNICATE?

The authentic sense of freedom of the press is freedom to print, that is the right of citizens to publish their opinions rather than newspapers' surveillance of the government. As Kant wrote in 1793 in his article in *Berlinische Monatsschrift*, every citizen should have the right to "make his opinion publicly known regarding what appears to him to be a wrong committed against the commonwealth by the enactments and administration of the sovereign. . . . *Hence the liberty of the press is the sole palladium of the rights of the people*" (1793/1914, 40; emphasis added).

Freedom of the press, though an extension of freedom of thought and speech, cannot be considered exclusively an innate right (which belongs to everyone by nature), but a combination of *innate and acquired* rights. Adopting, expressing, and publishing opinions represent *different* kinds of acts and, thus, personal rights—despite the fact that they all belong to the category of personal right. It is true that "*holding* a belief or opinion . . . does not itself impinge upon the freedom of anyone else, and the exercise of the right to freedom of thought is therefore simply an exercise of the innate right to freedom" (Guyer 2000, 238). However, *expressing* a belief or an opinion does not belong exclusively to the "inward domain of consciousness" of individuals, but always concerns other people, as J. S. Mill indicated. Still more, *publishing* opinions in the press (or other media) falls in the much more complex domain of the "combination among individuals," because it presupposes—in addition to the innate mental predisposition and ability of the individual—ample productive means, including the resources of others that are necessary for making opinions available to others or to the public (e.g., a printing office). As Kant explains:

> The author and the owner of the copy may both say of it with equal right: it is my book! but in a different sense. The first takes the book as a writing or a speech; the second as the mute instrument merely of the delivering of the speech to him or to the public, i.e. *as* a copy. This right of the author's, however, is no right in the thing, namely, the copy (for the owner may burn it before *the author's* face), but an innate right in his own person, namely, to hinder another from reading it to the public without his consent. (1785: 86)

The right to publish exceeds the innate *negative* right of the author to prevent others from receiving his opinion. It implies the right of access (which is a positive real right in Kant's terms) to the means—not any more merely his innate mental abilities—necessary to make an opinion deliverable to others. Mill noticed that the "liberty of expressing and publishing opinions may seem to fall under a different principle" than the liberty of conscience, "since it belongs to that part of the conduct of an individual which concerns other people" (Mill 1859/2001, 15–16), but then he decided not to separate the former from the latter because it is no less important than the liberty of thought. One could say he renounced treating the liberty of expressing opinions as a liberty different from the liberty of thought for "strategic reasons"—to provide to the act of publication the same amount of *negative freedom* as to the act of thought, since it was negative freedom (tolerance, noninterference) which Mill was primarily concerned about, and the analogy with freedom of thought would make freedom of expression less contestable.[1] Similarly, Guyer (2000, 258) argues that "one person's *adoption or expression* of virtually any belief whatever does not give anyone else a right to intervene in the former's exercise of his freedom in this form" (emphasis added).

Notwithstanding, freedom from interference is only a negative definition; positive definition must relate to the categorical imperative. And even more, if we follow Kant, it is not merely freedom at stake, it is a *positive right!* Talking *positive rights* is quite a different matter. The personal right to publish, which implies the real right of access, may conflict with the property right, which is a real right concerning an external thing. The question then arises as to which of the two rights is superior?[2] Or which infringement is less of an evil: the limitation of the personal right of publication by the real right of property or vice versa? Consequently regulation is needed not only to secure the rule of law in the sense that nobody should constrain, or be constrained by, the opinions of others but also to secure the personal-real right of publication.

Judging by Rousseau's and Kant's words, the right of publication should have a superior status. Both Rousseau and Kant suggest that the (civil) right of property be based on, and (potentially) restricted by, public opinion, which can only exist under the provision of the principle of publicity; without publicity no public opinion can develop. Rousseau denoted public opinion as the most important type of law because the implementation of all other laws, including those regulating the property right, depend on it. Kant essentially followed Rousseau's idea, considering property right (except hereditary right to possession) constitutive of the civil state of society which, however, is created through public opinion. The conviction that the right to publish, which is—together with the duty of publicity to be carried out by the necessity of acting from respect for the law—central to the principle of publicity, is superior to the right of property does not imply that the latter may be abolished; yet it may be limited by public regulation in the ways suggested already by Rousseau, Kant, and Mill. If there is a case against the libertarian conviction that liberty is inconceivable without private property as the absolute right, it is the case of the press. Even Kant conceded that the condition for a citizen to be his own master was not necessarily private property (Kant 1793, 246).

A similar line of thought was taken by the UNESCO International Commission for the Study of Communication Problems chaired by the late Sean MacBride:

> The freedom of the citizen to gain access[3] to communication, both as recipient and contributor, cannot be compared to the freedom of an investor to make a profit from the media: the former is a fundamental human right; the latter permits the commercialization of a social need. (MacBride 1980/1984, 39)

The belief that the property right ought to be superior to the right to communicate is based on the erroneous consideration of freedom of the press as a real right concerning an external thing (newspaper), rather than a personal right concerning individual reasoning, writing, and publishing opinions, which is not determined by the ownership of things. If this belief lacks objectivity, however, it does not also imply that liberty in general is conceivable without (freedom of) private property, neither does it contradict the well-grounded warnings against the dangers of bureaucratization and legal overregulation brought about by socialism and expansion of social-welfare state based on the severe limitation, or even the abolition, of the private property right.

Kant's hesitancy about private property as the condition of being one's own master was reconsidered by Habermas in his "Further Reflections on the

Public Sphere." He derives the argument for the depoliticization of private property from the Enlightenment, specifically, Kant's notion of the sovereign as the body politic consisting of all citizens:

> After the universalization of equal civil rights, the private autonomy of the masses could no longer have its social basis in the control over private property. . . . Their private autonomy had to be secured through reliance on the status guarantees of a social welfare state. This derivative private autonomy, however, could function as an equivalent of the original private autonomy based on control over private property only to the degree to which the citizens, as clients of the social-welfare state, came to enjoy status guarantees that they themselves bestowed on *themselves* in their capacities as citizens of a democratic state. (Habermas 1992b, 434)

Similarly, Marx (1844b/1974, 354) argued that it was only the political rescission of private property in suffrage that de facto provided the full recognition of the *private* character of property.

Although the right of publication is not *primarily* a real right, it nevertheless implies a characteristic of real rights—a duty or obligation imposed on all others, the community, in respect to the external thing (i.e., communication means external to communicator). In contrast to real right, which does not necessarily assume physical detention of an external thing by the owner (because real right is a pure juridical connection), the right to publish opinion as essentially a personal right paradoxically implies the actual, physical use—but not necessarily legal possession—of an external thing: the *medium* of publication (communication). I cannot write without a pen (or computer), I cannot make a phone call without a telephone, I cannot address the public without having an appropriate communication means at disposal—a newspaper, a broadcasting studio publicly transmitting the program, or at least access to the Internet. Using some of these media may impinge on the same rights of others at least because the available *real* public space and time are limited (as in contrast to the imagined "public sphere"). This is true not only of the media but also of nonmediated interpersonal communication. As John Peters (1997, 6) wrote: "The limit of democratic theory, perhaps even its tragic flaw, is the neurophysiological fact that we cannot listen to more than one voice at a time."

This rough *natural* restriction of communication is further complicated by the *normative* restriction, since "democratic talk is not essentially spontaneous but essentially rule-governed, essentially *civil* . . . not necessarily egalitarian but it is essentially *public*" (Schudson 1997, 298–99, 301). Communication can only take a democratic shape if it conforms to specific *norms* that differentiate democratic (civil) communication from communication in its natural state. Norms of democratic communication refer to both the form and the content of communication. For example, democratic norms may define specific procedures of opinion expression; they may even require the withdrawal of some issues from conversation, such as religion or minority rights. Not the fact of communication itself, but the norms that govern it determine its specific democratic nature and functions.

The problem of natural and normative restrictions is perhaps best exemplified with the letters that readers write to newspaper editors. Small local newspapers may publish close to 80 percent of the letters they receive, as Jorgensen recently estimated, but large papers are "forced to scrap a much larger percentage." It is believed that *New York Times* publishes *less than 6 percent* of the letters received (2002, 70). Jorgensen's study based on interviews with a number of U.S. editors suggests that editorial criteria in the selection of letters[4] "often work against the diversity of expression. . . . The letters section can, at best, offer a necessary mechanism of accountability and legitimation for the newspaper, composed to maximise its success in the market" (p. 78). It is indeed strange how such a strong editorial selection can be seen as "hazy reflections of public opinion" or even "a public opinion thermometer"—a bias comparable to the belief that opinion polls "measure public opinion," while in fact they are its elemental part, its specific form of institutionalization (see Splichal 1999, 221–69).[5] In terms of public use of reason, there is no difference between journalists and authors of the letters to the editor: they (may) both equally contribute to public reasoning. In terms of access, of course, a huge difference exists between the former as professional authors and the latter, who are "skilled" readers but only casual writers. "Many journalists regard freedom of speech as freedom to express their own views or biases, or continue to define themselves as 'guardians' or 'leaders' of society, called upon (by virtue of their superior access to information and understanding of the situation) to be in the forefront of political developments" (Jakubowicz 1996, 63).[6] They often behave not as their *own* masters, but as the masters of the *situation*, as the "representatives" of the public with a free mandate controlling access to the mass media.[7] Habermas accepts this "situation" supposedly in agreement with the concept of deliberative politics: "the mass media ought to understand themselves as the mandatary of an enlightened public whose willingness to learn and capacity for criticism they at once presuppose, demand and reinforce" (1992a/1997, 378). Dewey was among the first to warn against such a division reflecting the revival of the Platonic notion that "philosophers should be kings" (1927/1991, 204):

No government by experts in which the masses do not have the chance to inform the experts as to their needs can be anything but an oligarchy managed in the interests of the few. And the enlightenment must proceed in ways which force the administrative specialists to take account of the needs . . . The essential need, in other words, is *the improvement of the methods and conditions of debate, discussion and persuasion. That is the problem of the public.* (p. 208; emphasis added)

Even the most rudimentary forms of political democracy, such as general elections and the principle of majority rule, Dewey believed, enable and involve (at least some degree of) deliberation, which would reveal social needs and problems.[8] Popular government is educative and stimulates the recognition of common interests. The majority rule on which it is based is one of the fundamental democratic norms, yet it is not an aim in itself, for its meaning can only come true in the specific discursive way in which the majority is established. Thus it is not majority rule itself that is contestable; rather, it may seem questionable because methods of majority *formation* are not properly developed. Dewey especially warned against two dangers: on the one hand, an escape into pure scientific or "scholastic" discourse dominated by experts, and on the other hand, reduction of a variety of "physical agencies of publicity" to sensationalism, appearing in advertising, propaganda, invasion of private life, and fragmentation in reporting (pp. 168–69).

Dewey pointed to the absurdity and infantilism of the belief that perfect freedom of thought and communication has been achieved because all legal restrictions on freedom have been removed. The mere removal of "negative conditions" does not suffice; what is rather needed is "positive freedom," which Dewey considered "not a state but an act which involves methods and instrumentalities for control of conditions" (p. 168). Similarly to Marx and many other social theorists of the late nineteenth and early twentieth centuries, who wrote that the main threat to freedom of the press is its subordination to the entrepreneurial freedom, Dewey thought that the main danger to democracy was represented by the tendency of politics to become just another business (p. 182). He saw the central problem concerning the formation of opinions in the public and distribution of knowledge among its members through the press in *political domination* and *subordination to big business*, which was reflected in the growth of "extra-legal agencies" competing with the government as the "nominal organ" of the public (p. 119). After all, it was not a *privilege* of freedom that was granted to the (political) press because of its commercial inducement; it was universal freedom of expression—because the press was deemed an irreplaceable means for a full realization of the personal right to express opinions in public—even if the latter was just a pretense for the former. Wolfgang Hoffmann-Riem (1986, 130) similarly argues that "the concept of individual self-fulfilment and of citizens' rights to self-government . . . has been a key determining influence on the historical definition of freedom of communication in Western Europe," in contrast to the present time that is characterized by the rise of an "economic interpretation" of press freedom merging "the right to communicate" with "the right to run a commercial business."

MASS MEDIA AND THE PERSONAL RIGHT TO PUBLISH OPINIONS

To be sure, the complexity of mass communication processes makes impossible simply extrapolating from the rather simple situation of using newspapers for public reasoning in the eighteenth and even nineteenth centuries to the complex mass mediated communication processes of the late twentieth or early twenty-first centuries. Habermas became aware of the fundamental importance of global economic, political, and technological changes for (the conceptualization of) publicity and the public sphere only much after the publication of *The Structural Transformation*, and in 1990 he added "three revisions" to the 1962 original edition.[9] He justified the revisions as resulting from developmental changes in the self-regulation of society in the period between early 1960s and late 1980s, which significantly affected (1) the private sphere and the social foundations of private autonomy; (2) the structure of the public (sphere) and the composition and behavior of the publics, and (3) the legitimization processes of mass democracies. He revised his earlier theory of "linear development" from a reasoning to a consuming public (what he termed "refeudalization of publicity") with the idea of the "ambivalence of the public," which he first developed in his theory of communicative action as the idea of the ambivalent—authoritarian and emancipatory—potential of communication (Habermas 1981, 574). This shift was believed to be the consequence of objective, empirical social changes, which also transformed the nature of the public/ness. Although Habermas stressed that this revision did not mean the withdrawal of the original intentions which guided him in *The Structural Transformation*, he did confess that his "revised model" was closer to the libertarian concept of public opinion and the critique of the "tyranny of the majority" found in Tocqueville and J. S. Mill than to the classical liberal theories of *the rule of public opinion*.

Habermas of 1992 criticizes his own 1962 "pessimistic" theory of publicness because he failed to see that the individual citizens and their interests cannot be simply replaced by corporate bodies and their interests, or even by the society as a whole; neither can a society be deliberatively steered as a whole, nor can a deliberative model serve as a model for all social institutions, let alone individual citizens (1992a/1997, 331, 305). The contemporary institutionalized processes of public communication are not only characterized by the abundance of diverse mass media, which dominate quotidian communicative experience of individuals, but are also surrounded by a variety of noninstitutionalized forms of communication (exclusively) based on the negative freedom of communication, without guaranteeing equality to the citizens, perhaps best represented by the Internet. In addition to the "legal institutionalization of the general conditions of communication for a discursive formation of will," Habermas specifically underscores the importance of "the introduction and testing of *novel* institutional arrangements that might counteract the trend toward the transmutation of citizens into clients," the latter being merely concerned with their short-term interests and characterized by an "unpolitical follower mentality" (1992b, 450).

The need of democratic communication concerns all forms of the public use of reason, not only the press or mass media in general. With *no* public use of reason in the media, which is based on the right of citizens to be heard, there is no democracy. With public use of reason *only* in the media, there is no democracy either: democracy also rests on the principle of dialogue, not only mass dissemination. As Habermas states, "Parliamentary opinion- and will-formation must remain anchored in the informal streams of communication emerging from public spheres that are open to all political parties, associations, and citizens" (1992a/1997, 171). The informal sphere of opinion formation and expression, which influences political decision making, has to be separated from the institutional sphere of formal political proceedings aimed at reaching decisions. The two spheres have to be constitutionally protected as autonomous spheres enabling discursive formation of will; neither of them must be, as Habermas emphasizes, "organized like corporate bodies," but they should differ in conditions of communication, which also lead to differences in terms of accessibility of the two spheres.

In the view of potential collision between the personal right to publish opinion and the property right (which is also reflected in Habermas's claim against corporate-like bodies), the sphere of mass mediated communication is particularly important. The importance of theorizing the mass media, within the general framework of the theory of publicness, is not only due to the significant influence media have in the systems of politics and economy in contemporary society, but also—and perhaps even more importantly— because the media in the modern (or strict) sense did not exist in the time when the grand theories of publicity originated. These new developments in the mass media domain may prove, from the practical point of view, one or other of the alternative hypotheses on the relationship between the two fundamental freedoms—freedom to communicate and freedom of ownership— and the proper civil rights.

The complexity of the questions of communication and democracy does not allow restricting them to mass communication only. Nevertheless, the questions related to mass communication are much more than just an exemplification. The importance of the mass media for contemporary democracies becomes quite clear when contemporary society and its communication networks are compared with the ancient and medieval societies, and the political and economic significance of the modern mass media is compared with that of other forms of communication. Democracy is believed to ensure to the people (all members of a collectivity) a certain degree of (political) equality and the fullest possible involvement in procedures for arriving at collective decisions about public affairs. Beyond doubt, both the understanding of "the people" and the scope of "public affairs" to be discussed by "the people" considerably varied over time, as did the significance of "public," nonpersonal (or impersonal) communication. Classical Greek democracy was marked by participation of all citizens in common life of the city-state, which was based on the equal right to speak in the sovereign assembly. Materialization of this right enabled citizens to develop and realize their capacities and skills. For ancient democracy, freedom of opinion and expression was universal in terms of then disposable communication technologies. Citizens' participation in the process of government was restricted only by their skill to use their reason in public.

In terms of personal rights, the fundamental difference between interpersonal and mass-mediated public reasoning is in the relation of individuals communicating to the external means of production and control. In immediate[10] interpersonal communication, such means are either (1) not necessary at all, as in face-to-face communication, (2) part of individual *consumer* technology (telephone, personal computer) or (3) are, by definition, part of political, that is, *public infrastructure* (e.g., public meeting halls, parliaments), so no collision with the real property right may emerge.

In mass communication, however, the personal right to publish opinions (which is a right philosophically but not yet practically) collides with real property right as a *matter of principle*: the proprietor's right to dispose of communication means as "external things" also includes the right to control the supply and the choice of *contents*. Why should a private proprietor of communication means prefer (or even want) to make contents serviceable for democratic public reasoning over his or her private interest in maximizing commercial profit, if this would be only his or her moral duty, whereas no such duty would pertain to proprietors of any other external thing? Why would he or she countenance and encourage minority opinions, as J. S. Mill requested, although that could be harmful for his or her business?

The answer is very simple: he or she would not do that at all unless required by law. In the United States and elsewhere, opposition from broadcasters is the major obstacle for any legislation that would reduce the level of profit in the broadcasting industry (Hoynes 1994, 171). If a communication medium is used as any other productive property, that results in a commercial enterprise. Any communication organization exposed to market regulation would be forced to respond to popular demand prevailing in the marketplace; it would hardly countenance the expression of dissenting or minority opinions. As Jan van Cuilenburg's empirical study revealed, "media markets are far better in producing reflection of *majority civic interests* and *consumer preferences* than equal openness to political and cultural innovations stemming from minorities." Thus he concluded that "in democratic societies, opinion dominance, lack of political and cultural competition and other forms of 'market failure' inevitably asks for *governmental policy* to enhance entrance of new and rivalry among existing ideas and opinions" (1998; emphasis added).

William Hoynes suggested five general principles of democratic media: social ownership, diversity, participation, interaction, and criticism (1994, 168–77). Social ownership is considered the most important because it ought to facilitate the implementation of the others. Yet the idea that the problem of "unfairness" of the marketplace can be resolved by replacing private with "social" property is misleading, mainly for two reasons.

On the one hand, such a transformation would not change the relations between individual media and the marketplace. There is little chance that legally abolishing the private property of the media would make them democratically reordered and genuinely socialized, since they would remain surrounded by the *private economy*, which substantially limits their production autonomy (Negt and Kluge 1973, 191). As a consequence, even public service media react to the environment as business companies: for example, the results of the measurement of audiences become a sort of "television money" that determines the value of programming; they are managed according to the same principles as any other company; and they are directly involved in transactions with private suppliers of programs and equipment that often operate monopolistically. Hence the idea of socialization denotes *the need to acknowledge the specific nature of communication* and to liberate the (public service) media from their subordination to the principles of a "free marketplace." The demand that the media should not be regulated by the principle of profit maximization does not refer to the *revocation* of property right, but to its *regulation*.

On the other hand, the transformation of property itself cannot democratize inner relations in the media. In his plea for the Great Community, Dewey convincingly argued against socialists who demanded that "industry should be taken out of private hands," stressing that "the public has no hands except those of individual human beings. . . . The same causes which have led men to utilize concentrated political power to serve private purposes will continue to act to induce men to employ concentrated economic power in behalf of nonpublic aims" (Dewey 1927/1991, 82). Thus the (re)organization of communications as public goods and services should not be equated with a sort of nationalization of private property and its transformation into state or public property because such a transformation cannot resolve the problem of concentration of power.

The quintessential question is whether mass media are indeed, and should be considered, *primarily* (rather than exclusively) means of human communication or are primarily "external things" with no specific inherent purpose and thus may be appropriated according to the right of property. The hypothetical acceptance of one or other alternative determines the answer to the question of the proper kind of regulation. The authentic idea of freedom of the press to enable freedom of expression is based on the former assumption. The main function attributed to the "public service" media is to enable associations, groups, and individual members of civil society to make their politically relevant *opinions* and *actions* publicly available and thus, at least potentially, politically influential.

The growing complexity of modern communications has generated radically different communication systems in comparison to that typical for classical Greek democracy. *Freedom of expression* guaranteed by contemporary democracies has not the same meaning and scope it had in ancient societies, when it was not only a negative but also *positive personal freedom* and a *right*, since no specific conditions beyond being a citizen were needed to make freedom of expression effectual. If it is related to the most complex modern form of communication—mass communication—it is obvious that freedom of expression remained a purely negative freedom. Three decades ago Jean D'Arcy published a seminal essay presenting the concept of the *right to communicate*, which went far beyond normative principles adopted by the international community. It was later included in the MacBride UNESCO report and defined as:

> Everyone has the right to communicate: the components of this comprehensive Human Right include but are not limited to the following specific communication rights: (a) a right to assemble, a right to discuss, a right to participate, and related *association* rights; (b) a right to inquire, a right to be informed, a right to inform, and related *information* rights; and (c) a right to culture, a right to choose, a right to privacy, and related human *development* rights. . . . The achievement of a right to communicate would require that communication resources be available for the satisfaction of human communication needs. (MacBride Report 1980/1984, 138)[11]

To make the classical concept of freedom of expression equivalent to modern complex societies and functional in terms of participation of citizens in political life, it should be rethought, reconceptualized, and most likely extended together with the extension of other specific rights, such as the right to be informed or the right to privacy. The further communication technologies or means developed in the direction of contemporary complex hi-tech mass media not only broadened temporal and spatial horizons and reduced the temporal and spatial distance between those communicating, but also required more specific communication capacities, skills, and means, and eventually even the ownership of communication means, in order to use them. The demand for an "extension" of the personal right to communicate due to new communication technologies and opportunities is correlative with the extension of the real property right, which was de facto extended as a consequence of the colonization of new territories and development of new production technologies. In contrast, modern mass media are often used primarily as a new tool of control or a new opportunity for trade than a new possibility of citizens for self-expression.

Specifically, the right to make opinions available to others as the core of the right to communicate is a right that must be based on one, and only one condition, as Kant emphasized—that the person is his or her *own master*, or a *citizen*. I may need *some* property, if we follow Kant, to prove that I am truly my own master—that I qualify for that right (although Kant himself had some doubts about this condition), but this does not imply that my civil right to publish opinion rests with my own specific kind of property; after all, such reduction would bring us eventually back to the natural state of self-sufficient primeval communities with no division of labor. I am qualified to publish my opinions qua citizen, not as the owner of a specific newspaper or any other *specific* thing. Consequently, if the media were used as just any kind of property to satisfy private interests, freedom of the press would be merely a privilege of a group of media owners—purely a means to decrease the level of equality in society. If the media are considered a means to realize civil right of publishing opinions, they have to be regulated accordingly. They have to be regulated in a way that would stimulate individuals and groups to organize and express their opinions. This does not mean that all the media should be regulated as not-for-profit usable "things," yet only such a status justifies *specific* rights that cannot be descended from the property right itself.

No substantial regulative changes in the sphere of the media and culture can be purely indigenous because it permeates through all pores of society; methods and instruments for control of *social* rather than individual conditions are needed. This is the central problem of any attempt to regulate the media in contemporary complex societies in a way to overcome citizens' unequal influence in the formation and expression of (public) opinions. The idea of a radical reregulation, which may imply reinstitutionalization of society, is not unknown from history. The importance of this process was probably expressed in the most pronounced way by Emile Durkheim in his quest for the "completion" of the principles of the 1789 Revolution in France:

> There is indeed no question which should attract more the attention of legislators and Statesmen: do not all the difficulties in which nations find themselves at the present time stem from the difficulty in *adapting the traditional structure of societies to these new and unconscious aspirations* which have been tormenting societies for a century? (Durkheim 1890/1971, 43; emphasis added)

Reinstitutionalization is a broad concept that spans from a "social reorganization," as Henri de Saint-Simon would name it, when one form of social organization has perished and a new one is being developed, to modest institutional changes. A clear example of a continuous reinstitutionalization is the codification of human *rights*: first legal rights protecting individual's "negative" freedom, followed by political rights of bourgeois revolutions (e.g., rights to assemble, associate, and participate in government) and by social and economic rights in the twentieth century, which should now be followed by communication and cultural rights, particularly those related to the mass media. The extension of human rights was based on the *univer-salization* of political norms and values, which gradually reduced the extent of external inequalities of citizens and thus fostered their empirical equality. This continuous innovative process of the system of rights demands its peri-odical rethinking and reinterpreting. For example, the struggle for freedom of thought and press, as well as other citizen rights, was "in its essence an ex-pression of the fight of the new-bourgeois, the national-bourgeois class that positions itself as the 'public'—and very often as the 'people,' or the 'nation'—for power, i.e., first for participation in the power of old classes and the monarchy which it restrains, and later increasingly for independent power" (Tönnies 1922, 128). Yet by strengthening its power, the ideas of the bourgeois class also become a *universal good* of the political public because the ruling class could not deny the subordinate class those rights it obtained for itself. This controversial historical process is reflected in diverse concep-tualizations of publicity as the momentum energizing the public(s) and pub-lic opinion, particularly in terms of competence and free access of citizens.

The process of universalization of rights is now facing a new obstacle: that of *globalization,* which challenges traditional European ideas of publicity. The new global institutions are international but not cosmopolitan in the Kantian sense of "world citizenship". the sovereign in the "transnational states," such as the European Union, is not the citizen but the nation-state (cf. Kant 1797, 455–56).[12] Although processes of globalization provide condi-tions for an international civil society of nongovernmental organizations and a cosmopolitan critical public (Bohman 1996, 89), they may also loosen the responsibility of the nation-states and their responsiveness to public opinion. Generally, attempts to (re)regulate the media internationally by virtue of the principle of publicity were even less effective than at the national level. Some self-regulatory efforts even have opposite effects, such as the recent cases of the European and World associations of *press councils.* The Alliance of Independent Press Councils of Europe (AIPCE) more resembles a Japan-ese "press club" system (see Hayashi 1998) with an exclusive, closed-shop atmosphere and personal relationships between representatives of media in-dustry and political powers, not making available their discussions to the general public, to say nothing of participation of the latter in their debates.[13] WAPC (World Association of Press Councils), the world counterpart of the AIPCE founded in 1992, faced a major crisis in 2000 when several national press councils stepped out in protest against the association's efforts to write an International Code of Ethics for Journalists and establish a "world press council" that would not allow for national specificities.

However "negative" (avoiding positive freedoms) and passive (reduced to the "right to receive") forms of national and international regulation may have been in the Western democracies during the last two centuries, thus having taken no risk of interference with the property right, they have clearly brought the libertarian tradition of the press to an end and revived the questions of the relationship between the media and other agents of power in the realms of the state, economy, and culture, and the public. The question of media regulation came to the fore of theoretical and practical-political debates because of their growing (in)direct and long-term consequences for individuals and societies. The general idea of regulation was deeply rooted in Dewey's concept of the public substantiated by the *need to regulate* remote and long-term consequences of human transactions. Mass media do not represent the only sector of public life that calls for public regulation in democratic processes. The twentieth century is an age of the growth of human rights and public law, and consequently of the creation of a variety of statutory regulations and bodies governing and controlling diverse matters of public concern and policy, for example, safety in the factory, public health, environmental protection, schooling, sexual and race relations, public services, commercial standards, transportation, communications, and the mass media.

The fundamental problem of media regulation is that of striking a proper balance between all different actors (to be) involved. The society as a whole—not in the sense of an undifferentiated whole, but as the totality of different actors—should be "in control" of the media, rather than any specific part of it. Power held by commercial groups and political agents must be limited in order to protect and increase the autonomy of the media and prevent coalitions between the media and the state or capital that go to the detriment of the public. In particular, as Habermas emphasizes, "we must distinguish the actors who, so to speak, emerge from the public and take part in the reproduction of the public sphere itself from the actors who occupy an already constituted public domain in order to use it," or between the actors, usually only laxly organized, who "emerge from" the public and those merely "appearing before" the public (Habermas 1992a/1997, 364, 375). For Habermas, this is not just a difference between the endogenous and exogenous actors. He assumes that "the public sphere together with its public must have developed as a structure that stands on its own and reproduces itself *out of itself*"—which is per se a valid assumption—*before* actors with strategic intent can illegitimately capture it, which would always enable those "latent forces" to recapture it. It is not clear, however, how "strategic actors" could be excluded from the *constitution* of the public sphere. If we only take the example of the press, this assumption seems untenable: the *constitutional guarantee* of (negative) freedom of the press also gives constitutional protection to private business of publishing newspapers. There is no public sphere without the press; thus historically the public sphere was "infected" by strategic (profit) interests almost with the very act of its constitution, as we can see from Marx's writings.

Nevertheless, taking Habermas's juxtaposition of "legitimate influence" versus "actual influence" seriously, the question appears, How can "actual influence" be brought closer to its "legitimate" model? Habermas's judgment seems to be too optimistic: "Public opinions that can acquire visibility only because of an undeclared infusion of money or organizational power lose their credibility as soon as these sources of social power are made public. Public opinion can be manipulated but neither publicly bought nor publicly blackmailed" (p. 364).[14] The trouble is that those "public opinions" are legitimized by the very fact that they appear in the mass media—the most trustful actor of all the actors appearing in front of the public! It makes sense, as Habermas proposes, to test empirically "the relation between actual influence and the procedurally grounded quality of public opinion," since actual influence of public opinion does not necessary coincide with legitimate influence. Yet his conclusion about the incorruptibility of public opinion refers only to the extreme case of immoral power sources, whereas—as the *empirical* evidence shows—at the same time the whole advertising and public relations industry is based on the now legitimate "infusion of money or organizational power" to promote opinions. Habermas's optimism assumes, as in a fairy tale, that the justice eventually always wins. My experience (more than pessimism) is saying that even in the long run this may not always be true.

PUBLIC USE OF REASON IN THE
GLOBAL HIGH-TECH MEDIA ENVIRONMENT

Habermas's 1990 "revisions" of the original (1962) edition of *The Structural Transformation*[15] clearly indicate—regardless of whether we are willing to grant validity to his arguments relating to the continuity in the (infra)structural *changes* of the public sphere and the processes of *integration* of state and society—the importance of implications of global technological, economic, and political changes for the public reasoning and the public sphere. Habermas revised his earlier pessimistic thesis of "refeudalization of publicity" with the idea of "the *ambivalent nature of the democratic potential of a public sphere* whose infrastructure is marked by the growing selective constraints imposed by electronic mass communication" (1992b, 457; emphasis added), formerly conceptualized in his theory of communicative action as the *ambivalent*—oppressive and emancipatory—*moments of communication* (1981, 574). Despite the changes in the public and communication spheres brought about by extrinsic actors trying to subordinate them to their purposive-rational goals, Habermas argues that, as a matter of principle, public opinion cannot be bought or blackmailed since the public sphere (together with its public) was historically established and can only be maintained by actors with purely communicative (avoiding any power except power of reason aimed at understanding) rather than strategic (purposive-rational) intent (1992a/1997, 364). In other words, the predominance of strategic actors must be counterbalanced by "the public" or else the public sphere would cease to exist. No less we may agree that, on the other hand, "the 'quality' of public opinion" is an empirically measurable variable that makes the measurement of the legitimacy of the influence of public opinion on the political system possible (1992a/1997, 362). Yet these abstract determinations cannot prevent the public (sphere) from a practical-historical collapse—a process engendered by the commodification of mass media and their transformation from Tarde's means of "*intellectual exchanges between minds*" into a new autonomous *system power*, along with the traditional state powers. Habermas concluded the original edition of *The Structural Transformation* (1962) with a pessimistic quote from C. Wright Mills's *Power Elite* about the decline of the public and the emergence of "a society of the masses," with "empirically usable criteria for a definition of public opinion" borrowed from Mills. But he overlooked Mills's most operational criterion essentially inherited from Dewey, centered on the (dis)ability of the media to animate *public discussion*:

> The public and the mass may be most readily distinguished by their dominant modes of communication: in a community of publics, discussion is the ascendant means of communication, and the mass media, if they exist, simply enlarge and animate discussion, linking one *primary public* with the discussions of another. In a mass society, the dominant type of communication is the formal media, and the publics become mere *media markets*: all those exposed to the contents of given mass media. (Mills 1956/2000, 304)

Mills compared and even tended to explain the eclipse of the public with the growth of corporate economy, characterized by phenomena such as (partly hidden) monopoly of control, mass advertising, "opinion business," and "competition between the manipulators with their mass media," where most of the people only "receive their propaganda." The question transcending the empirical measurement of quality of public opinion is, What is the nature of close relationship between the media and economy? It is not difficult to find out that it concerns the status of the property right versus the right to communicate discussed earlier.

Thirty years later, Habermas similarly directed his discussion "Civil Society, Public Opinion, and Communicative Power" (1992a/1997, 359–87) to empirical manifestations, not referring this time to empirical circumstances in which the media act but to "normative reactions" to those circumstances, synthesized by Michael Gurevitch and Jay G. Blumler in a list of functions mass media ought to perform in democratic political systems:

1. surveillance of the sociopolitical environment, reporting developments likely to impinge, positively or negatively, on the welfare of citizens
2. meaningful agenda setting, identifying key issues of the day, including the forces that have formed and may resolve them

3. platforms for an intelligible and illuminating advocacy by politicians and spokespersons of other causes and interest groups
4. dialogue across a diverse range of views, as well as between power holders (actual and perspective) and mass publics
5. mechanisms for holding officials to account for how they have exercised power
6. incentives for citizens to learn, choose, and become involved, rather than merely follow and kibitz over the political process
7. a principled resistance of the efforts of forces outside the media to subvert their independence, integrity, and ability to serve the audience
8. a sense of respect for the audience member, as potentially concerned and able to make sense of his or her political environment. (Gurevitch, Blumler 1990, 270; Habermas 1992a/1997, 378)

Habermas considers the media—representing an essential part of the "abstract public sphere of isolated readers, listeners, and viewers scattered across large geographic areas, or even around the globe" (1992a/1997, 374)—a mediating structure between the private sectors of the life world and functional systems and political system, which "ought to preserve their independence from political and social pressure" (p. 378). As he further suggests, access to the media should be allowed only to political and social actors "who make convincing contributions to the solution of the problems that have been perceived by the public or *have been put on the public agenda with the public consent*" (p. 379, emphasis added). He also claims that "the mass media ought to understand themselves as the mandatary (*als Mandatar*) of an enlightened public." Although he uses the term "the fourth power" (*die vierte Gewalt*, p. 376), he does not discuss the concept of the fourth power in any detail. He effectively (re)introduced the concept of the media as the fourth estate by emphasizing their autonomy and impartiality and their task of blocking "the tacit conversion of administrative or social power into political influence"—the task of *surveillance* adapted to the mass media in modern complex societies. In relation to the mass media, the whole idea of the public use of reason or the personal right to communicate would thus be minimized to "a sense of respect," which the media ought to have for the potentially concerned and sense-making "audience member," and the media seem to be alienated from the "social integrative power of communicative action . . . first of all located in those particularized forms of life and life worlds that are intertwined with concrete traditions and interest constellations in the 'ethical' sphere" (1992b, 444).

The public seemingly imploded into media *consumers*—a consequence quite incongruent with Habermas's own quest for "the introduction and testing of *novel* institutional arrangements that might counteract the trend toward the transmutation of citizens into clients" (Habermas 1992b, 450). I do not see how reducing media functions to mediation between different actors could solve *the* problem of the public, as Dewey stated it and Habermas assented to, namely, to increase social knowledge and inclusion of actors and areas of popular participation, and to improve methods and conditions of discussion in the public. Nor can autonomy of the media wield the principle of publicity as the supreme principle of right without *citizens* being *capable* and *allowed*, or rather *stimulated* to make their own judgments on the validity of publicly presented claims. I am not saying, though, that Habermas wanted to solve this problem. Obviously he did not; he only gave sociological insights into the processes by which contemporary mass media are constructed:

> The sociology of mass communication depicts the public sphere as infiltrated by administrative and social power and dominated by the mass media. If one places this image, diffuse though it might be, alongside the above normative expectations, then one will be rather cautious in estimating the chances of civil society having an influence on political system. To be sure, this estimate pertains only to a *public sphere at rest*. In periods of mobilization, the structures that actually support the authority of a critically engaged public begin to vibrate. The balance of power between civil society and the political system then shifts. (1992a/1997, 379)[16]

Similarly to Habermas, for example, Danilo Zolo argues that the neoclassical doctrine of democracy still lacks satisfactory explanatory power and calls for an entire reconstruction of democratic theory. Such a theory must take into account the fundamental changes in (the relationship between) the private and public spheres, as well as changes in the legitimization processes of mass democracies as suggested by Habermas, but in a much more critical way. There are two main reasons for such a critical reassessment: (1) The asymmetrical, noninteractive nature of mass political communication is developed to such a degree that the idea of "electronic democracy" has definitely become a utopia. (2) By its further dispersion—as a consequence of the "narcotizing dysfunction" of the mass media—the public sphere transformed itself into "a reflexive area, a timeless meta-dimension in which the 'real' public passively assists, as if in a sort of permanent television broadcast carried out in real time, in the exploits of an 'electronic' public" (Zolo 1992, 166). These two tendencies are taking on worldwide proportions and bringing about "a second structural transformation of the public sphere," which is global and more radical than the national ones analyzed by Habermas, because "the sovereignty of the political consumer—i.e. the autonomy, rationality and moral responsibility of the citizen called upon to pass sovereign judgement on the competition between parties—can now hardly amount to more than empty verbiage in the context of the massive spectacularisation of teledemocracy to which pluralistic competition between the parties . . . is being reduced" (Zolo 1992, 170).

All the changes we have experienced in the twentieth century do not justify in itself the rejection of the enlightened idea of publicity. As Dewey argued in the controversy with Lippmann, "Until secrecy, prejudice, bias, misrepresentation, and propaganda as well as sheer ignorance are replaced by inquiry and publicity, we have no way of telling how apt for judgment of social policies the existing intelligence of the masses may be" (Dewey 1927/1991, 209). These changes point toward the need for major changes in practical forms of publicity to preserve the democratic virtues embedded in the original idea(s) of publicity as universal norm to regulate public discourse. New forms of publicity surely cannot take rise without a broader process of reshaping the public sphere and, specifically, media institutions and forms of media representation. Dahlgren (1995, 11–16) rightfully emphasizes that an important role in this process play the total *social structure*, which includes all the institutional arrangements of society from social stratification to the entire educational system and its place in the social order, and different forms of *sociocultural interaction*—from nonmediated face-to-face communication or "the public sphere beyond the media" to the interface of media and citizens. Although new procedures of mediatization and representation, which dominate in postmodernity, and their social and political consequences may seem to suggest that we should leave off the universal Kantian concept of publicity, this turn would be so radical that the question is in place as to whether all the new diversified opportunities and practices of *reception* and *consumption* in (mass) communication still help *form* and *express opinions in public* and *by the public*, which authoritative institutions must take into account. Thus a more "conservative" approach focused on the counterfactual entity of publicity still seems to be more adequate, for without the central concept of publicity, the significance of the media for democratic political process is depleted altogether.

A democratic system should provide informed decisions on public issues, and this can only happen on the basis of an open information and communication system that allows for the personal right of public expression. The true sense of democratic regulation of communications is equal availability of influence on different forms of public communication, particularly mass media, to all citizens, so that no citizen would have more institutionally guaranteed influence over public (or collective) affairs than any other. Legal regulation should guarantee individuals' distinctiveness and uniqueness as the basis of their equality, for people are not equal in the sense, as Dewey (1927/1991, 150–51) stated, that each individual is actually substitutive for any other, but only as much as any distinctiveness and uniqueness of them is truly respected and valued, irrespective of physical and psychological inequalities.

Like any activity exhibiting influence, communication activity can be controlled internally or externally. Attempts at democratic regulation are often confronted with external sources of inequality of influence (e.g., inequality of income and wealth). Any universal provision of equal rights ensures equal availability of influence only under the provision that such external sources of inequality of influence do not exist. But this is not a very realistic condition. Clearly, the view on which the number of votes a citizen has should depend on his or her taxable income—an option Mill had in mind—or any other external inequality would be considered antidemocratic today because citizens would be unequal in terms of votes. Yet this is usually not the case with an unequal availability of other forms of influence in a number of activities in the public sphere. Citizens are extremely unequal in terms of their access to the media to publish their opinions or to participate in public discussion. These are typical examples of external sources of inequality where the abolition of legal restrictions (e.g., censorship) does not yet represent a "positive condition" for intellectual freedom. We can easily agree with James Bohman's estimate of democratic societies: "while greater inclusion in wider rights of citizenship has been achieved, social and economic inequalities seem to have widened, and the scope of political decision making seems to have narrowed as the effectiveness of the available regulatory mechanisms for self-rule now seems less likely to bring the process of globalization and technoscience under control" (Bohman 1999, 176).

Personal public use of reason cannot be realized and the right to communicate not achieved by a mere extension of the *control* paradigm established in relation between the media and political authorities as the fourth estate model to the relationship between media audiences and the media—so that audiences would be able to actually *watch* the media, rather than just receive their messages. The solution is the (re)organization of the public sphere according to the principle of *cooperation*, as "a cooperative product of communication and reciprocal influence" (Cooley 1909/1983, 121). The idea of the *division of labor* might be more appropriate to assure specialization and independent actions of different power and public actors, and their mutual interdependence, than the principle of the "separation of powers" that can only ensure an effective mutual control. Whereas the idea of the separation of powers is based on mutual mistrust, the idea of division of labor presumes mutual trust and cooperation. At the same time, any regulation has to stimulate an increase in individuals' *knowledge* and widen *access* to the public sphere to groups remote from parliamentary institutions. The empowerment of individuals with "communicative power" would pave the way for an effective social communication and public use of reason.[17] An increase in individual communicative power would stimulate the development of a more democratic institutional framework making the public use of reason central to the possibilities of democratic reforms. From this perspective, the concept of freedom of the press has definitely proved insufficient as an ethical and legal principle.

In *normative* terms, this calls for a "radical democratization" not only of the *media* but also of political and economic systems representing the *soci-*

etal context of the media. According to a model proposed by Krüger (1991), such a democratization ought to be three-dimensional: (1) The *public use of the media* should allow for a symmetric change between the diverging perspectives of participants and observers. If not, the potentially public media would degenerate into economic enterprises or propaganda departments of the state or political parties. (2) Institutional autonomization of *political competition* should be counteracted by the following: (a) the recognition of the public media as the fourth, "soft" or symbolic-argumentative power, so as to preclude their subordination under one of the three classic powers (legislative, executive, judicial); (b) an ever renewed federalization of all four powers to limit their drive toward centralization; (c) lowering the thresholds of citizen participation in democratic political competition; (3) *economic competition* should be socioculturally regulated: (a) through the political separation of powers; (b) through the limitation of the costs of bureaucratization caused by (a); (c) through the extension of the customary models of code-termination, for example, by the inclusion of representatives of the public.

Krüger apparently proceeds from a Benthamian rather than Kantian idea of publicness, but he goes beyond the simplistic fourth estate model of the press by stressing the mediating role of the media both between different "powers" and between "diverging perspectives of participants" generally. The quest for the media as the symbolic-argumentative power brings to light the problem of expertise. Essentially, no public discourse can be purely rational and knowledge-based because it always involves opinions, evaluations, and anticipations which, even if informed by knowledge, are subject to interests, contingencies, and errors. Nevertheless, as Dewey argued, the first condition of a positive freedom is the development of knowledge and science, which ought to become accessible to everyone in the most appropriate way. The public can be democratically organized only if three conditions are fulfilled, according to Dewey: (1) freedom of social inquiry and of distribution of its results, (2) public education, and (3) complete publicity in respect to all issues concerning the public (1927/1991, 169). The first step in the formation of knowledge is systematic social inquiry, which has to be followed by the spread of its results through the media to stimulate and extend the scope of public dialogue. Dewey did not believe in *independent* experts, most certainly not in the social sciences, but rather emphasized two kinds of *dependence*: they could rule as a means in the hands of capital or they would have to affiliate themselves with the masses and help them participate in power. Clearly contradicting his own assessment of the role of experts in the formation of the public, which is among the most critical parts of his argument, is an almost blind faith in the autonomous and impartial "social inquiry." His idea to make the media *distributors* of results of social inquiry does not really solve the problems of partiality, lack of knowledge, and exclusion; it only moves them from the media to another level: experts.[18]

Dewey emphasized the importance of access of the public to the forums defining public needs that public knowledge should address, but he did not address the establishment of credibility and legitimacy of experts producing that knowledge through social inquiry. In terms of regulation, it does not make any difference whether the "forums" are outside of the media or (in) the media themselves (or both). He insisted in the fundamental importance of citizens' education and their participation in public deliberation and decision making for any democratic system—not for the sake of its efficiency, but for reasons similar to Kant's conceptualization of the principle of publicity: to achieve individuals' self-dependent *reasoning* and *social justice*. He pleaded for a genuine participatory democracy not as the most efficient, but as the most educative form of government. Yet educativenees of democratic processes even does not guarantee efficiency in terms of participatory involvement of citizens: a greater capacity of citizens in acquiring rights, which is based on an increase in the general level of education, does not guarantee a higher level of materialization of those rights. Even the possibility of acquiring communicative power largely depends on the reduction of *external* (primarily economical) inequalities in individuals' education, knowledge, wants, and customs.

The success of new regulatory ideas does not depend primarily on new technological possibilities, increase in the communicative power, and the feasibility of theoretical assumptions, but rather on the power relations between key actors in society. An illustrative solution to the problem of unequal access might be the institutionalization of the "*fair* marketplace of ideas" (Brighouse 1995), which "transforms" the personal right to publish opinion into the right of opinion to be published. In contrast to the naive marketplace of ideas discussed earlier, the regulation should allocate *equal time and space to each specific view* presented, or to each "public policy option," rather than to each individual or opinion agent. This is an idealization; in practice, space could normally be allocated only to political actors (e.g., parties) or tendencies (interest groups, movements), that will de facto organize the allocation of space to each issue. In other words, if a number of individuals or parties hold the same opinion, they would receive altogether only "one unit" of time or space in the media.

This is not a new idea. In theoretical terms, it represents an operationalization of Cooley's idea of public opinion as a process of representation in the sense that "the preponderant *feeling* of the group seeks definite and effectual expression through individuals specially competent to give it such expression" (1909/1983, 124). Looking in the opposite way, *competence* of an individual does not imply special personal right—based on external restraints, as it is the case of the media under the fourth estate model—but is a privilege to be "used" by social groups. In practical terms, ideas to encourage heterogeneity of media contents were well known already at the beginning of the twentieth century. Hayes argued in 1926 that the U.S. government should regulate by law the publication of newspapers in order to support the development of an informed public opinion, so that each newspaper would be obliged to give an equal amount of space to each of the four leading political parties in the last elections for the presentation of their ideas (in Wilson 1962, 81). Similar ideas can be found in Tönnies (1922). Many European countries regulate in this way not only public broadcasting but also the press and the Internet during election campaigns. The ethical principle of "fair and balanced" reporting reflects the same basic idea of the need for content diversity in the media reflecting the diversity of interests, orientations, and needs among citizens. Yet a substantial discrepancy exists between media *flattering* citizens (or rather consumers)—by *corresponding* and, however fugitively, *representing* their interests—and citizens' self-dependent access to the media. A similar level of discordance exists between the comprehensive meaning of the universal ethical principle of publicity and its legal operationalization(s) that ought to assure its practical enforcement as a citizen right to communicate.

The idea of *public service* is (still) central to the democratization of the media, particularly broadcasting media; moreover, it is a "natural" setting for the realization of citizens' right to communicate. The idea of public service appeared even before the emergence of radio, as a consequence of the subordination of newspapers to powerful political and/or commercial interests in the late nineteenth century. Many press reformers pleaded for "security valves in public life" based on charitable funds, which ought to limit the dependence of newspapers on political parties and advertisers, prevent sensationalism, and empower "voices of people [to] find their direct expression in the newspaper" (Tönnies 1922, 575). Tönnies believed, following the American sociologist J. W. Jenks, that "we will never have a newspaper which will report completely independently about problems of public life unless we have a newspaper that will be independent of circulation and advertising business" (1922, 184), and he recognized the need for radical reforms of the press to improve the quality and ethical standards of journalism and to make newspapers a *genuine organ of public opinion.*[19]

Since its first institutionalization in Europe, public service broadcasting was attributed democratic functions that the press has been progressively losing due to its increased political and commercial dependence. In addition to the goals justified by "public" interest—such as the promotion of national culture and integration, providing contents for minorities and specific groupings such as children, universality and quality programming in the fields of information, education and entertainment—public service broadcasting was always considered also a forum of public debates on political issues and a mechanism of surveillance of political authorities. It was not considered merely an institution established with the consent of the people through their representatives acting for the permanent good of the people—in analogy with the representative government as defined by Edmund Burke—but also designed to enable and stimulate individuals as *citizens* to take active part in mediated civic discussions and agenda setting aimed at influencing actions of authoritative institutions, that is, to participate in the formation and expression of public opinion (Splichal 1999, 34). The latter function of the media has never been fully materialized in practice for both societal and technological reasons. The development of advanced technologies of computer mediated communication and global computer communication networks may shape differently— but not determine—the future of democratic communication, fostering the optimistic conception of cosmopolitan citizenship supplementary to the citizenship framed by nation-states. Optimism is not based on the trust in an unlimited power of new technologies to democratize society but, just the opposite, on the belief that political and economic systems can be changed in the way to make it possible for an individual participatory use and collective citizen (public) control of communication goods.

The Internet is particularly appropriate to initiate processes of casting away prejudices preventing relevant problems from appearing in the agenda of public opinion. Indeed, with the new interactive virtual spaces it has created, the Internet substantially increased the feasibility of citizens' public use of reason activating tendencies and capacities of *innovation* and change. Specifically, the Internet had a constitutive role in the development of an informal global communication network of individuals, organizations and movements, which create a sort of international civil society leading toward a genuinely cosmopolitan public. The Internet brought about a new form of publicness—mediated and dialogical at the same time—supplementary to the mediated publicness constructed by traditional mass media. Whereas the mass media primarily extended the possibilities of passive *visibility* (i.e., of one being made visible by producers of media contents), the Internet is based on widespread active *participation*. In contrast to the Internet, traditional mass media favor and facilitate primarily reception and consumption through *imitation* owing to the market mechanisms and tendency of profit maximization that stimulate only publication of ideas and news stories that would not annoy or confuse their consumers. Whereas traditional media often help block innovation, particularly when they are heralds of particularistic interests of powerful interest groups behind them, the Internet is pluralistic in terms of both producers and users, and diversified in terms of content by its very nature—due to its decentered structure. If the concept of public/ness has been determined by the internally confined model of a community gathering by the end of the twentieth century, as Bohman (1996, 106) suggests, the rise of the Internet definitely helped transcend this limitation.

From the late nineteenth century, the industrialized, profit-oriented press progressively "occupied" the premodern public spaces and privatized them.

Whereas every citizen has had access to the public space of the ancient *agora* to speak to, and be heard by, his fellow-citizens, privately owned newspapers—while they substantially expanded the "public space" beyond the limits of physically attainable spaces—severely limited the possibility of an active citizens' participation in the newly created (virtual) public space. The right to communicate—if enacted—may now legally reopen general access to public spaces formerly restricted to elites in control of the press and other mass media. The Internet already tenders practicable online services such as electronic chat rooms and discussion forums that enhance political deliberation in practice.

Compared with the traditional media, however, the Internet is much less capable of digesting ideas and presenting them in a form that would influence the authorities to heed them. The Internet is not controllable; it proved essentially inaccessible to any (national) regulatory attempts (e.g., if national authorities forced an Internet provider to remove some Web pages, their producers could move them to another provider outside of the country). However, it can also hardly perform the role of a watchdog or create moral obligations in a way similar to the traditional media. The Internet is neither a Panopticon controlling its users/producers nor a public opinion tribunal controlling the traditional branches of power. Internet technology enables dialogical communication that can hardly be restrained by external surveillance, but at the same time it can hardly assure any response. While the Internet presents new opportunities for social interaction, it also stimulates "fragmentation" and "reparochialization" (Slevin 2000, 181). Nevertheless, the Internet is a perfect communicative environment that enables reflexive reasoning of participants—to detach themselves from the subjective personal conditions of their judgment and reflect on it from a universal standpoint, as Kant has suggested two centuries ago.

Yet without the traditional mass media, the public sphere would lack the most effective channel correlating the public(s) with power actors appearing before the public and deriving their legitimacy from it. This (am)bivalent relation between the public and the state mediated through the media is constitutive of publicness. If properly regulated, it is also the precondition necessary for the advancement of the principle of publicity as the supreme ethical and organizational principle, superior to property right and freedom of the press that is based on it. Mass media have the central significance in the creation of an institutional (infra)structure enabling the organization of the general interest both nationally and internationally (globally). The present lack of such an effective communication structure and practical impediments to its creation should become the central issue in the ongoing discussions on media democratization.

Historical changes that I have delineated show that freedom of the press "profaned" the principle of publicity. While the principle of publicity denotes a *universal* belief in freedom and autonomy of human nature and reason, the concept of freedom of the press exemplifies primarily support for the independence and freedom of a privileged social "estate," both in the sense of Marx's "urban estate" (i.e., the new bourgeois class) and in the sense of the press as the fourth estate. The struggle for freedom of thought, freedom of the press, and other civic rights and liberties was essentially an expression of the rise of the new, national bourgeois class—having identified itself with "the society," "the people," or "the nation"—and its struggle for power. The idea of the fourth estate accurately pointed to the fact that newspapers emanated from a new, predominantly bourgeois class (estate) and thus had a different source of legitimacy, so that it actually could have represented an important form of control over the traditional branches of state power, but only as long as the press developed as a critical pressure against the old ruling estates of feudal Europe. The bourgeois democratic revolutions suppressed the differentiation in sources of political and social legitimacy, since the same source—the people—legitimized all state powers. In such a situation the press preserved different sources of legitimacy—as an *organ of the public* and a capitalist *nonstate enterprise*, but the further autonomization of the press into a particular "estate" based on the power of capital effectively alienated freedom of the press from the universal principle of publicity and specifically from personal positive freedom to express and publish opinions.

Despite the pressure of democratic social movements, however, the developments after the constitution of the bourgeois public sphere and democratic state, and particularly the development of modern mass media—reflected in institutionalized forms and pressures to hinder the range and diversity of opinions in circulation or privileged dissemination of preferred opinions—do not "give rise to healthy institutional structures for the public sphere" (Dahlgren 1995, 12). The principle of publicity was originally conceived as a critical impulse against injustice based on secrecy of state actions *and* as an enlightening momentum substantiating the region of human liberty and making private citizens equal in the public use of reason. The idea of freedom of the press as the "fourth estate" only sustained the surveillance dimension of the universal principle of publicity. However, the fourth estate model of publicity fails to materialize both key dimensions of the Kantian principle of publicity—it neither guarantees the rightfulness of political decisions nor stimulates the public use of reason. In fact, it cannot guarantee the rightfulness of public enactments *because* it does not stimulate the public use of reason, since only a public capable of reflexive, critical reasoning acquired in public discourse can make reliable judgments. The fourth estate reasoning is based on Tocqueville's partial argument that the sovereignty of the people and the liberty of the press are correlative: if citizens have the right to participate in the government of society, "everyone must be presumed to be able to choose between the various opinions of his contemporaries and to appreciate the different facts from which inferences may be drawn" (1835, chap. 11). Tocqueville did not realize, however, that correlatively to the "sharing in the government"—which not only includes citizens' active right to cast a vote but also the passive right to be elected—freedom of publication should include not only the passive right to receive but also the active right to express opinions.

The concepts of public service media and, to a lesser extent, the model of social responsibility of the press attempted at recuperating the dimension of reflexive reasoning in publicity, but with very limited success. Social changes emanating from convergence of information and communication technologies, and economic, political and cultural globalization, call for new forms of social-cultural regulation that would fully recognize the universal principle of publicity. Forms of regulation aimed at capacitating the media—as *members* of the Benthamian "Public Opinion Tribunal"—to control all political (trans)actions are important, but they cannot ensure citizens of participation in deliberative processes. The necessary (though not yet sufficient) conditions of public deliberation are personal involvement and reflective distance: the two components of the process are mutually conditioned and restrained. It is not a disinterested individual who would claim the right of expressing opinions, but rather a citizen conscious of long-term consequences of transactions that are under discussion, who is able to rationalize his or her own involvement, consider arguments of others, and emancipate from prejudices. Personal right to express opinion in public is substantiated by personal involvement. Rational discussion without personal involvement may even degenerate into an "enlightened" absolutism— a position easily adopted by "neutral," "objective," and "disinterested" media of the fourth estate class. In fact, media are never merely means of transmission or "intermediaries" between two parties (e.g., authorities and audiences); they are always the constituting part of the "mediation" (deliberation). Bentham was right when he regarded them as "members" of the public opinion tribunal rather than its means.

Reforms of political, economic, and social regulatory practices are needed to open citizen access to the public sphere and mass media, which can only be based on the legal recognition of the generic human right to communicate, division of labor, and the principle of cooperation—in contrast to the market-driven principles of economic and political competition, separation of powers, and freedom of the press as a separate ("fourth") power. The "right to communicate" and the "fourth estate" model of the principle of publicity are incompatible under the prerogative of the *right to property*. However, under the prerogative of the right to communicate—which does not exclude the property right, but regulates it—the surveillance concept of publicity becomes equivalent to the dimension of "the principle of the legal order" in Kant's principle of publicity, with the only difference being that

Bentham's supreme principle of the maximization of the people's happiness is "replaced" with Kant's principle of rightfulness. Without such a broadening of the deliberative space for the exercise of citizenship bestowed by the right to communicate, *in situ* citizens will remain mere consumers of the modern media with an occasional experience, perhaps, of participating in "the public of the letters to the editor."

NOTES

1. A similar strategic analogy has been used in the opposite way to justify the opposite cause—the right to express opinions was presented as inseparable from the right to enforce opinion in such a manner that it would be commonly approved, that is, imposed on others, which would eventually resulted in a war of all against all—in order to make the claims for freedom of expression untenable (see Molivas 2000, 252–53).

2. Aristotle already strictly differentiated between the form of government whose end is *freedom* and the form of government in which men rule by reason of their *wealth*. The former he named *democracy* and the latter *oligarchy*. In democracy, all citizens being equal, they distribute the offices of state among themselves by lot, whereas under oligarchy there is a property qualification for all offices.

3.It was largely owing to the MacBride Commission that the idea of access to the media became one of the central issues of academic and grassroots discussions in the late 1970s and early 1980s.

4. Jorgensen (2002) identified four main selection criteria: the rules of relevance (responses to items already published), brevity, and entertainment (long letters are boring, not attractive for readers and do not enhance commercial success), and the rule of authority (privileging prominent and experienced senders).

5. Habermas rightly claims that "public opinion is not representative in the statistical sense. . . . it must not be confused with survey results," but I think he is wrong in suggesting that "political opinion polls provide a certain reflection of 'public opinion' only if they have been preceded by a focused public debate and a corresponding opinion-formation in a mobilized public sphere" (1992a/1997, 362). Opinion polls are essentially not an instrument of research or a kind of scientific endeavor, that is, not external to "public opinion" that would exist before a polling procedure starts; polling is rather an institutionalized component of public opinion itself, despite the fact it does not stimulate "cooperatively negotiated interpretations," but this is also the case with the mass media (see Splichal 1999, 221–70). "Numbers" presented as "polling results" are (not) trusted or believed, and consequently influential in the same way as any other individual or corporate actors in the public sphere—and according to Habermas, *influence* is the flagship of public opinion.

6. In the former Yugoslavia, the right to publish opinions became a constitutional right of citizens in 1963. In the 1980s, this right—together with the rights of reply and correction—became quite broadly used by citizens (mostly in the press). An important precedent occurred in a lawsuit when the Supreme Court of Slovenia ordered the main daily newspaper in Slovenia, *Delo,* to publish an article by a citizen criticizing a

high political functionary (1985). This case has become a rather celebrated one for both editors and journalists, as well as (critical) citizens, for it indicated the autonomy of both the press and judiciary system from party politics. However, when after the downfall of Yugoslavia in 1991, the Slovenian Ministry of Information proposed amendments to the former Law on public information adopted in 1985, it suggested "to cut out the provisions related to the publication of opinions." The ministry admitted that "this citizen right represented a great achievement of civilization under the conditions of a one-party system." However, it argued that "in a plural society and developed information market such a citizen right, or duty of the media, is an anachronism; the media will be forced to publish opinions important for the public primarily because of the pressure of competition." That view has been strongly supported by the Association of Journalists of Slovenia (Splichal 1991, 321).

7. This "situation" is a typically perverted one if compared with the normatively defined "situation" constitutive of the public sphere, where individuals are supposed to "encounter each other in a *situation* they at the same time constitute with their cooperatively negotiated interpretations" (Habermas 1992a/1997, 361), since here the situation is constituted only by the media as "representatives" of the public.

8. The same idea can be later found in Habermas (1992b, 449), who believes that "the rule to abide by majority decisions can be interpreted as an arrangement squaring a formation of opinion that seeks truth and is discursive as circumstances permit with the temporal constraints to which the formation of will is subject. Within the discourse-centered theoretical approach, decision by majority must remain internally related to a practice of rational debate."

9. The "revisions" first appeared in the introduction to the German Suhrkamp edition published in 1990.

10. The question of differences between the mass mediated and immediate forms of communication is far from being trivial, particularly with the development of computer-mediated communication and the Internet. By *immediate communication* I mean all forms of human communication, where communication is not controlled in terms of time and choice of subject by a human mediator set between individual communicator as citizen and recipients (regardless of the number of the latter). In that sense, computer-mediated communication is a form of immediate communication in the case of e-mail and open chat rooms, but it is a mediated form of communication in the case of electronic newsletters. The main conceptual difficulty is caused by personal Web sites, which may fall in either category. This difficulty has no implication for my theoretical discussion of freedom of the press relative to the right to publish opinions, but it must be resolved for any practical application.

11. The MacBride Commission recommended that "communication needs in a democratic society should be met by the extension of specific rights . . . [which are] all elements of a new concept: the right to communicate. In developing what might be called a new era of social rights, we suggest all the implications of the right to communicate be further explored" (MacBride 1980/1984, 216). Political reaction by the leading developed nations to the policy of UNESCO expressed in the criticism of the MacBride Report, which was part of broader debate on the New Information and Communication Order (NWICO), was atrocious. Incited by aggressive propaganda in the Western media against UNESCO, the United States and the United Kingdom withdrew from the organization in 1985.

12. Habermas is right in suggesting that the historical fact that both democracy and the nation-state developed in the same process should not prevent us from seeing the difference between the two. Based on such an abstraction, for example, the idea of the European state beyond the nation-state(s) appears as a feasible "identity formation," provided that the following conditions are met: (1) the emergence of the European civil society, (2) the construction of a European political public, and (3) the formation of an appropriate political culture (Habermas 2001, 64). The fulfillment of these conditions should be seen as a progressive historical process toward a "European republic" that goes beyond Kant's federal "community of the peoples of the earth" as a "negative surrogate" for the nation-state. At present, however, the institutions of the European Union cannot be regarded as originating from the sovereignty of "European citizens."

13. For example, the AIPCE Web site is only accessible to authorized (i.e., nonprivate) persons, which clearly makes the association anything but a promulgator of the principle of publicity. In June 2000, I was denied access when I applied as a university professor (I had to identify myself), with the argument that "the AIPCE site is intended as a discussion area for press councils and other related organizations in Europe."

14. Habermas, in contrast, denotes his earlier critical judgment that no resisting power and critical potential in mass public existed in the *Structural Transformation of the Public Sphere* (1962) as "too pessimistic" (1992b, 438).

15. The English version of the new introduction was published in Habermas 1992b.

16. Habermas modestly noted in another essay published at the same time (1992b, 439) that he has "paid only sporadic attention to . . . the diversified literature in sociology of political behavior."

17. According to Andrén's normative definition, "*a person has communicative power* to the extent that s/he (1) has consciously developed opinions and attitudes of his own; (2) s/he knows how to express his opinions and attitudes in adequate ways; (3) s/he has access to media where he can express his opinions and attitudes; (4) by (3) s/he can reach a large and/or influential audience or a particular audience which he wants to influence; (5) by (4) s/he will, in fact, influence the opinions, attitudes, or behaviors of other citizens in accordance with his intentions" (1993, 61).

18. One only has to look at the severe controversies over positive and critical science, or public opinion polling, to realize that even in (social) sciences there is no such thing as complete "objectivity" or "impartiality."

19. Tönnies argued for the separation of the press from political parties and advertising agencies because the development of the press as a moral and cultural power presupposed its autonomy from political actions of the state and economic actions of society in the first place. According to Tönnies, the reform should enact ideas and suggestions proposed by a German American, Ferdinand Hansen: (1) in every city the best instructed and educated men should found a completely independent newspaper; (2) all recognized political parties would retain space to introduce and explain events; (3) the newspaper should be independent of advertisers; this would be secured by large circulation, since there would be no need for a party press; (4) only trustworthy firms would receive space for advertising; (5) voices of people would

find their direct expression in the newspaper; (6) sensationalism would be excluded; (7) the major articles would be so unbiased, without passion, and objective so that introduced opinions would be accepted with attention and trust; (8) the newspaper should have its own network of correspondents (Tönnies 1922, 575).

References

Albig, William. 1956. *Modern Public Opinion*. New York: McGraw-Hill.

Alvis, John. 1999. Foreword to Milton's Political Writings. In John Milton, *Areopagitica and other Political Writings*, x–xix. Indianapolis: Liberty Fund.

Anderson, Brian A. 1983. "Mill on Bentham: From Ideology to Humanised Utilitarianism." *History of Political Thought* 4, no. 2: 341–56.

Anderson, David A. 2002. "Freedom of the Press." *Texas Law Review* 80: 429–530.

Andrén, Gunnar. 1993. "A Concept of Freedom of Expression for Superindustrialized Societies." In *Communication and Democracy*, edited by S. Splichal and J. Wasko, 55–68. Norwood, N.J.: Ablex.

Aristotle. 350 B.C. *Rhetoric*. Translated by W. Rhys Roberts. At: classics.mit.edu// Aristotle/rhetoric.html.

Ayish, Muhammad I. 1998. "Communication Research in the Arab World: A New Perspective." *Javnost/The Public* 5, no. 1: 33–57.

Beaud, Paul, and Laurence Kaufmann. 2001. "Policing Opinions: Elites, Science, and Popular Opinion." In *Public Opinion and Democracy: Vox Populi—Vox Dei?* edited by S. Splichal, 55–84. Cresskill, N.J.: Hampton.

Beniger, James R. 1986. *The Control Revolution. Technological and Economic Origins of the Information Society*. Cambridge, Mass.: Harvard University Press.

Bensaude-Vincent, Bernadette. 2000. *L'opinion publique et science*. Paris: Institut d'édition Sanofi-Synthélabo.

Bentham, Jeremy. 1776. *A Fragment on Government*. At: www.ecn.bris.ac.uk/het/bentham/government.htm.

———. 1781/1996. *Principles of Morals and Legislation*. Copyright James Fieser (jfieser@utm.edu). At: www.la.utexas.edu/research/poltheory/bentham/bsp/index. html.

———. 1787/1995. *The Panopticon Writings*. Edited with an introduction by M. Božovič. London: Verso.

———. 1791/1994. "Of Publicity." *Public Culture* 6, no. 3: 581–95.

——. 1820. *On the Liberty of the Press and Public Discussion.* At: www. la.utexas.edu/research/poltheory/bentham/bsp/index.html.

——. 1822/1990. *Securities against Misrule and Other Constitutional Writings for Tripoli and Greece.* Edited by P. Schofield. Oxford: Clarendon.

——. 1830/1983. *Constitutional Code.* Vol. 1. Edited by F. Rosen and J. H. Burns. Oxford: Clarendon.

Blumer, Herbert. 1969. *Symbolic Interactionism: Perspective and Method.* Berkeley: University of California Press.

Blumler, Jay G. 1991. "Broadcasting Policy in a Changing Information Environment." *Bulletin of Institute of Journalism and Communication Studies* [University of Tokyo] 43: 1–13.

Bohman, James. 1996. "Die Öffentlichkeit des Weltbürgers: Über Kants 'negatives Surrogat.'" In *Frieden durch Recht: Kants Friedensidee und das Problem einer neuen Weltordnung,* edited by M. Lutz-Bachmann and J. Bohman, 87–113. Frankfurt: Suhrkamp.

——. 1999. "Citizenship and Norms of Publicity: Wide Public Reason in Cosmopolitan Societies." *Political Theory* 27, no. 2: 176–202.

Boyce, George. 1978. "The Fourth Estate: The Reappraisal of a Concept." In *Newspaper History from the Seventeenth Century to the Present Day,* edited by G. Boyce, J. Curran, and P. Wingate, 19–40. London: Constable.

Brighouse, Harry. 1995. "Political Equality and the Funding of Political Speech." *Social Theory and Practice* 21, no. 3: 473–500.

Brucker, Herbert. 1951. *Freedom of Information.* New York: Macmillan.

Bryce, James. 1888/1995. *The American Commonwealth.* 2 vols. Indianapolis: Liberty Fund.

Bücher, Karl. 1893/1901. *Industrial Revolution.* New York: Henry Holt.

——. 1926. *Gesammelte Aufsätze zur Zeitungskunde.* Tübingen: Laupp'sche Buchhandlung.

Burke, Edmund. 1769/1967. *Selected Writings and Speeches of Edmund Burke on Reform, Revolution, and War,* edited by R. J. S. Hoffman and P. Levack, 46–112. New York: Knopf.

——. 1770. *Thoughts on the Present Discontents.* Project Gutenberg Etext. At: uiarchive.uiuc.edu/mirrors/ftp/ibiblio.unc.edu/pub/docs/books/gutenberg/etext02/thdsc10.txt.

——. N.d. *Selections from the Speeches and Writings of Edmund Burke.* At: uiarchive.uiuc.edu/mirrors/ftp/ibiblio.unc.edu/pub/docs/books/gutenberg/etext02/spweb10.txt.

Calhoun, Craig. 1996. "Social Theory and the Public Sphere." In *The Blackwell Companion to Social Theory,* edited by B. S. Turner, 429–69. Oxford: Blackwell.

Carlyle, Thomas. 1840/1966. "The Hero as a Man of Letters." In *Heroes, Hero-Worship, and the Heroic in History.* Lincoln: University of Nebraska Press.

Coleman, John. 1983. "John Stuart Mill on the French Revolution." *History of Political Thought* 4, no. 1: 89–110.

Cooley, Charles Horton. 1909/1983. *Social Organization: A Study of the Larger Mind.* New Brunswick, N.J.: Transaction.

Cuilenburg, Jan van. 1998. "Diversity Revisited: Toward a Critical Rational Model of Media Diversity." In *The Media in Question: Popular Cultures and Public Interests,* edited by K. Brants, J. Hermes, and L. van Zoonen, 38–49. London: Sage.

Curran, James. 1978. "The Press as an Agency of Social Control: An Historical Perspective." In *Newspaper History from the Seventeenth Century to the Present Day*, edited by G. Boyce, J. Curran, and P. Wingate, 51–75. London: Constable.

Dahl, Robert A. 2000. *On Democracy*. New Haven: Yale University Press.

Dahlgren, Peter. 1995. *Television and the Public Sphere: Citizenship, Democracy, and the Media*. London: Sage.

Darnton, Robert. 1984. *The Great Cat Massacre and Other Episodes in French Cultural History*. New York: Vintage.

Dewey, John. 1927/1991. *The Public and Its Problems*. Athens: Swallow.

———. 1938/1987. Experience and Education. In *The Late Works*. Vol. 13. Edited by Jo Ann Boydston. Carbondale: Southern Illinois University Press.

Dovifat, Emil. 1931/1967. *Zeitungslehre*. Berlin: Walter de Gruyter.

Downing, John. 1984. *Radical Media: The Political Experience of Alternative Communication*. Boston: South End.

Durkheim, Emile. 1890/1971. The Principles of the 1789 and Sociology. In *The Phenomenon of Sociology*, edited by Edward A. Tiryakian. New York: Appleton-Century-Crofts.

Ellis, M. A. 1906. "Variations in the Editions of J.S. Mill's *Principles of Political Economy*." *Economic Journal* 16 (June): 291–302.

Engels, Friedrich. 1849. "Der erste Pressprozess der *Neuen Rhenischen Zeitung*" (The First Trial of the *Neue Rheinische Zeitung*). In *Marx-Engels Werke*, 6:234–39. Berlin: Dietz Verlag.

Foucault, Michel. 1977. *Discipline and Punish: The Birth of the Prison*. New York: Pantheon.

Fowler, Mark S., and Daniel L. Brenner. 1983. "A Marketplace Approach to Broadcast Regulation." In *Mass Communication Review Yearbook 4*, edited by E. Wartella and D. C. Whitney, 645–95. Beverly Hills, Calif.: Sage.

Gaonkar, Dilip Parameshwar, with Robert J. McCarthy Jr. 1994. "Panopticism and Publicity: Bentham's Quest for Transparency." *Public Culture* 6, no. 3: 547–78.

Garnham, Nicholas. 1992. "The Media and the Public Sphere." In *Habermas and the Public Sphere*, edited by C. Calhoun, 359–76. Cambridge, Mass.: MIT Press.

Gauthier, Candace Cummins. 1999. "Right to Know, Press Freedom, Public Discourse." *Journal of Mass Media Ethics* 14, no. 4: 197–212.

Gerhardt, Volker. 1995. *Immanuel Kants Entwurf "Zum ewigen Frieden." Eine Theorie der Politik*. Darmstadt: Wissenschaftliche Buchgesellschaft.

Ginsberg, Benjamin. 1986. *The Captive Public: How Mass Opinion Promotes State Power*. New York: Basic.

Gleason, Timothy W. 1990. *The Watchdog Concept: The Press and the Courts in Nineteenth-Century America*. Ames: Iowa State University Press.

Gordon, Jill. 1997. "John Stuart Mill and the 'Marketplace of Ideas.'" *Social Theory and Practice* 23, no. 2: 235–49.

Guizot, François. 1851/1861. *History of the Origin of Representative Government in Europe*. London: H. G. Bohn.

Gurevitch, Michael, and Jay G. Blumler. 1990. "Political Communication Systems and Democratic Values." In *Democracy and the Mass Media*, edited by J. Lichtenberg. Cambridge, Mass.: Cambridge University Press.

Guyer, Paul. 2000. *Kant on Freedom, Law, and Happiness*. Cambridge: Cambridge University Press.

Habermas, Jürgen. 1962/1995. *The Structural Transformation of the Public Sphere: An Inquiry into a Category of Bourgeois Society.* Cambridge, Mass.: MIT Press.

———. 1965/1980. *Teorija i praksa* [Theorie und Praxis]. Beograd: Kultura.

———. 1981. *Theorie des kommunikativen Handelns.* Frankfurt: Suhrkamp.

———. 1990. Vorwort zur Neuauflage [Foreword to the new edition]. *Strukturwandel der Öffentlichkeit.* Frankfurt: Suhrkamp.

———. 1992a. *Faktizität und Geltung: Beiträge zur Diskurstheorie des Rechts und des demokratischen Rechtsstaats.* Frankfurt: Suhrkamp. In English, *Between Facts and Norms: Contributions to a Discourse Theory of Law and Democracy.* Translated by W. Rehg. Cambridge: Polity, 1997.

———. 1992b. "Further Reflections on the Public Sphere." In *Habermas and the Public Sphere,* edited by C. Calhoun, 421–61. Cambridge, Mass.: MIT Press.

———. 2001. "Warum braucht Europa eine Verfassung?" *Deutschland,* December 2001–January 2002: 62–65.

Hamada, Basyouni Ibrahim. 2001. "Islamic Cultural Theory, Arab Media Performance, and Public Opinion." In *Public Opinion and Democracy: Vox Populi—Vox Dei?* edited by S. Splichal, 215–40. Cresskill, N.J.: Hampton.

Hardt, Hanno. 1979. *Social Theories of the Press: Early German and American Perspectives.* Beverly Hills, Calif.: Sage.

———. 1996. "The End of Journalism: Media and Newswork in the United States." *Javnost/The Public* 3, no. 3: 21–41.

Hayashi, Kaori. 1998. "The Home and Family Section in Japanese Newspapers." *Javnost/The Public* 5, no. 3: 51–63.

Hegel, Georg Wilhelm Friedrich. 1821/2001. *Philosophy of Right.* Kitchener, Ont.: Batoche.

———. 1830/1971. *The Philosophy of History.* Kitchener, Ont.: Batoche.

Held, David. 1987. *Models of Democracy.* Cambridge: Polity.

Hobbes, Thomas. 1651/1992. *Leviathan.* Cambridge: Cambridge University Press.

Hoffmann, Ross J.S., and Paul Levack. 1949/1967. Introduction to *Burke's Politics: Selected Writings and Speeches of Edmund Burke on Reform, Revolution, and War,* i–xxxvii. New York: Knopf.

Hoffmann-Riem, Wolfgang. 1986. "Law, Politics, and the New Media: Trends in Broadcasting Regulation." *West European Politics* 9, no. 4: 125–46.

Hoynes, William. 1994. *Public Television for Sale: Media, the Market, and the Public Sphere.* Boulder, Colo.: Westview.

Hunt, F. Knight. 1850. *The Fourth Estate: Contributions Towards a History of Newspapers, and of the Liberty of the Press.* London: David Bogue.

Hutchings, Kimberly. 1996. *Kant, Critique, and Politics.* London: Routledge.

Ingelhart, Louis E. 1987. *Press Freedoms: A Descriptive Calendar of Concepts, Interpretations, Events, and Court Actions from 4000 BC to the Present.* New York: Greenwood.

Jakubowicz, Karol. 1996. "Civil Society and Public Service Broadcasting in Central and Eastern Europe." *Javnost/The Public* 3, no. 2: 51–69.

James, Michael. 1981. "Public Interest and Majority in Bentham's Democratic Theory." *Political Theory* 9, no. 1: 49–64.

Jorgensen, Karin Wahl. 2002. "Understanding the Conditions for Public Discourse: Four Rules for Selecting Letters to the Editor." *Journalism Studies* 3, no. 1: 69–81.

Kant, Immanuel. 1781/1952. *The Critique of Pure Reason*. Translated by J. M. D. Meiklejohn. Great Books of the Western World 42. Chicago: Encyclopaedia Britannica.

———. 1784. "An Answer to the Question: What Is Enlightenment?" At: www. totalb.com/~mikeg/phil/kant/enlightenment.html#1.

———. 1785a/1952. *General Introduction to the Metaphysic of Morals*. Translated by W. Hastie. Great Books of the Western World 42. Chicago: Encyclopaedia Britannica.

———. 1785b. "Of the Injustice of Counterfeiting Books." At: www.hkbu.edu.hk/ ~ppp/fne/essay3.html. In German, "Von der Unrechtmässigkeit der Buchnachdrucks." *Berlinische Monatsschrift* 1: 403–17. At: www.ub.uni-bielefeld.de/diglib/ Berlinische_Monatsschrift/index-e.htm.

———. 1786. "Was heisst: Sich im Denken orientiren?" *Berlinische Monatsschrift* 2: 304–30. At: www.ub.uni-bielefeld.de/diglib/Berlinische_Monatsschrift/index-e.htm.

——— 1788/1952. *The Critique of Practical Reason*. Translated by T. K. Abbott. Great Books of the Western World. Chicago: Encyclopaedia Britannica.

———. 1790/1952. *The Critique of Judgment*. Translated by J. C. Meredith. Great Books of the Western World 42. Chicago: Encyclopaedia Britannica.

———. 1793/1914. "The Principles of Political Right." In *Eternal Peace and Other International Essays*, 27–54. Boston: World Peace Foundation. An abridged translation of the article "Ueber den Gemeinspruch: Das mag in der Theorie richtig sein, taugt aber nicht für die Praxis." *Berlinische Monatsschrift* 2 (1793): 201–84. At: www.ub.uni-bielefeld.de/diglib/Berlinische_Monatsschrift/index-e.htm.)

———. 1795/1983. *To Perpetual Peace*. In *Immanuel Kant: Perpetual Peace and Other Essays*, 107–44. Cambridge, Ind.: Hackett.

———. 1797/1952. *The Science of Right*. (*The Metaphysics of Morals, Part One*). Translated by W. Hastie. Great Books of the Western World 42. Chicago: Encyclopaedia Britannica.

———. 1798/1979. *The Conflict of the Faculties*. Translated by M. J. Gregor. New York: Arabis.

Kellner, David. 1990. *Television and the Crisis of Democracy*. Boulder, Colo.: Westview.

Key, V. O., Jr. 1967. *Public Opinion and American Democracy*. New York: Knopf.

Knies, Karl. 1857/1996. *Der Telegraph als Verkehrsmittel: Über der Nachrichtenverkehr überhaupt*. München: Verlag Reinhard Fischer.

Krüger, Hans-Peter. 1991. "Radical Democratization." *Praxis International* 11, no. 1: 18–36.

Lasswell, Harold D. 1948/1971. "The Structure and Function of Communication in Society." In *The Process and Effects of Mass Communication*, edited by W. Schramm and D. F. Roberts, 84–99. Urbana: University of Illinois Press.

Lazarsfeld, Paul F., and Robert K. Merton. 1948/1971. "Mass Communication, Popular Taste, and Organized Social Action." In *The Process and Effects of Mass Communication*, edited by W. Schramm and D. F. Roberts, 554–78. Urbana: University of Illinois Press.

Le Bon, Gustave. 1895/2001. *The Crowd: A Study of Popular Mind* [Psychologie des foules]. Kitchener, Ont.: Batoche. At: www.ecn.bris.ac.uk/het/lebon/Crowds.pdf.

Lenin, Vladimir I. 1902. *What Is to Be Done?* At: www.marxists.org/archive/lenin/ works/download/what-itd.pdf.

Lippmann, Walter. 1922/1991. *Public Opinion*. New Brunswick, N.J.: Transaction.

Locke, John. 1689/1996. *Letter concerning Toleration*. Internet Encyclopedia of Philosophy. At: www.utm.edu/research/iep.

———. 1690. *An Essay Concerning Human Understanding*. At: socserv2.mcmaster. ca/~econ/ugcm/3ll3/locke/Essay.htm.

Macaulay, Thomas B. 1827/1999. *Hallam: "The Constitutional History of England, from the Accession of Henry VII to the Death of George II." By Henry Hallam*. 2 vols. At: www.elecbook.com/ebmacaul.htm.

———. 1828/1992. "Mill on Government." In *Political Writings*, by James Mill, edited by T. Ball, 271–303. Cambridge: Cambridge University Press.

MacBride Report. 1980/1984. *Many Voices, One World: Communication and Society Today and Tomorrow*. Abridged ed. Paris: UNESCO.

MacKinnon, William A. 1828/1971. *On the Rise, Progress, and Present State of Public Opinion, in Great Britain, and Other Parts of the World*. Shannon: Irish University Press.

Marx, Karl. 1842a/1974. "Die Verhandlungen des 6. rheinischen Landtags: Debatten über Pressefreiheit und Publikation der Landständischen Verhandlungen." In *Marx-Engels Werke*, 1:28–77. Berlin: Dietz Verlag.

———. 1842b/1974. "Bemerkungen über die neueste preussische Zensurinstruktion." In *Marx-Engels Werke*, 1:3–25. Berlin: Dietz Verlag.

———. 1843/1974. "Rechtfertigung des ++−− Korrespondenten von der Mosel." In *Marx-Engels Werke*, 1:172–99. Berlin: Dietz Verlag.

———. 1844a/1974. "Zur Kritik der Hegelschen Rechtsphilosophie." In *Marx-Engels Werke*, 1:201–336, 378–91. Berlin: Dietz Verlag.

———. 1844b/1974. "Zur Judenfrage." In *Marx-Engels Werke*, 1:347–77. Berlin: Dietz Verlag.

———. 1847/1974. "Das Elend der Philosophie. Antwort auf Proudhons 'Philosophie der Elend.'" In *Marx-Engels Werke*, 4:63–182. Berlin: Dietz Verlag.

———. 1848. "Der preussische Pressgesetzentwurf." In *Marx-Engels Werke*, 5:240–42. Berlin: Dietz Verlag.

———. 1849a/1974. "Der erste Presseprozess der *Neuen Rhenischen Zeitung*." In *Marx-Engels Werke*, 6:223–34. Berlin: Dietz Verlag.

———. 1849b. "Zensur." In *Marx-Engels Werke*, 6: 351–52. Berlin: Dietz Verlag.

———. 1857–1858/1974. *Grundrisse der Kritik der politischen Oekonomie*. Berlin: Dietz Verlag.

———. 1859/1974. "Zur Kritik der politischen Oekonomie." In *Marx-Engels Werke*, 13:3–160. Berlin: Dietz Verlag.

Marx, Karl, and Friedrich Engels. 1845/1973. "Die deutsche Ideologie." In *Marx-Engels Werke*, 13:9–532. Berlin: Dietz Verlag.

———. 1848/1998. *The Communist Manifesto*. London: Verso.

McQuail, Denis. 1994. *Mass Communication Theory: An Introduction*. 3rd ed. London: Sage.

Merton, Robert K. 1949/1993. "Manifest and Latent Functions." In *Social Theory*, edited by C. Lemert, 328–34. Boulder, Colo.: Westview.

Mill, John Stuart. 1838/1859. "Bentham." *London and Westminster Review*, August 1838, revised in 1859 in *Dissertations and Discussion*, Vol. 1. At: www.ecn.bris.ac.uk/het/bentham/bentham.

———. 1847. *The Principles of Political Economy*. 3rd ed. At: www.ecn.bris.ac.uk/het/mill.

———. 1859/2001. *On Liberty*. Kitchener, Ont.: Batoche.

———. 1861/2001. *Representative Government*. Kitchener, Ont.: Batoche.

———. 1863/2001. *Utilitarianism*. Kitchener, Ont.: Batoche.

———. 1873. *Autobiography*. Available from the University of Adelaide Library, Electronic Texts Collection.

Mills, C. Wright. 1956/2000. *The Power Elite*. Oxford: Oxford University Press.

Milton, John. 1644/1999. *Areopagitica*. In *Areopagitica and other Political Writings*, 1–51. Indianapolis: Liberty Fund. At: www.dartmouth.edu/~milton/reading_room/areopagitica.

———. 1648/1999. "Mr. John Milton's Character of the Long Parliament." In *Areopagitica and Other Political Writings*, 447–54. Indianapolis: Liberty Fund.

———. 1659. "A Treatise of Civil Power in Ecclesiastical Causes; Showing That It Is Not Lawful for Any Power on Earth to Compel in Matters of Religion." At: www.dartmouth.edu/~milton/reading_room/civil_power/index.html.

Molivas, Gregory. 2000. "From Religion to Politics: The Expression of Opinion as the Common Ground between Religious Liberty and Political Participation in the Eighteenth-Century Conception of Natural Rights." *History of Political Thought* 21, no. 2: 237–60.

Montesquieu, Charles de Secondat. 1748/1966. *The Spirit of the Laws*. With an introduction by F. Neumann. New York: Hafner, 1914. Translated by T. Nougat. London: G. Bell & Sons. At: www.constitution.org/cm/sol.txt.

Müller-Doohm, Stefan. 1972. *Medienindustrie und Demokratie: Verfassungspolitische Interpretation-Sozioökonomische Analyse*. Frankfurt: Athenäum.

Narveson, Jan. 1994. "Freedom of Speech and Expression: A Libertarian View." In *Free Expression: Essays in Law and Philosophy*, edited by W. J. Waluchow, 59–90. Oxford: Clarendon.

Negt, Oskar, and Alexander Kluge. 1973. *Öffentlichkeit und Erfahrung: Zur Organisationsanalyse von bürgerlicher und proletarischer Öffentlichkeit*. Frankfurt: Suhrkamp.

Noelle-Neumann, Elisabeth, and Winfried Schulz, eds. 1971. *Publizistik*. Frankfurt: Fischer.

Park, Robert F. 1904/1972. *The Crowd and the Public*. Edited by H. Elsner Jr. Chicago: University of Chicago Press.

———. 1921. "Sociology and the Social Sciences: The Social Organism and the Collective Mind." *American Journal of Sociology* 27, no. 1: 1–21.

———. 1921/1967. "Social Control." In *On Social Control and Collective Behavior*, edited by R. H. Turner, 209–24. Chicago: University of Chicago Press.

———. 1938. "Reflections on Communication and Culture." *American Journal of Sociology* 44, no. 2: 187–205.

Parsons, Talcott. 1942/1954. "Propaganda and Social Control." In *Essays in Sociological Theory*. Glencoe, Ill.: Free Press.

Peters, John Durham. 1997. "Why Dewey Wasn't So Right and Lippmann Wasn't So Wrong: Recasting the Lippmann-Dewey Debate." Paper presented at the International Communication Association, Montreal, May 1997.

———. 1999. *Speaking into the Air: A History of the Idea of Communication*. Chicago: University of Chicago Press.

Peterson, Theodore, Jay W. Jensen, and William L. Rivers. 1965. *The Mass Media and Modern Society*. New York: Holt, Rinehart and Winston.

Plato. 360 B.C.E./1901. *The Republic of Plato*. Edited and translated by B. Jowett. New York: P. F. Collier & Son. At: etext.lib.virginia.edu.

Plato. 360 B.C.E./1871. *Phaedrus*. Translated by B. Jowett. At: uiarchive.uiuc.edu/ mirrors/ftp/ibiblio.unc.edu/pub/docs/books/gutenberg/etext99/phdrs10.txt.

Poster, Mark. 1984. *Foucault, Marxism, and History: Mode of Production versus Mode of Information*. Cambridge: Polity.

Powe, Lucas A. 1991. *The Fourth Estate and the American Constitution: Freedom of the Press in America*. Berkeley: University of California Press.

Qur'an. 622 C.E. *The Noble Qur'an*. At: www.usc.edu/dept/MSA/quran/049.qmt.html.

Rinderle, Peter. 2000. *John Stuart Mill*. Munich: C. H. Beck.

Rivers, William L., and Wilbur Schramm. 1969. *Responsibility in Mass Communication*. Rev. ed. New York: Harper & Row.

Rogers, Lindsay. 1949. *The Pollsters: Public Opinion, Politics, and Democratic Leadership*. New York: Knopf.

Ross, Edward A. 1901/1969. *Social Control: A Survey of the Foundations of Order*. Cleveland: Press of Case Western Reserve University.

―――. 1917–1918. "Social Decadence." *American Journal of Sociology* 23: 620–32.

Rousseau, Jean-Jacques. 1750. *Whether the Re-establishment of Arts and Sciences Has Contributed to the Refining of Manners*. At: www.ucl.ac.uk/history/ courses/europe1/weeks/rou1.htm.

―――. 1755. *A Discourse on Political Economy*. At: projects.ilt.columbia.edu/ pedagogies/rousseau/.

―――. 1762a. *The Social Contract or Principles of Political Right*. At: www. constitution.org/jjr/socon.txt.

―――. 1762b. *Emile, or, on Education*. At: projects.ilt.columbia.edu/pedagogies/ rousseau.

Sabine, George H. 1961. *A History of Political Theory*. 3rd ed. New York: Holt, Rinehart and Winston.

Schäffle, Albert. 1875. *Bau und Leben des socialen Körpers*. Tübingen: Verlag der H. Laupp'schen Buchhandlung.

Schramm, Wilbur. 1971. "The Nature of Communication between Humans." In *The Process and Effects of Mass Communication*, edited by W. Schramm and D. F. Roberts, 1–61. Urbana: University of Illinois Press.

Schudson, Michael. 1997. "Why Conversation Is Not the Soul of Democracy." *Critical Studies in Mass Communication* 14, no. 4:297–309.

Searle, John R. 1995. *The Construction of Social Reality*. New York: Free Press.

Slevin, James. 2000. *The Internet and Society*. Cambridge: Polity.

Sparks, Colin. 1995. "The Media as a Power for Democracy." *Javnost/The Public* 2, no. 1: 45–61.

Spinoza, Benedict de. 1670/1883. *Theologico-Political Treatise*. Translated by R. H. M. Elwes. Mineola, N.Y.: Dover. At: users.erols.com/jyselman. At: www.spinoza.net/ Theworks/index.html.

―――. 1677/1883. *A Political Treatise*. Translated by A. H. Gosset. London: G. Bell & Son. At: www.constitution.org/bs/poltr-00.htm.

Splichal, Slavko. 1981. *Množično komuniciranje med svobodo in odtujitvijo* [Mass communication between freedom and alienation]. Maribor: Obzorja.

―――. 1991. "Komunikacijske pravice in svoboščine v slovenski demokratizaciji" [Communication rights and freedoms in the Slovenian democratization]. *Teorija in praksa* 5–6: 491–505.

———. 1999. *Public Opinion: Developments and Controversies in the Twentieth Century*. Lanham, Md.: Rowman & Littlefield.

Steintrager, James. 1977. *Bentham*. Ithaca, N.Y.: Cornell University Press.

Stephen, Leslie. 1900. *The English Utilitarians*. Vol. 1, *Jeremy Bentham*. At: www.socsci.mcmaster.ca/~econ/ugcm/3ll3/bentham/stephen1.html1.

Sumner, Colin. 1997. "Social Control: The History and Politics of a Central Concept in Anglo-American Sociology." In *Social Control and Political Order*, edited by R. Bergalli and C. Sumner, 1–33. London: Sage.

Stieler, Caspar. 1695/1969. *Zeitungs Lust und Nutz*. Bremen: Carl Schünemann Verlag.

Tarde, Gabriel. 1969. *On Communication and Social Influence*, edited by T. N. Clark. Chicago: University of Chicago Press.

Tindal, Matthew. 1698/1974. "A Letter to a Member of Parliament, Shewing that a Restraint Press is inconsistent with the Protestant Religion, and dangerous to the Liberties of Nation." In *Freedom of the Press: Six Tracts, 1698–1709*, edited by S. Parks, 1–32. New York: Garland.

Tocqueville, Alexis de. 1835. *Democracy in America*. Vol. 1. At: xroads.virginia.edu/~HYPER/DETOC/toc_indx.html.

———. 1840. *Democracy in America*. Vol. 2. At: xroads.virginia.edu/~HYPER/DETOC/toc_indx.html.

Tönnies, Ferdinand. 1922. *Kritik der öffentlichen Meinung*. Berlin: Julius Springer.

Trager, Robert, and Donna L. Dickerson. 1999. *Freedom of Expression in the Twenty-First Century*. Thousand Oaks: Pine Forge.

Turner, Bryan S. 1996. Introduction to *The Blackwell Companion to Social Theory*, 1–19. Oxford: Blackwell.

Varouxakis, Georgios. 1999. "Guizot's Historical Works and J. S. Mill's Reception of Tocqueville." *History of Political Thought* 20, no. 2: 292–312.

Waldron, Jeremy. 1987. Introduction to Karl Marx's "On the Jewish Question." In *"Nonsense Upon Stilts." Bentham, Burke and Marx on the Rights of Man*, edited by J. Waldron, 119–36. London: Methuen.

Weinberg, Julius, Gisela J. Hinkle, and Roscoe C. Hinkle. 1969. Introduction to *Social Control: A Survey of the Foundations of Order*, edited by E. A. Ross, i–lx. Cleveland: Press of Case Western Reserve University.

Williams, Raymond. 1962/1976. *Communications*. Harmondsworth, U.K.: Penguin.

———. 1978. "The Press and Popular Culture: A Historical Perspective." In *Newspaper History from the Seventeenth Century to the Present Day*, edited by G. Boyce, J. Curran, and P. Wingate, 41–50. London: Constable.

Wilson, Francis Graham. 1962. *A Theory of Public Opinion*. Chicago: Regnery.

Wirth, Louis. 1948. "Consensus and Mass Communication." *American Sociological Review* 13, no. 1: 1–15.

Wright, Charles R. 1959. *Mass Communication: A Sociological Perspective*. New York: Random House.

Zolo, Danilo. 1992. *Democracy and Complexity: A Realist Approach*. University Park: Pennsylvania State University Press.

Index

About the Author

Slavko Splichal is professor of mass communications and public opinion in the Faculty of Social Sciences, University of Ljubljana, director of the European Institute for Communication and Culture, and editor of its journal *Javnost–The Public*. He has been member of editorial boards of *Journal of Communication, Journalism Studies, Gazette, New Media & Society, Reseaux–The French Journal of Communication*, and *Zeszyty Prasoznaw-cze*. His recent English language books include *Public Opinion: Developments and Controversies in the Twentieth Century* (1999), *Ferdinand Tönnies on Public Opinion: Selections and Analyses* (coauthored with Hanno Hardt, 2001), and *Public Opinion and Democracy: Vox Populi—Vox Dei?* (editor, 2001).